This book is simply extraordinary. I doubt there is a person on the planet who knows both theological issues and time-management literature to the depth and extent Matt Perman does.

—John Piper, former Pastor for Preaching and Vision,
Bethlehem Baptist Church; author, *Don't Waste Your Life*

This amazing volume offers a wealth of practical, real-world productivity solutions, all framed within the context of the gospel. Matt provides the know-how and the know-who we need to be faithful stewards over the gifts we have been given.

—Michael Hyatt *New York Times* bestselling author; *MichaelHyatt.com*

A refreshing, lively, remarkably insightful, deeply God-centered approach to productivity. Everyone from any walk of life who reads this book will be helped and encouraged by it.

—Wayne Grudem, Research Professor of Theology and Biblical
Studies, Phoenix Seminary; author, *The Poverty of Nations*

The question isn't, What do I want to do for God? but, What does God want me to do? This book provides the framework for getting more done and making a bigger difference in your work.

—Mark Sanborn, author, *The Fred Factor* and
You Don't Need a Title to Be a Leader

This book is the fruit of experience as well as insight drawn from Scripture and common sense—without doing injustice to either. There is a lot of wisdom here.

—Michael Horton, Professor of Systematic Theology and Apologetics,
Westminster Seminary California; author, *The Gospel-Driven Life*

You will find in these pages a unique and remarkable combination of theological insight, biblical instruction, and practical counsel that will change the world if put into practice. I cannot recommend it more highly.

—Justin Taylor, Managing Editor, *ESV Study Bible*;
blogger, *Between Two Worlds*

A Christian companion to *Getting Things D*
—Hugh Whelchel, Executive Direc
and Economics; author

D0905974

Love your neighbor at work! This book shows you not only why you need to do this but also how. No matter who you are or what your work is, this is a reliable, exciting, and encouraging guidebook on getting things done, from a God-centered perspective.

—Brad Lomenick, President, Catalyst; author, *The Catalyst Leader*

This book is an engaging, motivating, and exciting vision for your work and the things you do every day, right along with helpful, clear, and practical instruction on how to become more effective with less stress. Want to be more productive for the glory of God? Read *What's Best Next.*

—Ed Stetzer, President, LifeWay Research; author, *Lost and Found; www.edstetzer.com*

Matt Perman approaches the task [of being productive at working] not only from his personal experience but from a Christian worldview. Follow his model to align what you do with God's purpose in your life—and in particular in your work.

—B. Joseph Pine II, coauthor, *The Experience Economy* and *Infinite Possibility*

What makes this book stand out is the way Matt Perman integrates all of this down-to-earth advice with the doctrine of vocation—how the gospel of Christ bears fruit in love and service to God and to our neighbors in every facet of life—a truth that animates every page.

—Gene Edward Veith, Professor of Literature, and Provost of Patrick Henry College; author, *God at Work*

Plain and simple: learning to effectively manage your time and tasks is one of the most practical and tangible ways you can love your neighbors, coworkers, family members, and the world at large. No one has articulated this better than Matt Perman in this unique book.

—Matt Heerema, owner and director, Mere Design Agency; Pastor, Stonebrook Community Church

EXPANDED EDITION

what's best next

HOW THE GOSPEL TRANSFORMS THE WAY YOU GET THINGS DONE

MATT PERMAN

ZONDERVAN

What's Best Next
Copyright © 2014, 2016 by Matthew Perman

This title is also available as a Zondervan ebook.

Requests for information should be addressed to:
Zondervan, 3900 *Sparks Dr. SE, Grand Rapids, Michigan 49546*

This edition: 978-0-310-53398-6 (softcover)

The Library of Congress catalogued the hardcover as follows:

Perman, Matt, 1976-
    What's best next : how the gospel transforms the way you get things done / Matt
Perman.
       pages cm
       Includes bibliographical references.
       ISBN 978-0-310-49422-5 (hardcover) 1. Work—Religious aspects—Christianity. 2.
Labor productivity. I. Title.
    BT738.5.P48 2013
    248.4—dc23   2013026880

All scripture quotations, unless otherwise indicated are taken from the ESV® Bible (The Holy
Bible, English Standard Version®). Copyright © 2001 by Crossway, a publishing ministry of Good
News Publishers. Used by permission. All rights reserved. Scripture quotations marked NASB
are taken from the *New American Standard Bible®*. Copyright © 1960, 1962, 1963, 1968, 1971, 1972,
1973, 1975, 1977, 1995 by The Lockman Foundation. Used by permission. (www.Lockman.org).

Any Internet addresses (websites, blogs, etc.) and telephone numbers in this book are offered
as a resource. They are not intended in any way to be or imply an endorsement by Zondervan,
nor does Zondervan vouch for the content of these sites and numbers for the life of this book.

All rights reserved. No part of this publication may be reproduced, stored in a retrieval system,
or transmitted in any form or by any means—electronic, mechanical, photocopy, recording, or
any other—except for brief quotations in printed reviews, without the prior permission of the
publisher.

Published in association with the literary agency of Wolgemuth & Associates, Inc.

Cover design: Faceout Studio
Interior design: Matthew Van Zomeren

Printed in the United States of America

---

16 17 18 19 20 21 22 /DHV/ 18 17 16 15 14 13 12 11 10 9 8 7 6 5 4 3 2 1

To the Lord, Jesus Christ,
for we are your workmanship,
created in you for good works (Eph. 2:10)

No man has a right to be idle. . . . [W]here is it that in such a world as this, health, and leisure, and affluence may not find some ignorance to instruct, some wrong to redress, some want to supply, some misery to alleviate?
— William Wilberforce, A Practical View of Christianity

Let your light shine before others, so that they may see your good works and give glory to your Father who is in heaven.
— Matthew 5:16

We are his workmanship, created in Christ Jesus for good works, which God prepared beforehand, that we should walk in them.
— Ephesians 2:10

Look carefully then how you walk, not as unwise but as wise, making the best use of the time, because the days are evil. Therefore do not be foolish, but understand what the will of the Lord is.
— Ephesians 5:15 – 17

Do all the good you can, by all the means you can, in all the ways you can, in all the places you can, at all the times you can, to all the people you can, as long as you ever can.
— John Wesley

Contents

Part 1
First Things First:
Making God Supreme in Our Productivity

Part 2
Gospel-Driven Productivity:
A New Way to Look at Getting Things Done

Part 3
Define: Know What's Most Important

Part 4
Architect: Create a Flexible Structure

Toolkit

Foreword

This book is simply extraordinary.

This is largely because of the way God has wired Matt Perman. His mind is saturated with biblical truth, and he is passionate, sometimes to a fault (as you will see in his personal stories), about being effective for the glory of Christ.

Those two traits have combined to produce a God-centered, Christ-exalting, Bible-saturated book that, without blinking, gets into stuff like Al Mohler's midnight productivity and Seth Godin's method for carving out time for work that matters.

I doubt there is a person on the planet who knows *both* theological issues and time-management literature to the depth and extent Matt Perman does. This combination is at times mindboggling.

Of course, I am totally biased—not dishonest, I hope, but biased. I've known Matt as his teacher, pastor, colleague, and friend for almost fifteen years. From hundreds of interactions on all kinds of issues, my judgment is this: Here is a theological mind that keeps pace with the best. Almost without fail, a conversation with Matt about any biblical or theological issue proves fruitful.

I'm also biased because I view his book as a colossal effort to push Christian hedonism—the theology I have trumpeted for forty years—into all the corners of life. In fact, Matt told me in an email at the last minute, "In a real sense, this book is really about the *horizontal* dimension of Christian hedonism." Yes. That's what I thought.

Which means that the book is really about how to be so satisfied in God that the power of this joy is released "to love people better in the midst of the current, very challenging environment of our modern, technological, constantly interrupted knowledge work era."

Matt says, "This book is also for those who do not share my faith perspective." If you doubt that a God-besotted book can be useful to a secular person, consider that Rick Warren's multi-million-copy-selling *Purpose Driven Life* begins, "It's not about you. ... If you want to know why you were placed on this planet, you must begin with God. You were born by his purpose and for his purpose." Matt's book takes that truth and gives it flesh for the sake of getting the best things done.

So I am happy to entice all kinds of people to this book. There are surprising tastes everywhere. Like:

> "The only way to be productive is to realize we actually don't have to be productive."
>
> "This book is also for screw-ups and failures!"
>
> "Serving is exciting. It's like steak, not broccoli."
>
> "Gospel-Driven Productivity is about ... bringing the gospel to all nations."
>
> "Productivity is the only long-term solution to world poverty."
>
> "Productivity is a fruit of the Holy Spirit."
>
> "The most important principle for being productive is Bible reading and prayer, before the day begins, every day."
>
> "Surfing the internet for fun at work makes you more productive, not less."
>
> "Productive things are things that pass muster at the final judgment—and hence receive the verdict 'eternally productive.'"

May God give this book wings for the glory of Christ and for the good of the world, and may it bring a blessing back on Matt Perman's head with wholeness and joy in every corner of his life.

—John Piper

Preface

Busting the Twelve Myths about
What It Means to Get Things Done

DO YOU UNDERSTAND PRODUCTIVITY in the right way? This book gives you a new way of understanding how to get things done and, beyond that, what it even means to get things done.

The ideas I advocate here are supported by the best research and the Scriptures, but many of them might seem new to you. Here are the top twelve myths this book seeks to overcome:

Myth #1: Productivity is about getting more done faster. When most people think of productivity, they think of *efficiency*—getting more things done faster. While efficiency is important, it is secondary. More important than efficiency is *effectiveness*—getting the right things done. Efficiency doesn't matter if you are doing the wrong things in the first place.

Truth: Productivity is about effectiveness first, not efficiency.

Myth #2: The way to be productive is to have the right techniques and tools. Using great tools and the most helpful techniques is a lot of fun. But, like efficiency, this is secondary. This book will give you the most helpful methods for improving your productivity, and will point you to some really cool tools. But one of the central tenets of this book is that the foundation of effectiveness is not first techniques or tools, but *character*. The only way to make the right decisions is first to be the right kind of person (Rom. 12:1–2; 2 Peter 1:5–11).

Truth: Productivity comes first from character, not techniques.

Myth #3: It is not essential to give consideration to what God has to say about productivity. I don't want to imply you have to be a Christian to get things done or to write on how to get things done.

Much of this is in the realm of common grace, and we can learn a lot from people of all perspectives.

The problem is if we stop there. For example, we often go about our planning as if it were just any other activity. But the Scriptures teach that to make plans without acknowledging God is not just wrong but *arrogant* (James 4:13–17). There are very significant things that we miss if we do not give serious consideration to what God has to say on these matters. One of the aims of this book is to show you what those things are, and that they are good news.

Truth: We cannot be truly productive unless all our activity stems from love for God and the acknowledgment that he is sovereign over all our plans.

Myth #4: It is not essential to make the gospel central in our view of productivity. The way to become productive is not to try harder, even if the focus of our efforts is the development of our character. The power behind our productivity comes from realizing that, through faith in the gospel, we are accepted by God in Christ apart from what we do. This puts wind in our sails and unleashes the power of the Spirit in our lives (Gal. 3:5).

Truth: The only way to be productive is to realize that you don't have to be productive.

Myth #5: The way to be productive is to tightly manage yourself (and others!). Sometimes we have the notion that people who care about getting things done need to be ultra-organized, rigidly scheduled, and inflexible. Nothing could be further from the truth. We are most productive not when we seek to tightly control ourselves but when we seek to unleash ourselves. Productivity comes from *engagement*, not control and mere compliance. This is why operating in our strengths is so important. Further, this approach to productivity naturally follows from a right understanding of the gospel.

Truth: Productivity comes from engagement, not tight control; when we are motivated, we don't need to tightly control ourselves (or others).

Myth #6: The aim of time management should be our peace of mind. Peace of mind is a good thing, but I'm going to argue that there is something far more important. The reason we should seek to be productive is to serve others to the glory of God, and not for the sake of personal peace and affluence. Ironically, however, peace of mind results when the good of others, and not our own peace of mind, is our first aim.

Truth: Productivity is first about doing good for others to the glory of God.

Myth #7: The way to succeed is to put yourself first. It is often thought that the way to succeed is to put yourself first and crush others. It turns out that not only is that an un-Christian ethic, but it also doesn't work. The biggest trend in the marketplace is, as Tim Sanders has put it, "the downfall of the barracudas, sharks, and piranhas, and the ascendancy of nice, smart people."[1]

Truth: We become most productive by putting others first, not ourselves.

Myth #8: We will have peace of mind if we can get everything under control. The problem with this idea is that it doesn't work. It is simply not possible to have everything under control, and so the quest to base our peace of mind on our ability to control everything is futile. Our peace of mind must be based on other grounds—namely, the gospel.

Truth: Basing our peace of mind on our ability to control everything will never work.

Myth #9: To-do lists are enough. I made this mistake for years. I read *Getting Things Done* (which I loved!) and created all sorts of next action lists, project lists, and someday/maybe lists, yet I rarely achieved "mind like water." Instead, my typical state could have been described as "mind like tsunami."

What I came to realize is that time is like space. Just as there is only so much stuff that we can fit into our closets, so also there is only so much stuff that we can fit into our days. If we don't think in terms of a basic schedule with slots for our main types of tasks, we end up in overload.

Truth: Time is like space, and we need to see lists as support material for our activity zones, not as sufficient in themselves to keep track of what we have to do.

Myth #10: Productivity is best defined by tangible outcomes. We often think of productivity as getting concrete things done—emails sent, widgets made, and assignments completed. These things are important, but they do not exhaust the scope of our productivity. More and more, productivity is about *intangibles*—relationships developed, connections made, and things learned. We need to incorporate intangibles into our definition of productivity or we will short-change ourselves by thinking that sitting at our desks for a certain number of hours equals a productive day.

Truth: The greatest evidence of productivity comes from intangibles, not tangibles.

Myth #11: The time we spend working is a good measure of our productivity. Being at our desks doesn't equal being productive, and organizations should no longer measure an employee's productivity that way. At the same time, other things take far longer than you would think: sometimes the best way to be productive is to be *inefficient.*

As a corollary to this, deadlines work well for execution tasks (the realm of personal management), but they do not work well for creative tasks and ambiguity (the realm of personal leadership). If we use deadlines and the efficiency paradigm for managing ambiguity, we often kill productivity rather than encourage it.

Truth: We need to measure productivity by results, not by time spent working.

Myth #12: Having to work really hard or even suffer in our work means our priorities are screwed up or we are doing something wrong. I'm not sanctioning the practice of making work an idol to which we sacrifice everything in our lives. Productivity is concerned with all areas of our lives—work, home, community, everything—because all areas of our lives are callings from God.

That said, people who work long hours often take it on the chin too much. The fact that someone is working a lot does not make that person a workaholic. Some people really enjoy their work and want to work a lot. This is not in itself workaholism. Sometimes it is the path God has placed before us. Where did we get the idea that we are exempt from suffering in our work lives? If we are suffering from and in our work, it does not necessarily mean we are sinning. (See 2 Cor. 11:23–29, where Paul even includes all-nighters among his many sufferings.)

Truth: We will (sometimes) suffer from our work, and it is not sin.[2]

You may believe some or all of these myths. This book will not only help you to see why these myths are wrong; it also will give you an alternative—a view of productivity centered on God.

Introduction

Why We Need a Uniquely Christian
View on Productivity

*Every Christian must be fully Christian by bringing God
into his whole life, not merely into some spiritual realm.*
— *Dietrich Bonhoeffer*

THIS IS A BOOK ABOUT GETTING THINGS DONE and making ideas happen, with less friction and frustration, from a biblical perspective.

Which immediately raises some questions.

Does God actually have anything to *say* about getting things done? Is it even possible to have a biblical perspective on such a practical subject like how to get things done? And should we even care about it as *Christians*, or is it unspiritual? Is God smiling on us when we are making ideas happen and being productive, or does he wish we were out sharing the gospel instead?

But first things first. We can't neglect what's right before us.

IT'S HARD TO GET THINGS DONE

Most of us feel that we have way too much to do and too little time to do it. As David Allen points out, the process of managing our work is often messy and overflows its banks. "Behind closed doors, after hours, there remain unanswered calls, tasks to be delegated, unprocessed issues from meetings and conversations, personal responsibilities unmanaged, and dozens of emails still not dealt with."[3] And as Scott Belsky notes, "While the tendency to generate ideas is rather natural, the path to making them happen is tumultuous."[4]

This is especially unfortunate because we are living in an incredibly exciting time in history. Many of us love our jobs and find the world of work exciting. We have more opportunities to do good than ever before, and more opportunities to do creative, challenging work than perhaps at any point in history.

But the process of getting things done is harder than it needs to be. Most of us are seeking solutions to this problem. But there is something we often overlook: What does *God* think about all of this? Does God have anything to say about getting things done, and if so, what? How should we think about this as *Christians*?

Unfortunately, many of us have had a hard time finding the answers to these questions. There is a shortage of teaching in the church on how to get things done, and we are all suffering for it. (Further, this is simply a subset of a much worse problem—the lack of a robust and interesting Christian doctrine of *work*.) There are many great secular books that we can greatly benefit from, but they don't show how this all connects to God.

It is my contention that in addition to the very helpful secular books that exist, we also need to develop a distinctly Christian understanding of how to get things done. We miss something important and amazing if we don't think about productivity from a specifically biblical perspective. I think the world misses something too.

THE PERPLEXING ABSENCE OF CHRISTIAN THINKING ON PRODUCTIVITY

It is odd that there is so little Christian teaching on productivity because, as Christians, we believe the gospel changes everything—how we go about our home life, work life, church life, community life, *everything*. Yet there has been little Christian reflection on how the gospel changes the way we get things done—something that affects all of us every day.

In fact, good productivity practices are often downplayed in the church at the altar of overspiritualization.

For example, shortly after I started my blog on productivity, a pastor at my church told me it was like I was "Einstein teaching first grade." He said it was a compliment, but it almost made me want to quit blogging![5]

Another time, I mentioned that I was having a difficult time figuring out how to manage my work and family life with the arrival of our third child. I was looking for practical help and guidance. Instead, he simply said, "It's only going to get harder."

How do you even respond to that?

I know he meant well. But I was looking for real help. Yet all I got was what seemed like an overspiritualized dismissal.

Many of us have experienced similar push-back from well-intentioned Christians when seeking to learn about practical subjects. A friend of mine who has a lot going on but is doing it all very well was told by one of his pastors that he should take it easy and not do too much because it "causes worry."

And sometimes when things get overwhelming, it is suggested that we need to "take a retreat with Jesus."

But maybe we've had enough retreats with Jesus. Maybe Jesus wants us to learn how to get things done. Further, we often come back from such retreats with loads of new stuff to do. How do we make those things actually happen? We need to know how to execute — how to get things done and manage ourselves. Developing a great vision for the next quarter or year or season of our lives and ministries will not help much if we don't know how to translate that vision into action.

In fact, I would argue that this downplaying of the practical is not only discouraging but actually an (unwitting) failure of *love*. It's a failure of love because part of the biblical conception of love is giving *practical help* to those who need it, and in our modern society this more and more needs to involve concrete insight on how to get things done and stay above water without burning out or ignoring your family.

WE NEED A CHRISTIAN APPROACH (... BUT NOT LIKE THAT)

Of course, there is a right way and a wrong way to develop a Christian approach to something. Unfortunately, Christians these days often have a reputation for taking the wrong approach.

For example, we've all heard of the proverbial "Christian" painter. He's the guy who goes around trying to get work painting your house not because he's a good painter, but simply because he's a Christian. He thinks that being a Christian makes up for the fact that he doesn't do good work.

That's not what I mean when I say we need to take a Christian approach to productivity!

So, if you want to get solid biblical instruction on how to get things done and understand the things you do every day in connection with your faith, where do you turn?

That's why I've written this book.

THE AIM OF THIS BOOK

My aim in this book is to reshape the way you think about productivity and then present a practical approach to help you become more effective in your life with less stress and frustration, whatever you are doing.

I want to help you live the life that God has called you to live, and to live it with maximum effectiveness and meaning. If you are an executive, I want to help you be a better executive. If you are a homemaker, to be a better homemaker. If you are a pastor, to be a better pastor. If you are a creative professional, to be a better creative professional. If you are a missionary, to be a better missionary. And if you don't know what life God has called you to live, I want to help you find it.

Along with that, I want to equip you to do good in radical, creative ways for the cause of missions, ending extreme poverty (it can be done!), and bringing justice to the oppressed. To do this you don't have to move to Africa but, because of technology, can be involved from right where you are. I want to show you that serving God in the things you do every day *and* going beyond to be engaged in God's global purposes is the life of greatest joy and peace—*not* seeking personal peace, affluence, wealth, or success.

This book is also for those who do not share my faith perspective. Since the gospel is the truth of how God reconciled us to himself, fundamental to doing anything in a "gospel-driven" way is doing it in a way that builds bridges with those who do not share our faith, taking their needs into account and writing in a way that can serve them rather than *simply* writing for other Christians.

Hence, even if you are not a follower of Christ, there is much in this book that you can benefit from. My hope is that seeing what the Scriptures have to say about a concrete subject like productivity will encourage you to consider the claims of Christ, who is at the center of this book. But whichever way you choose, I'm glad you are reading this book and I hope you find it helpful.

WHY WE NEED TO CARE—GREATLY—ABOUT PERSONAL PRODUCTIVITY

We are going to see many new reasons to care about getting things done in this book, and a new twist on some common reasons. Here are a few I want to highlight at the start.

1. Bad productivity approaches are annoying! People are crying out for better approaches to getting things done. They are frustrated not only with the amount they have to do and the difficulty of balancing it all, but also with the approaches they've been taught (or just made up) to get their work done.

It is my contention that bad approaches and productivity systems (and having no system is itself a system!) are one of the chief causes of our frustration. With a bad system, it's hard to get things done with a sense of confidence, relaxed control, and purpose.

The frustration of bad productivity approaches is not a small matter that we can just work around, for we can't run our lives without *some* sort of approach to getting things done. The issue is not whether we have an approach to personal productivity; the issue is whether our approach is a good one or a bad one.

2. Managing ourselves well is foundational to all we do. The importance of these things becomes even more clear when we realize that our ability to lead, manage, spend undistracted time with friends and family, and do everything else we do depends largely upon a skill that goes *underneath* all of those things and makes them all possible—the cross-functional skill of knowing how to manage ourselves.

For example, on the work side of life, Peter Drucker points out, "Executives who do not manage themselves for effectiveness cannot possibly expect to manage their associates and subordinates."[6] He then adds, "Management is largely by example. Executives who do not know how to make themselves effective in their own job and work set the wrong example." Likewise, Steven Hayward points out that "rare is the successful leader or executive with a chaotic mind or chaotic habits."[7]

We weren't made to simply respond to stuff all day, but to take action and move things forward. If we don't give attention to the discipline of personal effectiveness but instead let the flow of events determine what we do, we will likely fritter ourselves away doing all sorts of urgent things that come our way while never getting to the truly important things.

On the personal side of life, few have captured the tragic effects of poor personal management better than Mark Schultz in his song "Do You Even Know Me Anymore?" The second verse is especially poignant: "I turned around to see my son; well I remember his first birthday; now he's twenty-one. I missed his life; I missed it all."

That's tragic. A lot of times we blame this on misplaced priorities. For example, lots of people like to take shots at the poor guy who spent too much time at the office. But I'd like to say a (partial) word in his defense. I think one of the chief reasons some people spend "too much time at the office" is actually because they don't know *how* to do any different. Learning the skill of getting things done helps us avoid this fate.

As we will see in this book, managing yourself well involves more than just getting more done faster. It also involves knowing what the right things to do are—the realm of personal leadership. If we aren't heading in the right direction in our personal lives, we may accomplish our goals only to find out that we were going down the wrong road the whole time.

Mark Schultz gets at this idea in his song as well. The speaker reflects on how time has passed and wonders how he got where he is. Then he says, "I dreamed my dreams; I made my plans; but all I built here is an empty man." He had his plans, but they didn't take him where he thought.

In order to avoid the tragedy of the empty self, we need to know our purpose and direction in life. The last thing anyone wants is to end up having it all, only to realize they have nothing (cf. Luke 9:23–25).

3. A good productivity approach enables us to be more effective in doing good for others. As Christians, we are here to serve (Matt. 20:25–28). When we are being productive, we are actually doing good works, which is part of the purpose for which God created us (Eph. 2:10). A good approach to getting things done reduces the friction in doing good and also *amplifies* our ability to do good. The result is that we can be of more benefit to others with less snags, stress, and confusing systems.

In other words, getting things done, making ideas happen, and being productive are all ways to make a difference in people's lives. As Christians, we ought to care about this and be excited about it, for it is not only exciting in itself, but one of the chief ways God is glorified in our lives.

4. Knowing how to get things done is a component of our sanctification. Since productivity includes serving people and doing good works, it is actually a component of sanctification and Christian discipleship.

Growing in holiness doesn't mean running to the hills to make your own clothes and grind your own wheat until Jesus comes, but living the everyday life that is right in front of you for the glory of God. And, interestingly, our everyday life is the arena of projects and tasks and goals and calendars and email and meetings and strategic planning and all of these very "practical" things—that is, productivity. Since our everyday lives are the arena of our sanctification, knowing how to get things done thus puts us squarely in the realm of sanctification and discipleship. It is therefore a critical tool for living the life God calls us to in this current era.

5. Knowing how to get things done enables us to fulfill God's call to *make plans* for the good of others. This is one of the most exciting reasons to me. The biblical call on our lives is not to do good randomly and haphazardly. Rather, God calls us to be proactive in doing good—even to the point of *making plans* for the good of others.

For example, Isaiah 32:8 says that "he who is noble *plans noble things, and on noble things he stands.*" We often think of doing good simply as something we are to do when it crosses our path. But Isaiah shows us that we are also to *take initiative* to conceive, plan, and then *execute* endeavors for the good of others and the world. (And this requires, of course, actually knowing *how to plan* and actually make our plans happen!)

6. Knowing how to get things done is a component of a complete worldview. When we think of a Christian worldview, we typically think of theology and philosophy. But theology and philosophy are not the only components to a holistic worldview, for no worldview is complete without a perspective on how to live in the world. Thus, part of our worldview must include the issue of "how to get things done." This includes the disciplines of personal management, personal leadership, organizational management, and leadership.

7. Managing ourselves well enables us to excel at work and in life. As Christians we might be tempted to downplay this idea, but it matters! Knowing how to make yourself effective will also likely have benefits in terms of your career advancement. As time management expert Julie Morgenstern notes, "Workers who can consistently decide with clarity and ease which tasks are most important when under pressure are the most prized in every organization. Highly focused in pressure-cooker situations, they rise to meet the challenges of an opportunity-saturated workplace that demands tough calls at every step. Not surprisingly, these employees are also the most calm."[8]

Introduction

THE ROAD TO THIS BOOK

I've always cared about getting things done, but I didn't always give much thought to having a good *process* for getting things done. For a while, this worked. I went through all of college and seminary without even using a calendar, let alone a to-do list (though I did create a list of assignments once). Yet at one point in seminary I took forty-eight hours (sixteen classes) in a nine-month period, and one semester I completed all of my assignments in the first six weeks so that I could have the rest of the semester free from obligations. I used the time to work more and, I think, to do more reading.

But then I started my first full-time job at a ministry called Desiring God, and my first task was not so small: launch a nationwide radio program while managing the church bookstore and conference bookstores at the same time. Shortly after that, leading the web department was added to my plate as well.

In these circumstances, I found that my default practices for getting things done just didn't work. If I was going to do my job well (or even stay afloat), I realized that I had to become more deliberate about how I got things done.

Up to that point, my focus had been learning the Bible and theology. In college I spent most of my days reading theology, talking about it with my friends, writing articles to remember what I was learning, and debating atheists and Jehovah's Witnesses for fun. This helped me gain a firm theological grounding. I then went to seminary because I liked studying the Bible, wanted to add formal study on top of all the studies I had already done on my own, and wanted to prepare for ministry. Now I was in ministry, and I found that there had actually been a gap in my preparation—I hadn't learned about the discipline of personal productivity.

Since I had always read a lot, I decided to find the key books on productivity and then develop an overall approach and system to keep track of what I have to do and stay focused on what is most important.

The two linchpins of my system were David Allen's *Getting Things Done* and Stephen Covey's *First Things First*. I found that Covey was stronger at the higher levels (mission, values, and roles), whereas Allen was stronger at the lower levels (projects and actions). So I created an approach that integrated the two, together with my own insights.

With this productivity approach, I was able to run those three departments at the same time while leading a complete redesign and reengineering of our ministry website on the basis of sound principles of usability. The release of the new website was a turning point for our ministry, and within four months our most important web stats nearly quadrupled.

Learning more about productivity eventually had a surprising side effect, however: my workload increased even more! David Allen says, "The better you get, the better you'd better get" and that was exactly my experience. Being at a ministry where resources are limited and funds are scarce, I made up for the lack not only by using the productivity methods I had learned to work smarter but also by just plain working harder and longer since I loved my job so much.

At one point, for example, I was regularly pulling ninety-hour weeks. Often I pulled two all-nighters in a row; one time I even pulled three all-nighters in a row (my personal record).

I believe there is value in working hard and in working a lot, and I enjoyed it. But that pace was simply not sustainable. Even when I brought my hours down, I was still relying too much on brute force and high energy to get things done. Also, my wife and I had two young kids by this time, and it just wasn't going to be possible to keep doing this. I wasn't even altogether sure my life was going in the direction that I wanted it to.

This pressed me to refine my approach to give a greater place to prioritizing—an approach that focused not primarily on doing more things in less time but rather on doing the right things in a flexible way. It was at this point that I also realized that I had to be more deliberate about thinking biblically about this issue.

The pushback I had received from some in the ministry when I developed my productivity approach was discouraging, but it also helped me. After my pastor made the unfortunate "first grade" comment about productivity, for example, I asked myself what he was really trying to say. My conclusion was that what he really meant to say was simply this: Don't leave all of your theological learning behind; make sure you think about all of this explicitly in relation to God.

My solution was to go back and look more fully at what the Scriptures have to say about productivity and how we have to anchor our understanding of getting things done within the full biblical vision of the Christian life altogether. This involved looking afresh at what the

Productivity Highlights
(and Lowlights!) in My Life

I tend to overload myself, which is part of what led me to seek a productivity approach that is both God-centered and minimizes the friction in getting things done:

High school: Produce and star in a fifty-six-minute movie with a friend of mine who aspires to a career in filmmaking. It is a huge success (for our school!). As is my custom, I seek to follow it up by making not one but two more movies—at the same time, and along with my friend who is also making another movie, for a total of three. I almost overwhelm myself and can't run track that spring as a result, but the movies get done.

College: Attend college on a presidential scholarship with a full ride which, when combined with the other scholarships I get, means I actually get paid to go to college. Spend fourteen hours a day reading, writing, and discussing theology and the Bible with my friends. I leave hardly any time to study for my actual classes, but keep the scholarship with, I think, the smallest GPA margin ever.

First job after college: Almost get fired from my first job because my desk is "too neat," which probably means I'm "not busy enough." A few weeks later, I actually get fired for refusing to illegally sell insurance without a license. The job wasn't a good fit—this is a blessing.

First vacation after college: At some point shortly after college, embark on a mountain bike journey on the White Rim Trail of the Canyonlands with one of my brothers. It's a three-day, 100+ mile ride. Most people have someone drive a jeep with supplies behind them. But we take all our supplies in our backpacks and hook eight gallons of water on to each of our bikes, not realizing that each gallon weighs eight pounds—thus adding sixty-four pounds of weight. This makes it painful and excruciating to ride up and down all the hills. By the end of the first day, we are too exhausted to keep going. We have to carry our bikes up a thousand-foot cliff on a trail meant for hiking in order to get out of the canyon.

Seminary: Take sixteen classes (forty-eight hours) in a nine-month period and do so without using a calendar or to do lists, with the exception of a single list of all my assignments for the second semester. In that semester, finish every assignment in the first two months.

First job after seminary: My first full-time job after seminary is to launch a nationwide radio program while redesigning a major website at the same time. Realize that playing it by ear is not sufficient and decide to get a planner. At one point I'm running three departments at once and regularly working ninety-hour weeks. Regularly pull all-nighters, at one time pulling three in a row.

Redesign of a major ministry website: After developing my productivity approach, launch a complete redesign of a major ministry website. Web stats almost quadruple within four months.

Scriptures have to say not only about productivity but also about work, justice, mercy, and love (which are far more related to productivity than we often think).

Second, I took to the road to interview major Christian leaders on how they got things done. (You will see highlights throughout this book.) Third, I continued to do a lot of reading, and finally, I continued to refine my approach based on what I had learned and through lots of trial and error. Hence, in this book you are going to hear not just about what works but also about some of the pitfalls and interesting mistakes I made as I developed this approach. I hope that I can spare you some of the difficulties I went through!

The key for me was going back to the Scriptures. It wasn't until I more fully understood God's purposes for our lives and how they relate to the things we do every day that I was finally able to prioritize more effectively, get off the hamster wheel, and feel confident that the things I was getting done were actually the things God wanted me to get done.

GOSPEL-DRIVEN PRODUCTIVITY

The result of my quest is what I call *Gospel-Driven Productivity*. (That's just a fancy name for what the Bible has always taught about getting things done.) Gospel-Driven Productivity (GDP) is centered on what the Bible has to say about getting things done while at the same time learning from the best secular thinking out there—and seeking to do this with excellence and original thought, rather than simply taking over secular ideas and adding out-of-context Bible verses. This is what, I believe, God calls us to do.

The essence of GDP is this: We are to use all that we have, in all areas of life, for the good of others, to the glory of God—and that this is the most exciting life. To be a gospel-driven Christian means to be on the lookout to do good for others to the glory of God, in all areas of life, and to do this with creativity and competence. Further, being gospel-driven also means knowing how to get things done so that we can serve others in a way that really helps, in all areas of life, without making ourselves miserable in the process through overload, overwhelm, and hard-to-keep-up systems.

In other words, we are to put productivity practices and tools in the service of God's purpose for us, which is that we do good for others, in all areas of life, to his glory.

There are three preliminary things to recall before I summarize what we will see in each part of the book:

1. *This is about all areas of life.* This isn't just about your work life, though it is about that. Our personal lives should be given just as much attention and intentionality as our work lives. This book aims to help you in all areas of your life, because every area of your life is a calling from God.

2. *Getting "things" done is a slight misnomer.* The reason is that God calls us to do more than just get things done. He calls us to build people up and do many intangibles just as much as we are to do concrete, immediately measurable things. When I talk about getting things done, I almost always have this wider sense in mind.

3. *The importance of structure and method.* I've read a lot of books on productivity that have many great tips, but which I found hard to apply because there wasn't a clear and simple way to

relate them together. I've sought to avoid that here by reducing everything to a few principles and a four-step process. This will enable you to integrate the tips together and more easily apply them to your situation.

Why We Need to Begin with God

Part 1 shows us why it's so hard to get things done, why the typical ideas about efficiency don't work, and how the only way to be ultimately productive is to live our lives for God.

Guiding Principles for a Productive Life

What happens when we look at productivity in light of God and the gospel? Part 2 answers this question and shows how the gospel changes the way we get things done altogether.

This section unpacks the key purposes and mindsets behind GDP. One of the most important things we will see is that the chief guiding principle for being productive is actually *love*. It may seem counterintuitive, but seeking the benefit of others before ourselves is not only what God requires of us but also is the way to be most productive. This is true not just in our personal lives, but also in our work lives. *Generosity* is at the heart of true productivity in all areas of life. This is what the Scriptures teach and, interestingly, what the best business thinkers are also showing. Further, a life of doing good for others is actually the most exciting life, for God calls us to find ways of doing good with a sense of creativity, competence, and adventure.

We also will look at how the only way to be productive is to realize we don't actually have to be productive (our goal is to please God, not appease God), and how the gospel continues to give us peace of mind even when everything is blowing up around us.

The DARE Model

Parts 3–6 are the practical heart of the book. They give us the process behind gospel-driven productivity. We will see that there are four steps for leading and managing yourself for effectiveness: define, architect, reduce, and execute.

1. *Define.* This means not only knowing where you are going, but also knowing your criteria for deciding that altogether. This

is not just a matter of clarifying your values. It is a matter of identifying the right values to have, and basing our lives—our entire lives, especially right here at the center—on those values that God and his Word lift up as central.

This brings us into the realm of mission, vision, roles, and goals. The essence of defining can be summarized this way: Define what's most important in your life based on what God says, not first on what you (or others) think. This is the only way to build a life that lasts and thus is truly productive (Matt. 7:21–27; Prov. 3:5–6; 14:12).

2. *Architect.* Once you've identified the most important principles, goals, and ongoing priorities in your life, you can't just leave it at that. You have to weave these things into the structure of your life through a basic schedule, or time map, because intentions are not enough. A bad (or nonexistent) structure for your life will undo the best of intentions. Setting up a flexible framework for your life also frees you to be less dependent on lists, which was an especially welcome benefit to me once I figured this out. The essence of the architecture step can be summarized this way: Structure your life by living your life mainly from a flexible routine, not a set of lists.

3. *Reduce.* After creating this structure, often you'll find that making everything fit is the biggest obstacle. This doesn't necessarily mean you've architected wrong; it just means you need to reduce. You need to know what's most important (define), weave it into your life (architect), and then get rid of the rest (reduce).

   But you don't get rid of the rest by simply letting balls drop. Rather, you do it by creating systems and using tactics that ultimately expand your capacity. This brings us into the realm of the core practices of day-to-day time management, including delegating, eliminating, automating, and deferring (the DEAD process we will learn), as well as how to turn time killers back on themselves by harnessing them rather than being defeated by them.

   The essence of reducing can be summarized this way: Reduce on the basis of what's most important, not on the basis of misguided notions of living a minimalistic life, and do this by implementing systems that enable you to ultimately expand your capacity overall.

4. *Execute.* This is the stage of making things happen in the moment. It is easy to think of execution as synonymous with productivity, but in reality it is actually only the last step. When you have done the previous steps (define, architect, and reduce), the path is clear for efficient and enjoyable execution. This section will look at the best tactics for making things happen every day.

Conveniently, these form the acronym DARE—which reminds us of the all-important guiding principle that underlies all of this, which is that we should have a *sense of adventure* in doing good. That is, we should be radical and risky and creative and abundant in using our effectiveness to make life better for others. (And, that this is the most exciting life.)

The Results

Part 7 will show us that we need to understand productivity not simply in the sense of personal productivity but also in a broader sense—seeing it as about making our organizations, cities, and society as a whole more productive as well. We will also see that one of the chief things we should seek to do with our increased productivity is to take action to help lift the poor out of poverty, because this is at the heart of the righteousness God requires.

Most of all, we will look at what the Bible teaches about the results of GDP in the world. We will see that as we are productive in a gospel-centered way, God transforms our workplaces, communities, cities, and the entire world for the advancement of the gospel and the good of the world.

In other words, the ultimate result of GDP is the transformation of the world socially, economically, and spiritually, to the glory of God. For as we seek to do good for others to God's glory, the light of the gospel shines through our words and deeds. The result is the transformation of the world. As Martyn Lloyd-Jones said, "If only every Christian in the Church today were living the Sermon on the Mount [which is the anchor of GDP], the great revival for which we are praying and longing would already have started."[9]

Introduction

A WORD ON DOING THIS ALL WRONG

This book is also for screwups and failures! No gospel-centered approach to productivity would be worth its salt if it didn't have at its root what the gospel itself has at its root: helping imperfect people. There is a place for mistakes, screwups, and failures here, not to mention the times when circumstances almost inevitably create chaos and challenges in our lives that are beyond our control.

Likewise, I'm not going to promise that everything will go perfectly for you if you simply master the things I'm talking about. The mark of a truly helpful approach to productivity—and life—is that it keeps you oriented and keeps you going even when everything around you seems to be falling apart. This is a productivity approach for imperfect people in an imperfect world, but with a perfect God who is leading them to what one day will be a renewed world of perfect joy, peace, and righteousness.

BEING PRODUCTIVE IN READING THIS BOOK

Last of all, let me say a word on how to use this book as productively as possible. When a book is simply a long block of text, I find that it makes it hard to grab quick nuggets at a glance. For some subjects, that's great and I enjoy it. But when reading about productivity, we need our books to give us quick access to the core insights. So that's how I've designed this book.

I have designed this book so you can feel productive in reading it, and so that if you want, you can open the book to almost anywhere and find some helpful, immediately applicable things. That's why there are lots of headings, call-out boxes along the way with key tips, a summary box at the end of each chapter, and a toolkit at the very end.

So does God have anything to say about getting things done? Yes, quite a bit. Let's take a look.

PART 1

First Things First

MAKING GOD SUPREME IN OUR PRODUCTIVITY

What does it profit a man if he gains the
whole world and loses or forfeits himself?
—Luke 9:25

CHAPTER 1

Why Is It So Hard to Get Things Done?

How the world of work has changed; and introducing the villains

The knowledge worker cannot be supervised closely or in detail. He can only be helped. But he must direct himself, and he must direct himself toward performance and contribution, that is, effectiveness.

— Peter Drucker, The Effective Executive

WHY IS IT SO HARD TO GET THINGS DONE?

A reader of my blog and a highly successful woman in the business world recently said to me: "I am so overwhelmed right now with my work. The worst part is that I still haven't found a system for managing everything that works well for me and that I'm happy with."

Another friend of mine, this time someone who works at a ministry, recently posted on Facebook: "Is this for real? I'm leaving the office at a normal time!? Too bad it doesn't count when you bring work home."

Most of us can relate. We have too much to do and not enough time to do it. We feel overstressed, overworked, and overloaded. And thanks to new technology and media, we have more coming at us than we ever did before. But the problem is deeper than this. The root of the challenge lies in a major shift our society has undergone in the nature of work itself.

THE RISE OF KNOWLEDGE WORK

What Is Knowledge Work?

Until a few decades ago, we were predominantly an industrial economy. In that era, work was clearly defined for most people. If you were a farmer, for example, you had fields to plow, cows to milk, and equipment to fix. The work was hard and might involve long days, but (most) tasks were generally straightforward and self-evident. (Not to mention that you probably had someone show you the ropes before you took over full responsibility.)

With the shift to a knowledge economy, the nature of work has changed. Unlike in the industrial era, in which tasks were generally self-evident, the essence of knowledge work is that you not only have to *do* the work but also have to *define* what the work is.

For example, if you are painting your house (a form of manual labor), you can see right away where to brush next. But when you get a hundred emails a day (a form of knowledge work), most of which do a pretty poor job of getting to the point, the next actions don't usually come to you predefined. You have to figure out *what* to do with each email, then figure out how to fit that in with all the rest of your work that you have had (or have yet) to define.

Most of us haven't paid sufficient attention to the skill of defining our work clearly. This is why it so often feels like our workdays never stop. When you don't have your work clearly defined, there can never be any finish point.

Knowledge Work

"Knowledge work" is a term coined by Peter Drucker, which means work that consists primarily of creating, using, and communicating knowledge, as opposed to manual labor. Any work whose focus consists of generating ideas, communicating, and leading (which includes your personal life and family) is knowledge work.

What Is Unique about Knowledge Work?

Knowledge work is about creating and utilizing knowledge, but it is more than that. For when your work consists in creating and using knowledge, there is an important consequence: by definition, it must be primarily self-directed.

Peter Drucker points this out well: "The knowledge worker cannot be supervised closely or in detail. He can only be helped. But he must direct himself, and he must direct himself toward performance and contribution, that is, effectiveness."[1]

The freedom this gives us is a fantastic thing. But there is also a challenge.

What Is Challenging about Knowledge Work?

Some people think that knowing how to get things done is obvious—that it just comes naturally to people and that therefore we don't need to spend much time on it.

But that's not the case. In more than fifty years of consulting, Peter Drucker pointed out that he never found a "natural," someone who is instinctively effective. *Every* effective person he encountered—and as perhaps the greatest consultant and business thinker of the twentieth century, that's a lot—had to work at becoming effective.

Brilliant insight, hard work, and good intentions are not enough. Effectiveness is a distinct skill that must be learned. Some people are more inclined to it than others, and everyone is naturally built to be capable of effectiveness, but effectiveness is something we learn—like reading.[2] Drucker says it well: "To be reasonably effective it is not enough for the individual to be intelligent, to work hard or to be knowledgeable. Effectiveness is something separate, something different."[3]

Scott Belsky, founder of Behance (whose mission is "to organize the creative world") and author of *Making Ideas Happen*, makes the same point. Belsky's focus has been the creative world (also a form of knowledge work), where there is often a notion that if you have a great idea, it will naturally turn into reality. In contrast, Belsky writes, "Ideas don't happen because they are great—or by accident. The misconception that great ideas inevitably lead to success has prevailed for too long.... Creative people are known for winging it: improvising and acting on intuition is, in some way, the haloed essence of what we do and who we are. However, when we closely analyze how the most successful and productive creatives, entrepreneurs, and business people truly make ideas happen, it turns out that 'having the idea' is just a small part of the process, perhaps only 1 percent of the journey."[4]

Belsky adds later, "The ideas that move industries forward are not the result of tremendous creative insight but rather of masterful stewardship."[5]

So it takes more than just enthusiasm, great ideas, native talent, and hard work to get things done. It takes a method.

THE VILLAIN OF AMBIGUITY
Ambiguity in Defining Our Work

Knowledge work therefore brings us face to face with the first villain in this story: ambiguity. Ambiguity is not necessarily a villain in itself. It is a good thing that knowledge work has at its essence creating clarity out of ambiguity and making good decisions (i.e., determining what's best next). But when we don't know how to *do* knowledge work, ambiguity becomes a villain because it ends up frustrating us, making life harder, and sometimes defeating us. It's like jumping in the pool without knowing how to swim. Jobs today are not as clear as they were in the industrial era, yet we haven't been taught the skills of navigating this context, learning how to define our work, and managing ourselves for effectiveness.

Further, the most effective knowledge era strategies don't drop from heaven fully defined. We have to figure them out—and that happens by trial and error. As a society, we are still figuring out the best practices for navigating knowledge work—which means we encounter a lot that don't work and many problems along the way.

There are other factors as well:

- We change jobs more frequently.
- We have more nonroutine tasks than ever before.
- Many in highly specialized vocations, such as doctors, engineers, web developers, business analysts, pastors, and so forth, are taught in great detail how to do the activities of their job itself (thankfully!), but they aren't taught much about the *process* for managing their work, managing others, and leading others.

So with the shift from the industrial era to the knowledge era, we now need to decide more than ever what to do, when to do it, and how to do it.

Ambiguity in Defining the Direction of Our Lives

The issue of ambiguity doesn't simply affect us at the level of defining our work; it also affects us at the level of defining the direction of our lives. Our current era is unlike any in history. We have more choices and opportunities before us regarding what to do with our lives than we can even comprehend. Many of us (myself included) have found it hard to know what to do with our lives. And when we've sought out guidance on how to navigate that territory, there hasn't been much to find.

Many are still on that journey, trying to figure it out as they go. That can work, but it's a tough road. Others are blowing it altogether. Too many Christians in their twenties are living in their parents' basements playing video games. That aside, too many people at all stages of life are unclear on what they should be doing. We need to know how to make good choices at this level without expecting to have a map that tells us every detail. This is also part of what it means to manage ourselves, and part of what we will cover later in the book.

THE RISE OF MASS CONNECTIVITY

The rise of knowledge work has happened over the last sixty or so years. We have experienced an even greater revolution over the past fifteen years or so: the rise of mass connectivity. Distance is no longer the barrier it once was. As Tim Sanders has put it, it used to be that "relationships were for the most part geo-bound, and only a handful of people comprised your entire business network."[6] Today, our networks run into the hundreds and thousands, and we can connect with people all over the world through email, Facebook, Twitter, and more.

And we can do this no matter what we are doing. We can be in the back yard camping, on a run (my least favorite time to receive calls), or in a meeting. We can even text internationally. When I was in China recently, it almost felt like I was hardly gone because I could stay in instant communication with my wife through texting (though, unfortunately, I racked up a pretty high bill).

The proliferation of technology has not only increased our daily load of information; it has astronomically increased the rate of change in society and in the world of work altogether. As Tim Sanders notes, "before the information revolution, business changed gradually and business models became antiquated even more slowly. The value progression evolved over decades and double decades. You could go to college, get an M.B.A. and work for forty years, and your pure on-the-job knowledge stayed relevant."[7]

Today, however, our skills become outdated more quickly (except for the macro, *cross-functional skill* of getting things done!). We not only need to keep up with all the information coming our way on a day-to-day basis, but we also need to keep our skills and knowledge up to date with the massive changes that are rapidly occurring at the level of work and society.

This is a fantastic thing and has implications for how we do everything. It has also resulted in a whole lot more to manage—which leads to the second villain.

THE VILLAIN OF OVERLOAD

Just as something good (the rise of knowledge work) brought us head-to-head with the first villain, so also the rise of mass connectivity, though an excellent thing, brings us head-to-head with a second villain: overload.

Massive overload.

In 2008, the web contained one trillion pages. That has risen at an exponential rate, such that in 2013 the quantity of information on the internet began doubling every seventy-two hours. *Every* seventy-two hours—every three days—the amount of information online doubles.

In 2010, 95 trillion emails were sent (about 260 billion per day). That averages to about 153 emails per user per day (there were about 1.86 billion internet users at the beginning of 2010). Currently 92 million tweets are posted per day and 2.5 billion photos are uploaded to Facebook every day.

This amount of information is overwhelming—not simply at an aggregate level but at an individual level (I think most of those 95 trillion emails came to my inbox). We are all feeling this. It is almost impossible to keep up.

How do we make good decisions in the midst of this overload? And how do we keep this overload from sinking us? We can't just float along, like a ship without a rudder, expecting things to go well. We need to take initiative and learn how to navigate this and get things done in spite of the obstacles.

WE NEED TO LEARN HOW TO *WORK*

Here's the bottom line: We are using industrial era tactics for knowledge era work. And that doesn't work.

We need to give more focused attention to learning how to work. Not just the specific content of our jobs but the overarching, cross-functional skill of how to get things done in general—what David Allen calls "high performance workflow management."[8] This can make getting things done more relaxed, simple, and *possible*.

In other words, there are actually two components to doing our work. There are the job skills *themselves*—creating financial statements, writing web content, preaching sermons, leading meetings, and so forth—and then there is *the process of how to do work in general*.

We've done pretty well as a society at learning how to do the content of our jobs. But we haven't been so great at learning the overarching process of how to manage our work: how to keep track of what we have to do, make decisions about what's best to do next, keep from overcommitting ourselves, and do all of this in the midst of seventy-five emails, twelve phone calls, and eighteen interruptions a day.

In past eras, this wouldn't have been such a big deal. But today it is because of the rise of knowledge work and the consequent ambiguity, coupled with the overload that comes from mass connectivity.

EFFECTIVENESS CAN BE LEARNED

I mentioned earlier that effectiveness must be *learned*. Here's the good news: Drucker found that everyone who worked at becoming effective succeeded. And that's what Belsky found as well. Effectiveness has to be learned and, fortunately, *can* be learned.

If we are going to learn effectiveness, we need to do it right. Many people make a wrong turn here, however. In the next chapter, we'll learn what the answer is not.

The Box

Core Point

The reason it's so hard to get things done is that we have transitioned as a society from an industrial economy to a knowledge economy, but we haven't updated our strategies and tactics to align with the nature of knowledge work. The result is that we are unprepared to meet the challenges of ambiguity and overload.

Core Quote

When we closely analyze how the most successful and productive creatives, entrepreneurs, and business people truly make ideas happen, it turns out that "having the idea" is just a small part of the process, perhaps only one percent of the journey.

—Scott Belsky, Making Ideas Happen

Immediate Application

Do you know what your job is? Whether you are a student, in the workforce, or a stay-at-home mom, give thought to identifying the primary purpose of your work, then write it down.

Further Resources

David Allen, "A New Practice for a New Reality," chapter one in *Getting Things Done*
Peter Drucker, "Effectiveness Can be Learned," chapter one in *The Effective Executive*

CHAPTER 2

Why Efficiency
Is Not the Answer

How to avoid killing the knowledge worker

*Nothing is less productive than to make more efficient
what should not be done at all.*

—*Peter Drucker*

WHEN MOST PEOPLE THINK OF PRODUCTIVITY, they think of
efficiency—getting more things done in less time. This is a natural
response to the villain of overload that we saw in the previous chapter.
When we see so many things coming at us, our tendency is to speed
up. This isn't always bad, but if this is our first and primary solution,
it will backfire.

While efficiency is important, it works only when we make it secondary, not primary. It doesn't matter how efficient you are if you are
doing the wrong things in the first place. More important than efficiency
is *effectiveness*—getting the right things done. In other words, productivity is not first about getting more things done faster. It's about getting
the *right things* done.

WHY WE NEED TO PUT EFFECTIVENESS OVER EFFICIENCY
There are six things we need to know about efficiency and why it's the
wrong solution.

1. You can get the wrong things done. The summer before my
senior year of college, I had an internship as a claims representative at
a large insurance company. My role was to travel throughout my state

investigating storm damage claims, determining the amount of loss, and settling each person's claim.

One day toward the end of the summer, my boss had me investigate a fire claim. This claim was local, so it was going to be a quick trip and easy to do. All I had to do was go to the house, take pictures of the inside, and come back.

When I got to the house, the owner wasn't wearing a shirt and seemed slightly surprised to see me. But when I said I was from the insurance company to investigate the fire claim, he let me right in. I went through the whole house, taking pictures of each room, and then told him I'd be in touch. It was simple and quick.

When I got back to the office and gave the photos to my boss, however, he noticed a problem.

"What are these pictures?" he asked.

"The house you had me go to, with the fire claim."

"What? No they aren't." He got a good laugh, and so did the rest of the office, because it turns out I went to the wrong house.

Yes, I took pictures of the entire inside of the house for a damage claim that they had never filed.

Turns out the guy wasn't even insured with us. Why he let me in in the first place—let alone allowed me to take pictures of every room—I have no idea. And, in my defense, the house was a mess. Every room was disordered and filled with laundry and boxes and other stuff. I figured the reason it was in such disarray was because they were dealing with the fallout of the fire, and that the fire must have been limited to a single room and the main problem was minor smoke damage to the walls.

How wrong I was. (I still have the pictures, by the way.)

This little incident shows us why efficiency is not enough. The job was quick and easy, but none of it mattered because I was at the wrong house. I was efficient, but I wasn't effective. Likewise, if my wife asks me to go to the store to get a carton of milk, and I get there and back in record time but return with a carton of orange juice, I haven't been productive. I was efficient, but I wasn't effective.

Thus, more important than how much we get done and how fast we do it is whether we are getting the right things done at all.

2. Efficiency doesn't solve the problem. In many cases, efficiency doesn't even solve the problem of our hectic pace. As Stephen Covey writes, "Traditional time management suggests that by doing

The Virtue of … Inefficiency?

Sometimes the quest for efficiency is a red herring. Consider the example of the first lightbulb, described in *The Bottomless Well: The Twilight of Fuel, the Virtue of Waste, and Why We Will Never Run out of Energy*:

> Thomas Edison's first light bulb wasn't at all efficient. One 1905 observer complained that "the incandescent lamp is an extremely poor vehicle for converting electric energy into light energy, since only about 4 percent of the energy supplied to the lamp is converted into light energy, the remaining 96 percent being converted into heat energy." And the power plant that Edison built to light his bulb didn't convert even 10 percent of its heat into electricity.
>
> But the end-to-end losses of over 99 percent seemed worthwhile to produce such a wonderfully clean, compact, cool, and safe source of light. Efficiency was beside the point. As Jill Jonnes recounts in *Empires of Light*, gas and oil lamps didn't stand a chance against such a superior alternative.*

Sometimes a concern for efficiency undercuts what really matters. To have said "96 percent of the energy that goes into the lightbulb produces heat, not light, so let's get rid of this thing" would have missed the most important thing: we have light. And in a way that is far better than having to use oil lamps.

---

* Peter Huber and Mark Mills, *The Bottomless Well* (New York: Basic Books, 2005), 48.

things more efficiently you'll eventually gain control of your life, and that increased control will bring the peace and fulfillment you're looking for."[1]

But, as he and his coauthors rightly point out, "basing our happiness on our ability to control everything is futile."[2] It will never work. This is why many people are frustrated with most traditional approaches to time management. Simply speeding up doesn't help if you aren't going in the right direction in the first place.

It is good to exercise control over our environment. In fact, it's one of the purposes God gave us when he created us (Gen. 1:28). But especially in this fallen world, it's not possible to control everything. We will make mistakes, and sometimes things will simply be too much for us (cf. 2 Cor. 1:8–11). We need an approach to getting things done that acknowledges this and doesn't require us to keep it up perfectly or to see everything go our way in order to work. Anything else is doomed to futility and will only multiply our pain and frustration.

3. Becoming more efficient can actually make things worse. In fact, increasing your efficiency can actually backfire and make things worse. This is because when you become more efficient, you tend to do more things—and if you aren't doing the right things in the first place, you have just become an expert at doing more of what doesn't need to be done at all.

The best example here is from the world of energy. In their excellent book *The Bottomless Well*, Peter Huber and Mark Mills point out that historically it has been the case that as energy efficiency increases, we actually use more energy, not less. The reason is that as our electronic devices become more efficient, that clears the way for us to do more things with them, and so the amount of energy used goes up.

Now, I actually think this is a good thing when it comes to technology. But when it comes to our lives, it often isn't. If you become more efficient at getting things done, you will tend to do more. If you don't give thought to what that "more" is that you (often unconsciously) take on, you might just end up being incredibly efficient at completely useless things. Talk about the ultimate in unproductivity. As Peter Drucker said, "the most unproductive thing of all is to make more efficient what should not be done at all."

4. The quest for efficiency often undermines the true source of effectiveness in any organization—the people. It gets even worse than this. Not only can the quest for efficiency be wasteful (how's that for irony?); a quest for efficiency often undermines effectiveness as well.

For example, many organizations suffer from the myth that the best way to make a profit (or, for nonprofits, "steward donor money") is to be militant about cutting costs. The problem is that this is often done in ways that undermine their employees, making their work harder and more frustrating, thereby lowering morale. The lower morale, in turn, translates into lower overall productivity for the organization (and higher turnover, a very inefficient expense!).[3]

Worst of all is when the employees themselves are viewed as "cost centers" rather than for what they really are—the true source of value in an organization. When this happens, people begin to be treated like interchangeable parts, and the quest becomes finding the person who can do the work cheapest rather than the person who can do it best.

I've seen this happen firsthand, and it's not pretty. In one instance, some employees in an environment like this remarked, "We better not become too good at our jobs, or we'll be let go just like the people before us." What a shame.[4]

5. Efficiency is often the enemy of innovation. In addition to this, there seems to be an inverse relationship between efficiency and innovation: the more you focus on efficiency (beyond a certain point, at least), the less innovative you will be.[5]

6. The quest for efficiency often overlooks the importance of intangibles, which are now the main source of value in our knowledge economy. Tim Sanders rightly notes that "success in the future [which is now!] will be based on the fuzzy intangibles: the culture you nurture, the processes for managing information you set up for your people, the partnerships you form around technology's opportunities and challenges."[6]

Technology, hardware, and capital can be copied easily. What can't be copied easily is the culture and human capacity that create those in the first place—and does so in a way that engages not just functionally with people but also emotionally, so that people *want* what your organization offers. Effectiveness, in work and life, is thus more and more about the intangibles because effectiveness comes from *people* first, not things. Things are replicable; people aren't.

So many organizations miss this, and that's why they are miserable places to work. People become clock watchers, just putting in the time, because the organization doesn't care about them but cares only about what they can do. In my opinion that's not just unfortunate; it's unethical. It's not right to treat people that way because people are made in the image of God and are more than economic beings. They work for meaning as well as for a paycheck. Therefore, we ought to manage to the whole person, treating people *as people*, not as machines who are merely here to get a job done. And ironically, when you treat people this way, even though it is harder at first, you get higher productivity in the long run.

The tendency to focus only on immediate, directly measurable results is a huge fallacy in most organizations today. Way back in 1982, Tom Peters and Robert Waterman termed this "the numerative bias" and gave example after example of how a narrow concern for numbers leads managers and leaders to overlook the things that really make their products and services shine, and thus leads them to do things to "cut costs" and increase the bottom line that actually end up undermining their results in the long term.[7]

This is the great irony: defining productivity mainly in terms of immediate measurable results undermines the measurable results in the long run.

The time and energy and resources you invest in the intangibles is not lost; it is not a "cost of doing business." It is an investment that pays substantial returns in the long run. It's just that you can't always draw a direct and immediate line to the results. But the results are there, and the connection is there, just as the farmer who sows a crop in the spring sees results not immediately but in the fall, when it's time to harvest. So also we need to have this long-term view when it comes to our effectiveness and productivity, both as individuals and as organizations.

One of the biggest examples of investing for the long run for the knowledge worker is attending conferences. I believe that all knowledge workers should go to every conference they can because these are prime opportunities to connect with people and share ideas—the essence of knowledge work. But many think that going to a conference is a luxury or a bonus, something to do only if you can get your other, "real" work done.

But nothing could be further from the truth. Going to conferences is a key part of the work of any leader and manager. It is one of the many intangibles that define the essence of knowledge work in our day.[8]

USING EFFICIENCY RIGHT

The quest to cut costs and "be efficient" often ends up rendering people and organizations ineffective. I call this "superficial efficiency," and it is perhaps enemy number one to worker satisfaction and productivity in the workforce right now.[9]

The far greater priority than becoming more efficient is learning how to identify what's most important—that is, what's best—and then translate that into action. The mistake of superficial efficiency is that it sacrifices people on the altar of tasks. That's backward. As we will see later, efficiency exists so that you can serve others better, not sacrifice them to efficiency.

One of the best places for efficiency is being efficient with things *so that* you can be effective with people. If you become more efficient with things (for example, by setting up your computer, desk, workflow system, and files to operate in the most efficient way possible), you will have more time to give to being effective with people without feeling like you are always behind on your tasks.

The primacy of effectiveness, of course, leads to another question: If the answer to our problem is not getting more things done but instead getting the right things done (effectiveness), how do we know what the right things are? That's the next chapter.

The Box

Core Point

True productivity is not first about efficiency — doing things right and doing them quickly — but effectiveness — doing the right things.

Immediate Application

Are you focusing on effectiveness or efficiency? If you manage people, do you manage to the whole person and in light of the fact that people are more important than things?

Further Resources

Stephen Covey, "How Many People On Their Deathbed Wish They'd Spent More Time at the Office?" chapter 1 in *First Things First*

"The Wrong Way to Respond to a Recession": *http://www.whatsbestnext.com/2009/03/the-wrong-way-to-respond-to-a-recession/*

"Recessions Are Not for Hunkering Down": *http://www.whatsbestnext.com/2009/01/recessions-are-not-for-hunkering-down/*

CHAPTER 3

Why We Need to Be God-Centered in Our Productivity

To live your life without God is the most unproductive thing you can do: going beyond principle-centeredness to God-centeredness

> *I watched my days turn in to years, and now I'm wondering how I wound up here. I dreamed my dreams, I made my plans, but all I built here is an empty man.*
> —*Mark Schultz, "Do You Even Know Me Anymore?"*

WE SAW IN CHAPTER 1 that we are encountering two chief villains that make it hard to get things done: ambiguity and overload. As a result, we need to learn how to work, and as we saw in chapter 2, the approach we develop needs to focus on effectiveness over efficiency.

Just learning how to work, however, is still not enough because there is a third villain we haven't met yet. As much as we need to address ambiguity and overload, tackling them by themselves is not enough. We need to counter them in a way that also overcomes the third villain: lack of fulfillment.

THE QUEST FOR PEACE OF MIND

In many ways, the aim of time management can be boiled down to the quest for peace of mind—getting things done with less stress and finding greater fulfillment in what we do. Yet even on days when we get a lot done, we often still feel unfulfilled at the end of the day. We can even feel unfulfilled if we have a life that seems to have it all.

Time management expert Roger Merrill tells the story, for example, of a man who was vice president of a multinational corporation with a great family, home, and life in general, who nonetheless confessed to him, "My life is full of good things—a nice house, a nice car, a good job, a busy life. But when you asked us to think deeply about our lives, to come to grips with what matters most, it really brought me up short."[1]

Most of us can relate to that. Why is this? What's the problem?

Let's start with the question of why we so often feel unfulfilled at the end of the day, even when we've gotten a lot done.

WHY WE ARE SO OFTEN UNFULFILLED AT THE END OF THE DAY

The source of our lack of fulfillment is not just that the best of our intentions often get knocked away from us. The deeper reason is that we feel unfulfilled when there is a gap between what is most important to us (the realm of personal leadership) and what we are actually doing with our time (the realm of personal management).

You are satisfied with your day when there is a match between what you value and how you spent your time. On the other hand, when what you actually work on and accomplish during the day is mostly different from what really matters to you, you feel unfulfilled. Not because you didn't get much done—in many cases, you have—but because the things you were getting done weren't the things that you value.

In his book *First Things First*, Stephen Covey points out that the creation of systems in pursuit of time management has progressed through four generations in an attempt to solve this problem. While these generations build on one another and are sequential in a sense, each of these generations is still around today, and it is important to know which generation we tend to default to.

FOUR GENERATIONS OF TIME MANAGEMENT

The first generation of time management focused primarily on getting organized. The thinking here was that if you can get everything in order, you will have peace of mind. The main tools for this generation were lists and reminders, especially the daily to-do list.

The second generation incorporated reminders but took things up a notch by adding calendars and goal setting. The focus became not only keeping track of what is right before you but also looking ahead to the future, setting goals, and being explicit about achieving long-term aims.

Giving more thought to the future was a big step forward, but many people soon realized that it wasn't enough just to make commitments and set goals. They realized that our plans and goals need to accord with what matters to us. Hence, the third generation goes beyond setting goals and making long-term plans to identifying values and then connecting your planning and goals to those values.

Values clarification was a major advancement. As we mentioned earlier, if the things you are accomplishing are out of sync with your values, you won't feel productive or satisfied no matter how much you've done.

There is, however, one more problem: you can have the wrong values. Stephen Covey makes this case well, pointing out that there are certain realities that are true and significant in themselves, regardless of what we think. If your values are not in accord with these principles— the things that are truly important in life—you will not have true peace and fulfillment and joy.

Covey, therefore, sets forth a new approach to time management, which he calls a fourth-generation approach. The fourth generation is based not just on values, but also on *principles*.

The point is that instead of just determining whatever values you want, you need to base your values on correct principles: unchanging truths and ideals that truly represent what is most important, principles such as truth, justice, fairness, generosity, kindness, and equality. While values are subjective, principles are objective. The key to effectiveness is to value correct principles and weave them into your life. The fourth generation of time management is called principle-centered leadership,[2] and as Covey points out, it has major ramifications not only for personal management but also for organizational management and leadership.[3]

THE NEED FOR A FIFTH GENERATION: GOD-CENTEREDNESS

Covey has made an excellent contribution, and he gives us a lot of solid, common-grace wisdom. He is right that we can have the wrong values and that we need to value correct principles. This is important, and I think Covey is right that, unless we do this, our productivity ultimately becomes misguided. However, I want to argue that he doesn't go far enough. We cannot stay at simply being principle-centered; we need to go beyond being principle-centered to being God-centered.

The center of your life is your source of guidance, security, and meaning. To be God-centered, then, is to make God the source of your guidance, security, and meaning. It is to put him first in your life, to regard him as more important than anything else, to make his glory the chief aim of your life, to do everything you do to please and honor him, and to live your life in relationship with him.

Why We Need to Center Our Lives on God, Not Just Principles

The only way to find fulfillment and be productive in the ultimate sense is to center our entire lives—and therefore our productivity—on God. It is good to be principle-centered, but we need to go beyond being principle-centered to being God-centered. Consider a few reasons.

1. God is foundational to true principles. The problem with simply being principle-centered is that there is something more fundamental even than principles—namely, *God*. God is the source of all true principles.

Many people who read Covey automatically make this adjustment. When they read "principle-centered," they take it to mean "God-centered." It also is true that thinking in terms of principle-centeredness establishes true and real common ground among Christians and those who do not share the faith. For example, in leading a business, I don't think you need to make your business a formally "Christian business" to please God. God has given natural law (what is evident through conscience and nature) to guide secular society so that both Christians and non-Christians can engage in it together.

However, when we consider this individually in our own lives, and when we consider this as leaders of specifically Christian organizations (churches, ministries, faith-based nonprofits, families, and so forth), we ought to be deliberate about taking the further step to God-centeredness, and to being consciously and explicitly so.

For example, Proverbs 9:10 is one of the most well-known passages in the wisdom literature of the Bible. It states, "*the fear of the Lord* is the beginning of wisdom." Likewise, Proverbs 3:5–6 says, "Trust in the Lord with all your heart, and do not lean on your own understanding. In all your ways *acknowledge him*, and he will make straight your paths."

Or consider Ephesians 5:17, the fundamental New Testament passage on time management. This passage speaks of time management as not being chiefly about applying correct principles to our lives but being about understanding "the *will of the Lord*" and doing it. Productivity is specifically about doing "the will of the Lord." It's about specifically orienting our lives and decisions around God's will. We are to ultimately be Christ-centered, not just principle-centered.

This is life altering. The most important reality in the universe is not a set of principles, but a person. As a result, our aim becomes not simply to value certain truths but to please, honor, and love God. It makes productivity personal in the fullest sense, and makes our whole lives one of fellowship with God, rather than a following of principles. It gives us even more guidance than simply being principle-centered, for God is a living being.

2. God ultimately defines what the right things are to get done. It is popular to speak of productivity in terms of "getting the right things done." But what are the right things we need to get done? If God exists and has revealed himself, getting the right things done means doing the things *God* wants done—and in the way he wants them done.

3. God is "what matters most." Productivity books often talk in terms of accomplishing "what matters most." God is, by definition, the most important reality in the universe. Consequently, it makes sense that if we care about living in line with what matters most, we need to center our lives—and therefore our attempts at productivity—around him. Why would we center our lives around something less significant than the most important being in the universe?[4]

Why We Need to Center Our Lives on God over Ourselves

There are many centers you can have in your life other than principles. As Covey points out, you can be money-centered, work-centered, pleasure-centered, possession-centered, self-centered, even spouse-centered, family-centered, or church-centered. None of those are bad in themselves. They just aren't to be the center of our lives.

Perhaps the chief competitor to God-centeredness is simply making our own aims our center. This, then, leads us to be work-centered, or possession-centered, or pleasure-centered, or having any of those other centers.

So it's important to say that not only do we need to go beyond principle-centeredness to God-centeredness; we also need to avoid the trap of settling for any other center. In fact, a concern for productivity naturally points us to the need for us to put God's purposes at the center of our lives and productivity, rather than our own purposes. Consider a few reasons.

1. We will give an account to God of how we spent our time. The apostle Paul states, "For we will all stand before the judgment seat of God.... Each of us will give an account of himself to God" (Rom. 14:10, 12). This account has to do with all of our life, including how we treat people and operate at work (see Eph. 6:5–9) and not just the time we spend (or don't spend) at church.

This means that *God* is the ultimate measure and judge of our productivity. Things that do not pass muster at the final judgment are, by definition, not productive in an ultimate sense. On the other hand, passing the final judgment is the ultimate meaning of a productive life.[5] Hence, in order to know what is truly productive, we need to look to God first, not ourselves or even our own desires.

2. Excluding God is the ultimate in unproductivity. Jesus makes an important statement in Luke 9:25: "What does it profit a man if he gains the whole world and loses or forfeits himself?" Now that is the ultimate in unproductivity: gaining the entire world but losing yourself. Then what do you have?

If you get everything you want in this life, but do it apart from God and receive no eternal value from what you've done, have you been productive? Not in the slightest. Productivity cannot be accomplished apart from Christ. "I am the vine; you are the branches. Whoever abides in me and I in him, he it is that bears much fruit, for apart from me you can do nothing" (John 15:5). On the other hand, if you live a life that pleases God, in spite of the fact that you are persecuted and mistreated for it, have you been productive? Yes. For God will make up for this in eternity and reward you greatly. "Everyone who has left houses or brothers or sisters or father or mother or children or lands, for my name's sake, will receive a hundredfold and will inherit eternal life" (Matt. 19:29).

3. God offers ultimate productivity. When we are productive in Christ and for his sake, everything we do has an eternal impact. Literally everything. "In *everything* he does, he prospers" (Ps. 1:3). "Therefore, my beloved brothers, be steadfast, immovable, always abounding in the work of the Lord, knowing that *in the Lord your labor is not in vain*" (1 Cor. 15:58).[6] We are to *abound* (be productive) in the work of the Lord and, beyond that, we are to know that the abundant results of our work in the Lord will not be simply temporal but will last forever (they are not "in vain").

If we care about productivity, then it makes sense that we would want the things we do to have an eternal impact and last forever. That's the ultimate in productivity. We have this when we do everything we do for Christ, in his power, and for his glory. It is ultimately *unproductive* to look only at this life.

4. God answers our need for fulfillment. As Augustine said, God has made us for himself, and our hearts are restless until they find our rest in him. Or as Jesus said, "Whoever drinks of the water that I will give him will never be thirsty again. The water that I will give him will become in him a spring of water welling up to eternal life" (John 4:14). The chief villain of the story—lack of fulfillment—is answered and conquered only by God himself.

The ultimate reason to center your life and productivity on God is because Jesus is worth it. Jesus is what makes it "your best life now," if we were to talk in those terms (though I prefer "your best life—later").

5. God does a better job of planning our lives than we ever can. While it is important for us to make plans and work for those plans to succeed, we don't want to fall into the trap of planning our entire lives in meticulous detail, for this simple reason: we are finite and fallible creatures.

You don't want to be the one to plan your whole life, because God does a better job than you ever will. Again, there is a place for planning. But if your plans are never upset or disrupted, if all that happens to you is something you have planned, your productivity will be very limited. Some of the best, most productive moments in life are the things that we don't plan—the surprises of life.

THE ULTIMATE VILLAIN BEHIND ALL THE OTHERS

There is an even deeper reason why centering our lives on our own aims or even on correct principles cannot overcome the three villains of ambiguity, overload, and lack of fulfillment. For, from a biblical perspective, we can go deeper than simply acknowledging the presence of the villains and draw the curtain back behind the villains themselves.

The Bible tells us that creation is under a curse because of our sin. Here's what God said to Adam after he sinned in the garden: "Cursed is the ground because of you; in pain you shall eat of it all the days of your life; thorns and thistles it shall bring forth for you" (Gen. 3:17–18).

When we read that, we typically think of manual labor—that the curse that God placed on Adam was that manual labor would become exceedingly difficult. Farming would no longer produce abundant crops as easily, there would be droughts and floods, thorns would annoy us when we till the ground and walk through meadows, and gardeners would have to fight weeds.

Genesis 3, however, isn't the only place where the Bible describes the curse of the fall. The end of the Pentateuch, in Deuteronomy 28, gives us a more complete elaboration of the curse. It is interesting, then, that Deuteronomy speaks of "confusion" (v. 20) and "confusion of mind" (v. 28) as part of the curse, along with "frustration in all you undertake to do" (v. 20).

In other words, the curse of the fall didn't affect only manual work, as we often seem to think. The curse also affected knowledge work. Excessive ambiguity that prevents us from figuring out how to navigate is really a form of confusion; overload is one of many forms that "frustration in all that you do" takes. The inordinate challenges we face in knowledge work can be traced to the fall just as much as the challenges in manual work.

Sin especially lies behind the villain of lack of fulfillment. The reason we lack fulfillment is because we aren't fulfilling our true purpose—that is, because we have sinned and deviated from God's path. What a tragedy: we have a purpose (the highest possible—to reflect and glorify God), and yet we can't fulfill it. This is a terrible situation.

Behind the villains, then—behind all of them—is sin and the curse it brought onto the world.

The good news? The curse will be done away with. Christ has already dealt the decisive blow, and we will see the fullness of his victory when he returns.

But in the meantime, when it comes to issues of our work and how we can lessen the effects of the curse right now, what's the solution?

TO BEGIN WITH GOD MEANS TO BEGIN WITH THE GOSPEL

The solution, as we have seen, is to begin with God, to be God-centered in our productivity. This means that we need to serve God according to how he wants to be served, not how we think he should be served. We find out what God wants by looking to what he has revealed in the Scriptures.

What does the Bible say about how God wants to be served? This is an important question, for it's possible to begin with God in the wrong way. If we view centering our productivity on God as a matter of identifying his standards and then seeking to meet them through our own efforts, we have missed the point.

It is right and good to live according to God's standards, to be sure. But something needs to happen first, before we can even do that— something even more foundational. The problem is that, because of our sin, we have missed God's standards. The solution to this is not to try harder. The solution we need is *forgiveness*.

This is why it is especially important for our approach to productivity to be gospel-driven, based first on the provision that God has given in his Son for our sins, not on what we do for God. For if the challenges we are encountering are ultimately a result of sin and the fall, then the only ultimate solution to them is in the gospel—God's solution to our sin problem.

But does God really care about productivity? And can there even be a *gospel*-centered approach to a seemingly secular subject like productivity? Not everyone thinks there can be. That's the next chapter.

The Box

Core Point

We can be productive in an ultimate sense only if we center our productivity around God and the gospel.

Core Passage

Trust in the Lord with all your heart, and do not lean on your own understanding. In all your ways acknowledge him, and he will make straight your paths.

—Proverbs 3:5–6

Immediate Application

Where do you look to define what matters most? What would change if you looked to Christ to define what matters most in your life?

Further Resources

Timothy Keller, *Counterfeit Gods: The Empty Promises of Money, Sex, and Power, and the Only Hope That Matters*

Rick Warren, "What Drives Your Life?" Day 3 in *The Purpose Driven Life*

Steven Covey, "Possible Perceptions Flowing out of Various Centers," "Inside Out," and "Habit 2: Begin with the End in Mind," appendix A, chapter 1, and chapter 3 in *The Seven Habits of Highly Effective People*

John Piper, *Desiring God: Meditations of a Christian Hedonist*

CHAPTER 4

Does God Care about Getting Things Done?

Why knowing how to get things done
is actually an essential component of
sanctification and Christian discipleship

*Aimless, unproductive Christians contradict the creative,
purposeful, powerful, merciful God we love.*
—*John Piper,* Don't Waste Your Life

DOES GOD ACTUALLY CARE ABOUT getting things done? Is it spiritual to be productive, or does God wish you spent all your time at church instead? Is being productive actually a "Christian" thing to do?

We saw the need for a biblical view in the previous chapter. But to advocate for a biblical view on productivity raises some questions. For example, we might wonder whether God has anything to say about such practical things as our work. Or we might fear that if he does, he might have strange things to say (like "stop working hard and just pray," or something like that).

Sometimes as Christians we inadvertently give fuel to those strange notions. For example, one Christian author has said, "I think the need of the hour is for more holy ambition, not more training in workflow systems. Jesus didn't say much about organizing. He did say a lot about passion for what's most important. Passion is a far better prioritizer than any productivity system. Soul refreshment comes from seeing glory, not getting stuff done."

This is the tension we face as Christians when it comes to the issue of productivity. Most of us have found that it is harder to get things done than it ought to be. Yet, on the other hand, there is also this notion out there that productivity is not a very "spiritual" issue.

So before we look at how the gospel changes the way we get things done, we first need to look at how the gospel *doesn't* change the way we get things done.

To do this, we need to ask three questions:

1. Does God actually want us to be productive?
2. Does God want us to learn about managing ourselves well?
3. What does it mean to think Christianly about a secular subject like productivity?

DOES GOD WANT US TO BE PRODUCTIVE?

We aren't just marking time here on earth. God has given us purposes to fulfill, he requires us to fulfill them, and we will be held accountable for doing so. Productivity is not simply a subject that is fascinating or that helps make our lives easier. It is, at root, a biblical concern and a fundamental issue before God. The innate desire we have to be productive and do useful things is an echo of this.

The Creation Mandate: God Created Us to Be Productive

We see this first of all in the creation mandate: "Be fruitful and multiply and fill the earth and subdue it, and have dominion over the fish of the sea and over the birds of the heavens and over every living thing that moves on the earth" (Gen. 1:28).

This is the charter that God gave to the human race, and at the heart of it is the command to be productive and create culture. Notice, for example, the word "subdue." As theologian Wayne Grudem points out, "The word translated 'subdue' implies that Adam and Eve should make the resources of the earth useful for their own benefit, and this implies that God intended them to develop the earth so that they could come to own agricultural products and animals, then housing and works of craftsmanship and beauty, and eventually buildings, means of transportation, cities, and inventions of all sorts."[1]

We see people beginning to fulfill the creation mandate right away, as they began to grow food (Gen. 4:2), create cities (Gen. 4:17), play musical instruments (Gen. 4:21), and forge tools (Gen. 4:22), thus showing that we are to be productive in creating culture and meeting the full range of needs.

To be productive, in fact, glorifies God because when we are productive we are not only obeying him but imitating him. Wayne Grudem perhaps captures this best: "It may be that God created us with such needs because he knew that in the process of productive work we would have many opportunities to glorify him. When we work to produce (for example) pairs of shoes from the earth's resources, God sees us imitating his attributes of wisdom, knowledge, skill, strength, creativity, appreciation of beauty, sovereignty, planning for the future, and the use of language to communicate. In addition, when we produce pairs of shoes to be used by others, we demonstrate love for others, wisdom in understanding their needs, and interdependence and personal cooperation (which are reflections of God's Trinitarian existence)."[2]

This also helps us understand better the biblical response to the quote earlier that "soul refreshment comes from seeing glory, not getting stuff done." Biblically speaking, I say yes to the importance of passion and finding our refreshment in the glory of God. But, as C. S. Lewis points out in his sermon *The Weight of Glory*, our desire is not only to see glory but also to participate in the glory we see. This comes in part through reflecting it and imitating it, as any parent of young children knows. When we are getting things done, creating, and making ideas happen, we are not only fulfilling part of God's purpose for us but also reflecting his own character and attributes, which allows us to enjoy his character and attributes in a way that simply observing them does not.

The Parable of the Talents: Jesus Requires a Return on Your Life

Consider also the parable of the talents in Matthew 25:14–30. Illustrating the final judgment, Jesus tells the story of a man going on a journey who entrusts his property to his servants. One receives five talents and makes five talents more, another receives three talents and makes three talents more, and another receives one talent and buries it in the ground.

The first two were productive with what the landowner had given them. The last one was not. When the landowner returned, what was his response? Did he say to the third person, "You know, productivity isn't a very spiritual issue anyway, and it was only one talent. A single talent doesn't even matter"? Not even close.

The person who buried his talent was *rebuked* and called faithless. (Interesting—to play it safe is not more commendable to God but actually is considered faithless!) The other two, however, were commended. They took what they had received and made a return on it. They were *productive* with it.

Jesus' point is that God requires the same of us. The "talents" that he has given us are all that we have—our gifts, literal "talents," the ability to work and earn money (see Deut. 8:18), time, energy, opportunities, everything. When we reach the final judgment, we are not to give back to the Lord simply what we were originally given. We are to get a return on our lives and return to Jesus more than he gave us. And if we do this,

The Single Best Piece of Advice I Heard in All My Interviews

Mike Allen, of the Washington, DC, based news organization Politico, got right to the core of things and gave the single best piece of advice I encountered in all of my interviews.

Q: How would you define productivity?
A: Being a maximum steward of your time, talents, and resources.

Q: What are the biggest obstacles to your productivity?
A: The biggest obstacle is what I think afflicts all of us: the amount of input. The amount of data and inputs are a blessing, but a challenge to manage.

Q: For Christians who want to be productive and make the most of their time, what is the most important piece of advice you would give?
A: To every day think about what is the single thing you could do today that would serve God and your employer or audience or family. And if you think about one thing that you can do, you'll increase the odds that you'll do it. Just do it. Instead of putting it on a list, pick one thing and do it.

he will say to us, "Well done, good and faithful servant. You have been faithful over a little; I will set you over much. *Enter into the joy of your master*" (Matt. 25:21).

DOES GOD WANT US TO MANAGE OURSELVES WELL?

I would argue that the call to be productive (Gen. 1:28) also implies the need to learn *how* to be productive. Yet, this is a slightly different question from "Does God want us to be productive?" because one could presumably say "Yes, God wants us to be productive, but he doesn't want us to fiddle with things like workflow systems and productivity tips and tools."

The Importance of Intentionality

But what we see in the Scriptures is that productivity doesn't happen accidentally. We are called to be intentional in the way we live our lives. Note again, for example, Ephesians 5:15–17, the core New Testament passage on productivity: "*Look carefully* then how you walk, not as unwise but as wise, *making the best use of the time*, because the days are evil. Therefore do not be foolish, but understand what the will of the Lord is" (emphasis added).

We are not to breeze through life, taking whatever comes. We are to "look carefully" how we walk. You don't just walk through a store with your eyes closed, buying whatever you touch, and expect it to turn into a wardrobe. And neither should you do that with your life. Likewise, we are to "make the most" of the time. The time doesn't make the most of itself; we are to take back the time from poor uses and turn it to good uses.

Further, a concern for good use of our time is a characteristic that the Bible expects us to have. Consider Psalm 90:12: "Teach us to number our days that we may get a heart of wisdom." I like how the New American Standard Bible puts this: "Teach us to number our days, that we may present to Thee a heart of wisdom." Even our growth in wisdom and our ability to manage ourselves is something we do for God and present to him.

We saw in the previous chapter that a concern for time management should actually lead us right up to God. What we see here is that love for God should also lead us to be concerned with time management. As Peter O'Brien has said, "those who are wise will have a right attitude toward time."[3]

An Affirmation of Personal Effectiveness

The Scriptures get even more concrete on the issue of personal effectiveness. Notice how in Ephesians 5:15–16 Paul placed walking as "wise" people in parallel with "making the most of the time." We are to walk "not as unwise *but as wise*, making the most of the time."

Paul isn't simply saying here that the wise make the most of their time (though he certainly is saying that). He is actually connecting his exhortation to the central Old Testament theme of wisdom.

As most commentators point out, Paul is referring to the wisdom literature of the Old Testament as central to aiding us in discerning the Lord's will for our actions and making the most of our time: "Paul commends to the believers the vast Old Testament teaching about wisdom, especially as represented by the books of Proverbs and Ecclesiastes. There they can find ethical insight into God's will."[4]

In addition to pointing us to the wisdom literature generally, his exhortation here connects with several specific passages. One of those passages is Proverbs 6:6–8, where we are also told to "be wise": "Go to the ant, O sluggard; consider her ways, and *be wise*. Without having any chief, officer, or ruler, she prepares her bread in summer and gathers her food in harvest."

Paul's command that we walk "as wise" people in Ephesians 5:15 hooks up with Proverbs 6:6, where we see that managing yourself well, like the ant, is an essential component of wisdom.

What we see here is that in commanding us to walk as wise people, Paul is not simply commanding us to be wise in spiritual things (though that is there; cf. Prov. 11:30). He is also calling us to be wise in relation to how we live in this world—specifically, to be wise in how to lead and manage ourselves, just like the ant.

Knowing how to get the right things done—how to be personally effective, leading and managing ourselves well—is indeed biblical, spiritual, *and* honoring to the Lord. It is not unspiritual to think about the concrete details of how to get things done; rather, this is a significant component of Christian wisdom.

PRODUCTIVITY AND DISCIPLESHIP

What we see here is that there is no distinction between learning how to be productive and learning how to live the Christian life altogether, for both are about how we are to live in this world for the glory of God.

The way we go about handling our email, making appointments, running meetings, attending classes, and running the kids to where they need to go are not distinct from the everyday life of sanctification that God calls us to but are themselves a fundamental part of it. We are to "be wise" in them just as we are to be wise in the things that directly pertain to salvation; indeed, the way we go about them is an expression of our Christlikeness and sanctification.

THINKING CHRISTIANLY ABOUT PRODUCTIVITY

A Christian perspective on prayer makes sense, but what about a Christian perspective on getting things done? How can that even be?

The brief answer is that, as Christians, our faith changes our motives and foundations but not necessarily the methods we use.

For example, a Christian doctor and a non-Christian doctor will likely go about heart surgery in the same way, using the best practices they've learned from their training and experience. Both will also seek the good of the patient rather than their own ends. But the Christian has an additional motive: loving God and seeking to serve him. This is a difference that is fundamental but that can't necessarily be seen.

That's not always the only difference—sometimes there *are* variations in our methods (for example, the Christian doctor will likely pray before the surgery)—but it is the main difference.

Another change our faith makes is that it puts our work on a different foundation. We look to God for power to do all we do, including our work, and act not out of a desire to *gain* his acceptance, because we already have it in Christ.

With the issue of productivity, then, we will likely utilize the same best practices as non-Christians in things like processing workflow and emptying our email inboxes. But when it comes to the motive and foundation of our productivity, the gospel brings in some radical transformations.[5]

THE BEGINNINGS OF A NEW DEFINITION OF PRODUCTIVITY

What we've seen in this chapter gives us a new starting point for knowing what is productive and what the right things are to get done. At root, what we see is that productive things are things that pass muster at the final judgment—and hence receive the verdict of being "eternally productive."

First Things First

At the same time, this does not take us off into some spiritual never land, but actually underscores the importance of the things we do every day and knowing how to navigate our lives in this world, because it is *in* the things we do every day that we serve God and others.

We will see this more fully in the next section when we look more specifically at what God wants done.

The Box

Core Point

God wants us to be productive and even cares about things like productivity methods and secular thinking.

Core Quote

Paul commends to the believers the vast Old Testament teaching about wisdom, especially as represented by the books of Proverbs and Ecclesiastes. There they can find ethical insight into God's will.
— Zondervan Illustrated Bible Background Commentary on Ephesians

Core Passage

Go to the ant, O sluggard; consider her ways, and be wise. Without having any chief, officer, or ruler, she prepares her bread in summer and gathers her food in harvest.
— Proverbs 6:6–8

Immediate Application

Grow in your ability to get things done. (In other words, keep reading this book!)

Further Resources

Wayne Grudem, *Business to the Glory of God: The Bible's Teaching on the Moral Goodness of Business*
Leland Ryken, *Redeeming the Time: A Christian Approach to Work and Leisure*

PART 2

Gospel-Driven Productivity

A NEW WAY TO LOOK AT GETTING THINGS DONE

Wilberforce sat at his desk at that foggy Sunday morning in 1787 thinking about his conversion and his calling. Had God saved him only to rescue his own soul from hell? He could not accept that. If Christianity was true and meaningful, it must not only save but serve.
— *Charles Colson, preface to William Wilberforce's* A Practical View of Christianity

THE FUNDAMENTAL TRUTH behind this book is that *the gospel changes everything*. It affects the way we go about all areas of life—the workplace, business, the arts, culture, serving the poor, everything. We are to live all of our lives in a gospel-centered way. When we are driven by the gospel, we act in God's power and work for the peace and prosperity of everyone (Jer. 29:4–7). And God's call on us is to do this through all kinds of work, not just ministry work.

We saw in part 1 why we need to put God and the gospel at the center of our productivity. In this section, we will look at what happens when we do that. In brief, we will see that, when considered in light of the gospel, to be productive is to be abundant in doing good for others, according to our gifts and abilities. Productivity is about making a contribution and giving more than we get so that God gets the glory (not us).

How do we unleash ourselves to be maximally productive and effective in doing good while overcoming the villains of overload, ambiguity, and unfulfillment that we saw in part 1? That brings us to the essence of this book: Gospel-Driven Productivity.

Gospel-Driven Productivity (GDP) is an approach to personal productivity that is based on the Scriptures without rejecting good common-grace wisdom or being spiritually weird. It takes what the Bible and common grace teach us on this matter and puts it into a simple framework to help us apply it.

GDP can be broken down into two parts: (1) the overall vision for how to go about getting things done (the purpose, principles, and foundations) and (2) the basic process for making things happen.

Note that the overall vision is just as important as the process. Many times when we think about productivity we want to jump right to tips and tactics. But more important than knowing specific tips is having an overall vision for our productivity. This infuses the things we do with great meaning and gives us the guidance we need at the most important level: purpose and principles. Further, only with these things in mind will the tactics we use make the difference we intend.

This section is about the first part of GDP: the overall vision the Bible gives us for our productivity, which is rooted in the biblical vision of the Christian life altogether. We will see the purpose of our productivity (to glorify God by doing good for others), the guiding principles for our productivity (putting others first), and the ultimate foundation of our productivity (the fact that God accepts us through faith in Christ, apart from our productivity). Then, in part 3, we will transition to the basic process of GDP.

CHAPTER 5

Why the Things You Do Every Day Matter

God calls us to be abundant in doing good, but you don't have to run to the hills and leave the world to do this good

There is another that has made you, and preserves you, and provides for you, and on whom you are dependent: and He has made you for himself, and for the good of your fellow-creatures, not only for yourself.
　　　　　—Jonathan Edwards, Charity and Its Fruits

THE GOSPEL IS TO BE THE FOUNDATION for how we think about all of life. So what happens when we look at our productivity in light of the gospel? It's time to answer that question.

We saw in chapter 1 that to be productive means to get the right things done. Then we saw that, when we recognize the centrality of God, the right things are the things that God wants done. To be productive is to get done what God wants done. What, then, does God want done?

WHAT DOES GOD WANT DONE?

Good works. What God wants done are good works.

We see this right in Matthew 5:16, where Jesus sums up for us the entire purpose of our lives: "Let your light shine before others, so that they may see your *good works* and give glory to your Father who is in heaven" (emphasis added).

That is the purpose of the Christian life summed up for us in one sentence. The entire purpose of our lives—what God wants from us—is to do good for others, to the glory of God.

We also see this in one of the most important passages on productivity in the Bible—Ephesians 2:8–10: "For by grace you have been saved through faith. And this is not your own doing; it is the gift of God, not a result of works, so that no one may boast. For we are his workmanship, created in Christ Jesus *for good works*, which God prepared beforehand, that we should walk in them" (emphasis added).

Likewise, Titus 2:14 tells us that Jesus "gave himself for us to redeem us from all lawlessness and to purify for himself a people for his own possession who are *zealous for good works*" (emphasis added). And Jesus says in John 15:16, "You did not choose me, but I chose you and appointed you that you should go and bear fruit and that your fruit should abide."

Hence, good works are part of the purpose of our salvation. In one sense, then, we have been doubly created for good works. God created us to do good works, as we saw in the creation mandate, and now we see that we are also re-created in Christ to do good works.

Productive things, then, are things that do good. Productivity always has to be understood in relation to a goal, and God's goal is that we do good works. Hence, we can redefine productivity this way: to be productive is to be fruitful in good works.

DO ALL THE GOOD YOU CAN!

Note that God's goal for us is not simply that we do good works but that we be *fruitful* in good works. The notion of being fruitful in good works, rather than simply doing a few good works, is central to the biblical ethic. God's will is not simply that we do good but also that we be productive in doing good. In fact, the biblical ethic is that we do *all the good we can*.

The Scriptures teach that we are to do good "always" (1 Thess. 5:15) and to bear not just some fruit but "much fruit" (John 15:8). We are to "abound in every good work" (2 Cor. 9:8) and be "always abounding in the work of the Lord" (1 Cor. 15:58). We are to sow bountifully (2 Cor. 9:6) and be radically generous (2 Cor. 8:2; Prov. 11:24–25). We are never to withhold good from others when we have the opportunity (Prov. 3:27). And if we have riches in the present world, we are to make it a special point to be "rich in good works" (1 Tim. 6:17–19).

This is also Paul's point when he says that we are to make "the best use of the time" (Eph. 5:16). He isn't saying simply to use our time well. He is saying to maximize it. We maximize it by doing the Lord's will, which means doing good for others. Paul is saying, "Do all the good you can. Make the *most* of the time."

As John Wesley said, "Do all the good you can, by all the means you can, in all the ways you can, in all the places you can, at all the times you can, to all the people you can, as long as you ever can."

Or, in other words, to be productive is to do all the good you can.

Note a few things about this definition. First, we are to do all the good we *can*. We aren't called to do all conceivable good, which would be impossible for us, but rather to maximize the opportunities that *we* have. As Paul says in Galatians 6:10, "as we have opportunity, let us do good to everyone." We aren't called to do good that God has not put within our reach; to try to do so would be quite exasperating.

But, second, notice that we are to do *all* the good we can. Very often we seem to settle for a reduced view of the good that God has for us to do. But when we look around at the world, we see that there are far more opportunities to do good than we can imagine. If we aren't abounding in good works, the problem is likely not a lack of opportunity but a lack of desire. I love what the great evangelical social reformer William Wilberforce said: "No man has a right to be idle.... [W]here is it in such a world as this that health, and leisure, and affluence may not find some ignorance to instruct, some wrong to redress, some want to supply, some misery to alleviate?"[1]

That's the biblical ethic. We are not to be scant and scarce in our good works, or even nominal and mediocre, but abundant and liberal in doing good. We are not simply to do good for some people here and there; we are to do good for all people as often as we can and as much as we can.[2] While we cannot do all the good that is conceivable, the Scriptures do expect us to do a lot of good—that is, to abound in it.

Third, notice that we are to do all the good *we* can. Each of us is an individual, with unique talents and gifts. Productivity is not about trying to do good according to another person's style, or with gifts we don't have. As the parable of the talents shows, productivity is about taking

Christians Are to Be Useful People!

I like how Wilberforce puts this: "You are everywhere commanded to be tender and sympathetic, diligent and *useful*."*

That's intriguing—and exactly right. We hear often about the fact that we should be sympathetic and diligent, but we don't often hear people say "we should be useful." But it's true. Christians should be useful people.

It's not enough to be diligent and work hard. Your work has to actually benefit people. And that means you have to know what you are doing. You are to be *useful*—and usefulness takes competence.

---

* William Wilberforce, *A Practical View of Christianity* (1797; Peabody, MA: Hendrickson, 2006), 147.

the gifts and resources God has given each of us individually and making those talents useful for the good of others.

WHERE DO WE DO THIS GOOD?

Now, if the Christian life is about doing good, where do we do this good? Do we have to retreat to the hills? Live in a Christian bunker? Spend all day at church? Go to Africa? What exactly *are* good works?

The Unbiblical Separation

By default, and somewhat unconsciously, I think we tend to have a very narrow view of good works. We think that they are rare and special things that we do every once in a while, like going to Africa on a missions trip. Or we think of them in terms of the proverbial situation of helping an elderly woman across the street (which I've yet to come across). Either way, good works are conceived of as unusual and out-of-the-way things we do.

The result is that we live somewhat disconnected lives. Our good works are in one category of our lives, but the things of everyday life—things like commuting to work, raising our kids, and living in our communities—are over in another category, strikingly disconnected.

In GTD terms, this view tends to put good works on our someday/

maybe list. We think, "Yeah, I'd like to do some good works. Maybe I'll get the chance to do some next month."

The True Meaning of Good Works

But the Bible has a very different view of good works. According to the Scriptures, good works are not simply the rare, special, extraordinary, or super spiritual things we do. Rather, they are *anything we do in faith.*

I am a firm believer in doing hard things for the glory of God and the good of others. We should go to Africa and all manner of hard places to do good and advance the gospel. When I taught a class on theology several years ago at a seminary in Cameroon, West Africa, and my wife served at a clinic, it was one of the best (and hardest)[3] experiences of our lives (though I don't get the food staple they call "fufu"; it's basically corn with all the flavor beat out). But we also need to recognize that you don't have to leave the country or do other rare and special things to be doing good works.

You don't even need to volunteer at the soup kitchen.

You just need to live your life!

More specifically, you just need to go about all the things you already do — but do them in faith. That is, for the glory of God and the good of others. Good works are anything you do in faith. Let's look at this in two ways.

First, we know that good works are anything you do in faith through general statements of what God's will is. "Good works" are defined by God's moral will. Does God command us to do only extraordinarily difficult things like go to Africa or spiritual things like evangelism? Not at all! Those things are very important, but God commands us to love our neighbor as ourselves (Matt. 22:37–40; Rom.12:9). That means that anytime we do good for our neighbor, in faith, we are walking in good works. Here's another way to put it: What is a good work? Anything that does good and is done in faith.

Second, we see this through specific instances the Scriptures give us of good works. At one point I went through every New Testament passage I could find on good works. It was very surprising to see what the Scriptures refer to as good works.

For example, according to 1 Timothy 5:10 raising children is a good work: " … and having a reputation for good works: if she has *brought up children*, has shown hospitality, has washed the feet of saints, has cared for the afflicted, and has devoted herself to every good work."

Now, that's quite incredible—and surprising. Paul is talking here about qualifications for widows to be eligible for support, and he tells us that a primary condition is that they have a reputation for good works. Then he lists examples of good works to illustrate what he means. And he doesn't list "going to Africa" or even *simply* caring for the afflicted, but also includes *raising children* as an example of a good work. Parents, be encouraged. Raising children may often be an exhausting, thankless task, but it is highly valued in God's eyes because raising children is a good work!

Likewise, according to Ephesians 6:5–8, our daily work is a good work: "Slaves, obey your earthly masters with fear and trembling, with a sincere heart, as you would Christ, not by the way of eye service, as people-pleasers, but as servants of Christ, doing the will of God from the heart, rendering service with a good will as to the Lord and not to man, knowing that whatever good anyone does, this he will receive back from the Lord, whether he is a slave or free."

This is very interesting because this passage is in Ephesians—the same book where Paul had just said that God created us "in Christ Jesus for good works" back in 2:10. Now here, just a few chapters later, he uses the term "good thing" to describe our daily work. This seems to be a clear reference back to the "good works" of chapter 2.

What we see here, then, is that Paul is explicitly referring to the work we do as a "good thing," that is, as "good works"—when we do it as unto the Lord. And note that this is all-encompassing: "*Whatever* good thing each one does, this he will receive back from the Lord."

So what we see in Scripture is that "good works" are not just spiritual things we do, or hard and rare endeavors. They are anything we do in faith, which includes the mundane activities of everyday life like raising kids, going to work, and even tying our shoes.

A New Way to Look at Matthew 5:16

This allows us to understand Matthew 5:16, the charter for the Christian life, in a deeper way.

Recently, when I was at a Christian technology and leadership conference, I had the privilege of hearing Dan Cathy, president of Chick-Fil-A, speak. His message was quite interesting as it showed how the Sermon on the Mount was the foundation of their entire business philosophy.

Where Does the Bible Talk about Productivity?

When it talks about good works. *This changes everything.* It means:

- The things you do every day are good works—whether that is going to meetings, delivering mail, designing bridges, creating financial reports, developing marketing plans, or making chicken sandwiches.
- The purpose of what you do is to serve.
- The purpose of productivity tactics is to amplify your effectiveness in those good works.
- You don't have to quit your job to have a meaningful life.

At one point, he quoted Matthew 5:16 this way: "Let your light so shine before others that they may *see your clean parking lots* and give glory to your father in heaven." He replaced Jesus' phrase "good works" with the specific and concrete example of "clean parking lots."

Was he misquoting the verse?

Not at all. From what we've seen about good works, we can see that he was right on the mark. Since good works are the things we do every day in faith, then things like clean parking lots, swept floors, and even Chick-Fil-A chicken sandwiches can indeed be good works. That's exciting!

ENCOURAGEMENT FOR YOU RIGHT WHERE YOU ARE

Here's what this means: The things that we are doing every day when we are being productive—answering emails, going to meetings, making supper for the family—are not just things we are doing. They are good works.

When you are answering emails, you aren't just answering emails. *You are doing good works.* When you attend meetings, you aren't just attending meetings. *You are doing good works.* When you make supper for your family, you aren't just making supper for your family. *You are doing good works.* When you put the kids to bed, you aren't just putting the kids to bed. *You are doing a good work.*

The activities of our everyday lives are not separate from the good works that God has called us to. They are themselves part of the good works that God created us for in Christ. And, therefore, they have great meaning.

This is one of the main reasons I've written this book. I want you to see everything you do in a new light so that you can become an agent for good, right where you are, to the glory of God. Don't just try to get things done; seek to serve others to the glory of God in everything you do. More than that, be proactive and enthusiastic in doing good for others. Make plans for the welfare of others, and use all the things you learn from this book to make yourself more effective in carrying out those plans.

THE HEART OF PRODUCTIVITY

The fact that productivity is about doing good works also means that our productivity is first about others, not ourselves. A radical concern for others is to be at the heart of our productivity and at the heart of everything we do every day.

Hence, being productive is not just about getting things done. It's about *being a useful person*, making a contribution, and leaving things better than you found them. It's about always being on the lookout to do good for others and knowing how. Christians are to be known by their love—not just love in the abstract but in their everyday lives. And this is substantially shown through a concern for being of benefit to others in *all* that we do (not just some things that we do).

THIS IS EXCITING

To talk about service might seem boring to some. We've fallen into this notion that serving is boring, like broccoli.

This is because the concept of Christian morality has often been hijacked in our day by boring people—people who have reduced Christian morality to the *avoidance ethic* and its most degenerate form, the *boycott ethic*.

The avoidance ethic is the opposite of what I have outlined here. Instead of seeing the Christian life as about being proactive and abundant in doing good, it sees the essence of the Christian life as avoiding bad. It turns discipleship into the art of, as David Platt has said, "disinfecting Christians" rather than sending them out for real engagement in the world.

Who would get excited about a life that is mainly about avoiding things and holing yourself up in a Christian bunker, allegedly "safe" from the world?[4]

Another reason we easily fall for the fallacy that serving is boring is because Christians often wrongly pit obedience against joy. We act as though joy is simply extra credit in the Christian life, rather than itself a command that God has given us. As a result, emotions can be downplayed, and discipline and obedience are portrayed as things that often go against our inclinations. There is almost a notion of "you better obey, but you sure aren't going to like it."

In reality, and in contrast to both of these views, *serving is exciting.* We are exhorted in the Scriptures to be *zealous* for good works (Titus 2:14) and to *never flag* in our zeal (Rom. 12:11). A life of serving is a life of joy and adventure and excitement—far more exciting, in fact, than a life lived for yourself, no matter how many times you get to travel the world.

A NEW REASON TO GET THINGS DONE

Since getting things done is ultimately about serving and making a difference in people's lives, an entirely new reason to get things done comes to light: it enables us to serve others better. There are four specific ways it does this.

1. Reduce the Friction in Doing Good

First, good productivity practices *reduce the friction in doing good*, thus making doing good easier and more likely. For example, I have a series on my blog about how to set up your desk. I think it's pretty fun to have your desk set up well. But what's the ultimate reason a good desk setup matters to me? Because setting up your desk effectively helps you be more effective in serving others. It means that instead of having your stuff all over, getting in your way and creating friction in your life, you can operate in a smooth and efficient way to focus on what you really need to get done.

Likewise, why are productivity practices such a good thing? One reason is, of course, that they just make life a bit simpler for us. But another reason is that they enable us to be more fruitful in good works because we spend less time unnecessarily managing our stuff and more time getting things done.

2. Amplify Your Ability to Do Good

Second, good productivity practices *amplify our ability to do good*. When you know how to make good plans, for example, you are able to get more done, plain and simple.

This is not only something we see from experience; it is also something we see in the Scriptures. For example, Proverbs 21:5 says "the plans of the diligent lead surely to abundance." Planning leads to getting more done. Further, the "abundance" here is not just making money, though that is probably included. Since we have seen that the biblical ethic is ultimately about doing good, the meaning here is that planning (with diligence) enables us to be more abundant in doing good.

We see this especially when we consider this verse in light of 1 Corinthians 15:58, where Paul tells us to be "always *abounding* in the work of the Lord" (emphasis added). Paul commands us to abound in the work of the Lord, and Proverbs 21:5 says that planning helps us abound in whatever we do. Hence, part of obeying Paul's command that we abound in the work of the Lord is making use of good planning and productivity practices to help amplify our ability to do good and advance the gospel, both of which are the work of the Lord.

3. Free Up Time to Serve: A Better Use of the Four-Hour Workweek

Third, good productivity practices free up more time to serve. This is where I would differ, for example, with Tim Ferriss' very helpful book *The Four-Hour Work Week*. Ferriss shows how you can reduce the time you spend working while simultaneously increasing your output, so that you have more time available to do what you want. But the emphasis is placed on using this extra time to indulge in various pursuits like traveling the world or lying in a hammock while your assistant in India writes birthday cards to send to your friends.[5]

While I certainly don't have anything against traveling the world, I would suggest that it is far more exciting and honoring to God to use this extra time *to do good*. This might take the form of doing more good in our jobs themselves, using some of the time we've freed up to benefit our communities, or using that time to address large global problems (which all of us can now do through technology).[6]

To his credit, Ferriss does talk about serving later in his book, but it isn't the primary motivation for saving time. The subtitle of the book seems to show the primary emphasis: "Escape 9–5, Live Anywhere, and Join the New Rich."

4. Do Larger and More Challenging Good Works

Fourth, good productivity practices enable us to serve others better because they make certain good works possible that otherwise we couldn't do at all. This is because many of the good works before us are not only small and simple, but large and complex.

We often have this notion that serving mainly concerns activities like helping a friend move—things that may be challenging but do not require detailed skill to do.[7] And, of course, it is very important to do these kinds of things. Even giving someone a cup of water in the name of Jesus will not lose its reward (Matt. 10:42).

But in the modern world and with the proliferation of technology and the internet, many of the good works before us today are large and complex. They are things that we literally couldn't do without the right skills, even if we wanted to do them.

For example, if good works are anything we do in faith, that means that they even include building bridges and heart surgery. But these are things you can't do without specialized skills. Likewise, as we've seen, one of the specialized skills necessary to get things done in our era is the skill that goes behind all the others—the foundational skill of personal productivity.

With so many emails and requests and demands coming at us, if we don't develop the skill of personal productivity, there are many good works that we simply won't get to, or which will die an early death because we continually put them off in favor of the urgent over the important.

Good planning and productivity practices exist to make us more effective in doing good and advancing the gospel. Use them that way!

The Box

Core Point

The things you do every day have great meaning because, in doing them, you are doing the good works that God prepared beforehand for you. Further, doing good for others is not boring, like broccoli, but exciting, like steak. It is the path to the life of greatest joy.

Core Quote

No man has a right to be idle.... [W]here is it in such a world as this that health, and leisure, and affluence may not find some ignorance to instruct, some wrong to redress, some want to supply, some misery to alleviate?
—William Wilberforce

Core Passage

Let your light shine before others, so that they may see your good works and give glory to your Father who is in heaven.
—Matthew 5:16

CHAPTER 6

Put Others First: Love as the Guiding Principle for All of Life

We are most effective when we seek the good of others before ourselves; this is both biblical and what the best business thinkers are coming to realize

As a principle of love is the main principle in the heart of a real Christian, so the labour of love is the main business in the Christian life.
—*Jonathan Edwards,* Charity and Its Fruits

WE SAW IN THE LAST CHAPTER that the gospel gives us a new definition of productivity and a new goal for our productivity. To be productive means to be abundant in doing good, and the goal in all the things we do every day is to serve others.

But how do we actually do good for people? The vocations of our everyday lives are the chief arena in which we do good. But how do we actually go about doing good in this arena? Does it happen automatically?

Further, this is also about our joy. How do we go about getting things done in a way that maximizes our fulfillment? How can we be productive *and* happy?

Most things boil down to a few fundamental, core principles. This is almost always the best way to understand a subject. Productivity is no different. In order to maximize our productivity, there is a basic, underlying, governing principle we need to know.

This chapter gives us the guiding principle of Gospel-Driven Productivity, which is simply the guiding principle of the Christian life: put the other person first, and be on the lookout for ways to do this.

In other words, *generosity* is to be the guiding principle for our lives. This is both the right thing to do *and* the way to be most productive. It is the surprising, counterintuitive key to productivity.

Success in business and life does not come from crushing the weak, doing as little as you can get away with, and trying to get every dime you can out of people. It comes from the opposite: helping the weak, going the extra mile, and putting others first.

LOVE IS TO BE THE GUIDING PRINCIPLE OF OUR LIVES

Generosity is the outworking of an even more fundamental principle — namely, love. We can put it this way: Love is the guiding principle of the Christian life, and generosity is the chief way love manifests itself in the world of work, our communities, and society.

We see how love is central to our productivity right in the core New Testament passage on productivity, Ephesians 5:15 – 17. Paul writes, "Look carefully then how you walk, not as unwise but as wise, making the best use of the time, because the days are evil. Therefore do not be foolish, but understand what the will of the Lord is."

Paul defines "making the best use of the time" in terms of understanding and doing "the will of the Lord." And what is his will? This is not mysterious. Everyone, even non-Christians, knows what Jesus wants. What Jesus wants is *love*.

We know this, of course, from the Great Commandment, which is that we love God and love others (Matt. 22:37 – 40).[1] Interestingly, we also see it right here in Ephesians 5:15 – 17, for Paul had just told us at the beginning of this chapter what the Lord's will is: "Therefore be imitators of God, as beloved children. And *walk in love*, as Christ loved us and gave himself up for us, a fragrant offering and sacrifice to God" (Eph. 5:1 – 2; emphasis added).

The will of God is that we love others to his glory, and the ultimate reason we are to do this is because God is like that ("be imitators of God") and Christ is that way ("as Christ loved us and gave himself up for us"). So when Paul tells us that we make the most of the time by understanding the will of the Lord, his meaning is this: The way you make the most of the time is by loving others. Do you want to make the most of the time (Eph. 5:15–17)? Then walk in love (Eph. 5:1–2).

Hence, the overarching principle of the Christian life is that we are here to serve, to the glory of God. We are to be in this world not for what we can get out of it but for what we can give. According to the Bible, a truly productive life is lived in service to others. Being productive is not about seeking personal peace and affluence because God made us for greater goals. Jonathan Edwards nails this:

> There is another that has made you, and preserves you, and provides for you, and on whom you are dependent: and He has made you for himself, and for the good of your fellow-creatures, and not only for yourself. He has placed before you higher and nobler ends than self, even the welfare of your fellow-men, and of society, and the interests of his kingdom; and for these you ought to labour and live, not only in time, but for eternity.[2]

This is foundational to the entire Christian life: We are not our own (1 Cor. 6:19). We did not create ourselves, and we did not redeem ourselves. We doubly belong to God. And God has not made us merely to seek our own good. He created us for something far greater: to seek the good of others, and of society, and his kingdom. The true Christian lives for *these* ends, not his own comfort and welfare.

WHAT DOES IT MEAN TO LOVE OTHERS IN EVERYDAY LIFE?

When we think of going about our everyday lives, we don't often think of love. We tend to have an abstract, overly sentimental, or romantic view of love. So we need to understand what the Bible is really saying when it commands us to love others. It turns out that the biblical call to love others is actually very concrete.

To have love as the guiding principle of our lives means that our continual mindset in all we do should be "What will serve the other person?" It is not "What will serve *me*?" but "What will serve *them*?" The guiding mindset of our lives is to be: how can I do good for others? How can I benefit my neighbor?

In other words, the good of others is to be the motive and criteria for all that we do. The good of others is "what's best next."

Is Productivity a Fruit of the Spirit?

Yes—and this goes to the heart of this book. Most of the time when people look at the fruit of the Spirit (Gal. 5:22–23), they think in terms of character qualities. The fruit of the Spirit, it is thought, is about who you are, not what you do.

I certainly do not want to dispute the primacy of character in the Christian life. That is one of the key themes of this book: Who we are is more important than what we do, and the true basis of effectiveness in our lives is not strategies and techniques but character. But character always manifests itself in action (see, for example, James 3:13–18), and it turns out that the fruit of the Spirit does apply to what we do as well as who we are.

For, as we've seen, being productive is about doing good for others—creatively, competently, and abundantly. Understood in this sense, productivity is indeed a fruit of the Spirit, for this is actually the meaning of "kindness," which Paul lists as one of the chief fruits of the Spirit.

We often think of kindness in rather dull terms—simply as being "nice." But as Jonathan Edwards points out in his book *Charity and Its Fruits*, to be "kind" doesn't simply mean to be nice. Rather, it means to be proactive in seeking good for others. It means to be free and liberal in doing good. Hence, when Paul says that "love is kind," he means, as Edwards summarizes, that love "will dispose us freely to do good to others."[3]

As we've seen, that's exactly what productivity is. Hence, productivity is indeed a fruit of the spirit.

This simply comes from the Golden Rule, which Jesus says sums up the Old Testament and his teaching: "Do unto others as you would have them do unto you" (Matt. 7:12). This is simply another way of stating the Great Commandment to "love your neighbor as yourself" (Matt. 22:39).

How should we love others? The same way we love ourselves. Which means: take the energy you have for meeting your own needs and use that as the measure of the energy you use in seeking the good of others. Desire and seek the good of others with the same passion, creativity, and perseverance as you seek your own.

It boils down to one thing: How would I want someone else to treat me? And then the gospel amps it up: How did *Christ* treat me? Go do that.

More specifically, loving others means six chief things.

1. Have real goodwill toward the other person. Motives count. The essence of love is having real goodwill toward others—that is, truly wanting the best for them and *delighting* in it. Notice, for example, how Paul equates love and goodwill in Philippians 1:15–16: "Some indeed preach Christ from envy and rivalry, but others from *good will.* The latter do it out of *love.*" To do something out of love is to do it out of genuine concern for others.

2. Put the other person first. This means finding out what others need and making those needs your priority, not your own. Along with goodwill toward the other person, this is at the heart of what it means to love others.

This is the example that Jesus himself gave us: "Whoever would be great among you must be your servant, and whoever would be first among you must be your slave, even as the Son of Man came not to be served but to serve, and to give his life as a ransom for many" (Matt. 20:26–28). As Christians, we are to be in this world not for what we can get out of it but for what we can give. We are to serve, not dominate.

Paul also teaches this, basing his exhortation on the example of Christ: "We who are strong have an obligation to bear with the failings of the weak, and not to please ourselves. Let each of us please his neighbor for his good, to build him up. For Christ did not please himself ..." (Rom. 15:1–3).

He then expounds this further in Philippians 2:3–4, stating, "In humility count others more significant than yourselves. Let each of you look not only to his own interests, but also to the interests of others." And in 1 Corinthians 10:24, Paul states "let no one seek his own good, but the good of his neighbor."[4]

As we can see, putting others first is not simply an outworking of the command to love our neighbor as ourselves. It is even more fundamentally rooted in the gospel itself. We are to seek the interests of others first precisely because this is how *Christ* loved us.

Putting the interest of others first involves finding out what matters to *them.* It is not loving to impose our own grid onto others! We need to understand their situation and their needs accurately, and this comes from listening to them, not coming in with our assumptions. "If one gives an answer before he hears, it is his folly and shame" (Prov. 18:13).[5]

And we are to do this not just in large things but also in small things, even if it requires sacrifice. As Edwards notes, "The rule of the gospel is that when we see our brother under *any difficulty* or burden, we should be ready to *bear the burden with him* (Galatians 6:2)."

3. Be eager in meeting the needs of others, not begrudging and reluctant. If love is genuine concern for others, then we see that things done from love are done joyfully and eagerly, not backwardly and reluctantly.

In fact, as John Piper argues, the pursuit of joy in doing good is actually an essential component of virtue. At first this may sound selfish, but quite the opposite is true. Piper gives the example of taking his wife out for their anniversary. If she says, "Thanks so much; why did you do this?" and he responds with "It's my duty," she is not going to feel very loved! But if he were to say, "Because I love being with you and I couldn't imagine doing anything else," she feels loved and honored.

So also in all the good we do. If we don't do good eagerly and because we *want* to, we are missing an essential ingredient of love. Hence, pursuing joy in doing good is a moral obligation. As Paul teaches, we aren't simply to do good works, but be *zealous* for them: "[Jesus] gave himself for us to redeem us from all lawlessness and to purify for himself a people for his own possession who are zealous for good works" (Titus 2:14). Don't just do good works; be zealous, energetic, and eager in doing them.

The Christian Attitude in Doing Good	
Is	**Is Not**
Eager Enthusiastic Joyful Creative Gets a kick out of it	Reluctant Grudging Indifferent Bored Would rather be playing X-Box or Wii
Positive Examples	**Negative Examples**
Paul William Wilberforce Jonathan Edwards	Tightly controlled corporate structures Scrooge Third-world dictators

4. Be proactive, not reactive, in doing good. Don't simply wait for needs to come your way. The Christian ethic is to be on the lookout to identify needs proactively and then take action to meet those needs.

The importance of being *proactive* in doing good comes right from the Great Commandment. Jesus said, "Love your neighbor as yourself." How do we love ourselves? We are proactive in identifying our own needs and taking action. Therefore, we should be proactive in meeting the needs of others.

I don't, for example, wait until my car runs out of gas before I fill the tank. I keep an eye on the gas gauge and fill it up in plenty of time to avoid running out. Likewise, we should not wait until people ask before we do good but take the initiative to find out what people need and conceive of ways to meet their needs and make their lives better. We should look for opportunities to do good for people.

Here's how the great preacher Charles Spurgeon put it: "Let us *be on the watch* for opportunities of usefulness; let us go about the world with our ears and our eyes open, ready to avail ourselves of every occasion for doing good; let us not be content till we are useful, but make this the main design and ambition of our lives."[6]

In fact, this is not optional, but is part of what it *means* to be a loving person. I love how Edwards puts this: "A charitable person, whose heart disposes him to bounty and liberality, will be *quick-sighted* to discern the needs of others."[7] We are to be quick-sighted to discern the needs of others! Conversely, if we aren't readily seeing other people's needs, it is not simply a technical failure in the Christian life; it is selfishness. Edwards captures this well:

> A selfish man is not apt to discern the wants of others, but rather to overlook them, and can hardly be persuaded to see or feel them. But a man of charitable spirit is apt to see the afflictions of others, and to take notice of their aggravation, and to be filled with concern for them, as he would be for himself if under difficulties. And he is ready, also, to help them, and take delight in supplying their necessities, and relieving their difficulties.8

The older theologians and Christian social reformers spoke of this readiness to do good in terms of being forward to promote the good of others. Wilberforce puts it this way: "Are we acute to discern and forward to embrace any fair opportunity of promoting the interest of another?"[9]

5. Avoid a self-protective mindset and *take pains* to do good for others. We are to do good even if it requires a sacrifice on our part. Radical generosity, not self-protection, is the Christian ethic (Matt. 5:42; see also the parallel in Luke 6:32–36). We should be willing to make things harder on ourselves to make them easier on others.

In doing so, we are imitating God (Matt. 5:43–48). Our default mindset should not be "How do I protect myself and keep from being taken advantage of?" but rather "How do I demonstrate in my own life God's radical, abounding love for me?"

This means that the Christian life involves risk. The fact that something is risky is not an indication that God isn't in it. Sometimes that is the very indication that he *is* in it. Don't excuse yourself from doing good because it is risky or hard. We are to go to extremes to help others because Jesus went to extremes to help us.[10]

6. Be creative and competent in doing good, not lazy and shoddy. If we are about serving others, then we need to be competent in serving them because incompetence does not serve people. For example, if you are helping a friend remodel his kitchen, and you cut corners, will that serve him? You are making things easier for yourself *at his expense*; instead of going through the trouble to do it right, you are making something that will work less effectively for him down the road, transferring the burden from yourself to him (which is the opposite of Gal. 6:2).

Or at your job, if you haven't mastered the skills of your job or aren't seeking to do so, you aren't serving your employer and coworkers as well as you should. You might even be making the work of others harder. Mediocre work is not Christian! We are to love our neighbor as *ourselves*. We do not serve ourselves incompetently. We should not treat our neighbors—which includes our coworkers and employers—this way either. The help we offer has to actually help. "In everything the prudent acts with knowledge, but a fool flaunts his folly" (Prov. 13:16).

And we need to be creative because God is not simply a God of utility but also is a God of beauty. Putting thought into how we can serve people with creativity is simply an implication of the command to "love your neighbor as yourself." We don't do "just enough" to make things work for ourselves. Instead, if we are, for example, remodeling our kitchen, we'll do it in a way that is appealing to us. We probably won't go all out to make it top of the line, but we'll make it a place we'll like

Three Characteristics of Gospel-Driven Christians

1. Known by their love, and *also* sound in theology. Both/and, not either/or.
2. Engaged in their communities and workplaces and working for the good of others, not retreating to the hills to grow wheat until Jesus comes.
3. Not afraid of culture, but not compromising the gospel either. The gospel is unchanging, but it does need to be contextualized.

to be. And so it is in the initiatives we undertake for others—we are to go beyond merely what works and accomplishes the minimum. Go the extra mile, showing creativity and thoughtfulness.

We begin to see here the radical nature of the Christian ethic. We often reduce the Christian ethic to simply "work hard and be honest," but there is much more to it than that. We are to have a sense of adventure and creativity toward doing good. We are to always be on the lookout to do good and actually get a kick out of doing good.[11]

DOING GOOD SO GOD GETS THE GLORY

There is a wrong turn we can make here. We could think that the Christian life is merely about doing good; that somehow seeking to help others would make up for the fact that we ignore God in our lives or that it is sufficient to do good for others without the motive of love for God behind our love for others.

This would be a big mistake. God is supposed to be a part of our doing good. The mark of a godly life is a life that does good *with* God, not one that goes off on its own and does good without any consideration of him (Mic. 6:8). If our works are to be truly productive—that is, affirmed by God at the final judgment and last forever—they need to be done with a love for God at the center. Anything else is ultimately idolatry.

One of the chief things this means is that we are to do all we do not only in his power (1 Peter 4:10–11), but also as an offering to him through Jesus Christ (1 Peter 2:4). Edwards makes this point very well:

What is given, is given to that which the individual makes his great end in giving. If his end be only himself, then it is given only to himself, and not to God; and if his aim be his own honor or ease, or worldly profit, then the gift is but an offering to these things. The gift is an offering to him to whom the giver's heart devotes, and for whom he designs it.12

A great work is not given to God if God is not the great end in what you do or give. Good works without this motive of love for God may do much temporal good, which is commendable in its own right, but they will have no ultimate spiritual or eternal value because you've missed the most important point—God.

DOES THIS REALLY APPLY AT WORK?

But do love and generosity actually apply in the world of work? And is this really the best way to be productive in this life?

We'll start with the first question. Yes, this applies at work, for Paul writes: "Let *all that you do* be done in love" (1 Cor. 16:14, emphasis added). What things should we do in love? All things. Likewise, he says we are to "*always* seek to do good to one another and to everyone" (1 Thess. 5:15, emphasis added). How often are we to seek the good of the other person? Not just sometimes, but always.

Note also Paul's interesting statement in Romans 13:8. After speaking of our obligations in society, Paul says, "Owe no one anything, except to love each other, for the one who loves another has fulfilled the law." In other words: "Let all your debts—all your obligations to others—be debts of love." Love is to be the motive behind paying our bills, paying our taxes, mowing our lawns, and doing all the other things we do in the business and community arenas of our lives.

To exclude the world of work from the command to love our neighbor as ourselves is to make the same mistake we saw in the previous chapter on good works. The more complete and biblical view of good works that we have seen, in fact, necessarily entails that we also have this more comprehensive view of love. For if good works are everything we do in faith, including our work and the demands of our daily lives, then surely our work lives are not an exception to the command to love others as ourselves.

Further, if Christ, who has the highest position in the entire universe as Lord of all, uses his power and authority and position to serve, how can we think that we are relieved from the obligation to serve in our lesser positions?

So this is the right way to live, but does it *work*?

THIS IS (USUALLY!) THE BEST WAY TO BE PRODUCTIVE

Counterintuitively, putting others first is actually the best way to be productive at work (as well as in the rest of life).

The notion that success comes by putting yourself first is not only morally misguided; it is incorrect altogether. We see this in the Scriptures *and* from the best business thinkers.

In regard to the Scriptures, Edwards makes a strong case for this both in his book on love (*Charity and Its Fruits*) and in his classic sermon "The Christian Duty of Charity to the Poor." Regarding generosity, he points out that "there is scarcely any duty spoken of throughout the Bible, that has so many promises of reward as this, whether for this world or the world to come."[13]

Generosity is the way to be productive for eternity, because it is one of the chief ways that we lay up treasure in heaven (Luke 12:33). What we give (especially to the poor) is loaned to the Lord (Prov. 19:17), and the Lord does not default on his "loans." The Lord pays back everything that is "loaned" to him with great increase and even more abundance (Luke 6:38).

Generosity is also the best way to be productive in this life. Proverbs 11:24–25 tells us that "one gives freely, yet grows all the richer; another withholds what he should give, and only suffers want. Whoever brings blessing will be enriched, and one who waters will himself be watered." Isaiah 32:8, after telling us that those who are noble plan noble things, immediately adds "and *on noble things he stands*." As Edwards says, "It is easy for God to make up, and more than make up to us, all that we thus give for the good of others."

We also see that generosity is the way to be most productive from common grace. The best business thinkers have been making this case for decades, but many have still not caught up with it. The awareness that all of our work is about serving is a major trend in contemporary thinking that lines up with the biblical ethic. This is something that we should support, amplify, and build on as Christians.[14] Two authors who write for the secular arena brought this concept home to me. The first is Tim Sanders.

Love: The Killer App

Tim Sanders is the former chief solutions officer at Yahoo and author of several books, including *Love Is the Killer App*. Tim is a person of faith, but his book was written for the general market. It is informed by biblical thinking, but it is not a Christian book.

Sanders argues that "the most important new trend in business is the downfall of the barracudas, sharks, and piranhas, and the ascendancy of nice, smart people."[15] *Fast Company* captured this concept well in their blurb for the book: "Why faith beats fear, greed isn't good, and nice guys finish first."

Sanders argues that love is the new point of differentiation in business. He defines love as "the selfless promotion of the growth of the other."[16] It is significant that Sanders is calling for the *selfless* promotion of the other's growth. He is not saying "be of benefit to others with the ulterior motive that they will be of benefit to you in return." Tim does believe that will happen, but your aim of serving others in everything you do is not for the sake of what you can get. "In the old days, I would think, Who will pay me for my advice? Now I bestow my advice knowing that it's the giving that matters, not the tangible rewards."[17] Effectiveness does follow, he argues, but it begins by genuinely caring for others, not treating them simply as a means to your own ends.

This theme runs through his whole book: Don't make things about yourself first; your first aim needs to be the good of others.

That is the true meaning of "business ethics."

Networking: Making Others Successful

Keith Ferrazzi's book *Never Eat Alone* is the second book that really drove this point home to me. *Never Eat Alone* is by far the best book on networking out there (and networking is a critical skill if you want to be effective in the workplace).

When most people hear the term *networking*, they think of the networking jerk—the guy who doesn't care about other people, is just looking for what you can do for him, and is, frankly, boring.

What is so distinctive about Ferrazzi's book is that he emphasizes that networking is not about what you can get, but about what you can do for others. He is right on the same track as Sanders: "I learned that *real* networking was about finding ways to make *other* people more successful. It was about working hard to *give* more than you get."[18] What Ferrazzi says about networking is a good summary of what the Bible teaches about all of life: everything we do, including our work, is to be done for the sake of others.

He also argues that you will be more effective and successful this way: "I came to realize that first semester at business school that Harvard's hypercompetitive, individualistic students had it all wrong. Success in any field, but especially in business, is about working *with* people, not against them. No tabulation of dollars and cents can account for one immutable fact: Business is a human enterprise, driven and determined by people."[19]

Another word for what Ferrazzi is advocating is *generosity*: "Bottom line: It's better to give before you receive. And never keep score. If your interactions are ruled by generosity, your rewards will follow suit."[20]

We see this not just in networking but also in every single area of our work and community lives. For example, if you read up on effective blogging, you will find that the key principle is to put the reader first. If you read up on effective job interviewing, you will see that the key motive is to show how you can benefit your potential employer (and prove it by quantifying past results). If you read up on how to provide effective customer service, you will see that the chief principle is to benefit your customers. In every area of the world of work, seeking the benefit of others is the guiding principle of effectiveness.

IS THERE ANY DIFFERENCE IN THE BUSINESS WORLD?

Is there *any* difference between what love looks like in the world of work and what love looks like in our personal lives?

Certainly. I'm not arguing here that profit should be of no concern in the business world. My point is that in the arena of work we are to seek *more than* profit, not *other than* profit. We are to seek profit *in line with values*. In our personal lives, we are to do many things for which we will never be repaid on this earth (Luke 14:12–14). This is sometimes true at work, but the chief thing that makes business *business* is that we seek the good of others *in a way that is profitable*.

SLACK WORK IS A FORM OF VANDALISM

The Christian ethic of generosity and service puts all of our work in an entirely new light. It means, for example, that shoddy work is not simply shoddy work—it is a failure of love.

The Key to Effectiveness: Service

I recently asked Mike Allen of Politico, the Washington, DC, based news organization and author of a daily news report with 100,000+ subscribers, the most important thing we can do to be effective. His answer was exactly what we have been seeing in this chapter.

Q: What does it mean to be effective in your work?
A: Think about how you can serve the person above you and below you. Even if you are an intern, you can serve the other interns, and you definitely want to serve your boss. One of the things I teach young people is that the last shall be first. Sometimes what is perceived as the lowest job can be the best job. You might have to drive the boss, but then you will have more time with a great mind. Or a new person at the White House might carry the chief of staff's bag. The astute person will realize that this is a big deal.

Another thing I teach them, especially when I talk to reporters or those in PR, is to always think about what you would want if you were the other person. So if I'm the press secretary and you are the reporter, would you want to come back from lunch and find that you have six phone messages and three emails from me? Or would you rather have just one that summarizes everything? It's clear what you would want, so put yourself in the other person's shoes and do to them what you would want them to do to you.

In fact, the Bible actually teaches that slack work is a form of vandalism. Proverbs 18:9 brings this out when it says he who is "slack in his work is a brother to him who destroys." Slack work is like vandalism because it makes life harder for people — just like vandalism.

One summer after some especially heavy rains, three sump pumps went out on our street, all on the same day. I've come to believe that we live in a former swamp, because the water table is very high around our home. Our sump pump runs continually in the spring and summer. But even with the high water table and heavy rains, these sump pumps failed far more quickly than they should have. The reason, as we eventually learned, is that the builders decided to use the cheapest sump pumps they could find rather than spending a couple hundred dollars more to get higher quality pumps. The result of their poor workmanship was a flooded basement.

The builder was seeking to save himself a few hundred dollars on each house built, but in order to do so, he passed a far greater cost onto me, the owner. I paid with my time and an insurance deductible, and my insurance company paid for new carpet and baseboards. Our builder made life easier on himself at the cost of making it harder on us.

That is not what I would call good work. This is another example of the "superficial efficiency" we encountered in chapter 2. Though it seems cheaper at first, it costs more in the long run — with the cost being pushed off onto someone *other* than the one who saves a few bucks.

Christians are to be the opposite of vandals and slackers in their work. We are to do work that will truly benefit people by going the extra mile rather than just doing the minimum necessary. Excellence in our work is actually a form of generosity and *love*, and poor quality is a form of stinginess and selfishness. Shoddy work is not just shoddy work; it's a failure of love.

THE CHRISTIAN CHARGE FOR OUR WORK: EXCELLENCE AS A FORM OF LOVE

This means we are to be generous not just with the results of our work but also *in* our work. One of the best forms of generosity in our work is *excellence*. Excellence matters not only because it is right and exciting in itself, but even more significantly because it is a way of serving people.

Excellence at work chiefly manifests itself in two ways: caring about usability and caring about good design.

1. Usability: Create products that lift burdens, not products that create burdens. We are to care about usability because hard-to-use products make life harder for people, not easier. And the Christian ethic is to lift people's burdens — make their lives *better* — rather than create burdens for them by making their lives harder in order to save ourselves some time and effort in the design of our products.

This means caring about usability on your website, because usable websites not only will get you better results but also will serve your customers more effectively. It means that if you are in marketing, you need to create your marketing initiatives in a way that doesn't annoy people or seek to use them but instead will serve them even in the *way* you market to them.[21] If you build houses for people, build houses that won't start causing problems for people in three years. Instead, build houses that solve problems rather than creating problems after you are all done and have made your money. If you run a pizza restaurant, get quality ingredients for your toppings, rather than the dog food that disguises itself as sausage and hamburger at most pizza places.

2. Good design: Create products that people like. Likewise, we are to care about good design and involve *beauty* in what we do. We need to care about beauty and not just the utility of our products because people are not only rational but also emotional. We need to treat people as whole people. This means caring about beauty and the emotional side of human nature, not just utility. We need to create products for the whole person by appealing to the emotional side of people, not just the practical and utilitarian side.

THE INCREDIBLE, SURPRISING RESULT OF LIVING FOR THE GOOD OF OTHERS

I've argued that putting others first is not just the right way to live but also a more exciting way to live. We have also seen that it leads to the greatest possible productivity. But I want to close by focusing on one chief, amazing, incredible implication of living a life of good works for others: God will make your happiness his own charge.

Jonathan Edwards says this best:

> If you are selfish, and make yourself and your own private interests your idol, God will leave you to yourself, and let you promote your own interests as well as you can.
>
> But if you do not selfishly seek your own, but do seek the things that are Jesus Christ's, and the things of your fellow human beings, then *God will make your interest and happiness his own charge*, and he is infinitely more able to provide for and promote it than you are. The resources of the universe move at his bidding, and he can easily command them all to subserve your welfare.
>
> So that, not to seek your own, in the selfish sense, is the best way of seeking your own in a better sense. It is the directest course you can take to secure your highest happiness.[22]

That is breathtaking. Upon initially hearing that we are to put others before ourselves, we can fear that this means things are going to go bad for us. Who will look out for us?

It may seem like no one will, because so many people in the world are about achieving their own welfare first. But the answer is that you won't be left without anyone looking out for you. For *God himself* will have your back. And God is able to provide for you and support you better than any human, and certainly better than you are able to provide for yourself.

This doesn't mean that things will always go right for you. There is much suffering on the path to glory. But it does mean that God will always move heaven and earth to give you anything you truly need, that he is always and only seeking your good, that he will work all things for your good (Rom. 8:28), and that ultimately, he will make sure that one day you will enter his glory and live a life with him forever of indescribable and unlimited happiness.[23]

WHAT'S BEST NEXT?

The things we have seen allow us to answer this question now at the most significant level.

What's best next? Doing good for your neighbor. *That's* what's best next.

What will serve *others* and the display of God's glory best next? Do that. And, enjoy it.

The Box

Core Point

The chief guiding principle of effectiveness is to put the other person first in all that you do, including your work.

Core Quote

Am I desiring and seeking the temporal and eternal good of my neighbor with the same zeal, ingenuity and perseverance that I seek my own?

—John Piper

Core Passage

Always seek to do good to one another and to everyone.
—1 Thessalonians 5:15

Immediate Application

1. In everything you do, including the routine tasks of your work like answering the phone, responding to emails, going to meetings, or making dinner, make serving other people for God's glory your motive. "Let all that you do be done in love" (1 Cor. 16:14).
2. *Be on the watch* for opportunities to do good. Continually ask yourself, "What can I do to build this person up and make life better for them?"

Further Resources

Tim Sanders, *Love Is the Killer App*

Keith Ferrazzi, *Never Eat Alone*

Stephen Covey, "Seek First to Understand, Then to be Understood," Habit 5 in *The Seven Habits of Highly Effective People*

Jonathan Edwards, "Love Is Cheerful and Free in Doing Good" and "The Spirit of Charity the Opposite of a Selfish Spirit," lectures 5 and 8 in *Charity and Its Fruits*

CHAPTER 7

How the Gospel Makes Us Productive

The only way to be productive is to realize you don't have to be productive

[The Christian] knows therefore that this holiness is not to precede his reconciliation to God, and be its cause; but to follow it, and be its effect.
— William Wilberforce, A Practical
View of Christianity

The more a person counts as loss his own righteousness and lays hold by faith of the righteousness of Christ, the more he will be motivated to live and work for Christ.
—Jerry Bridges, The Gospel for Real Life

WILLIAM WILBERFORCE WAS ONE of the most productive people in history.

And, he was productive in the best possible way. The banner that waves over his whole life is that "he lived to do good."[1] He was so prolific in doing good that his biographers and friends noted that "he lacked time for half the good works in his mind"[2] and that "factories did not spring up more rapidly in Leeds and Manchester than schemes of benevolence beneath his roof."[3]

As is well known, chief among his good works was the massive social good of bringing an end to the slave trade and, ultimately, slavery itself in the British Empire.

WHY DID THE GREAT DOER WRITE A BOOK ON DOCTRINE?

So Wilberforce was immensely productive and lived to do good. He also wrote a very influential book seeking to reform the moral outlook of his nation. In light of that aim and his amazing practical bent, we might expect the book to focus chiefly on strategies for being more effective in our lives. Yet Wilberforce's book did not focus primarily on strategies for effective living. Rather, it was essentially on doctrine. And, specifically, its focus was on the doctrine of justification by faith alone.

Which is strange.

Why was one of the greatest social reformers and most productive people of all time so concerned about *doctrine*? Why did he care about it so much that, in the one book he wrote in the first part of his life—with the aim, in fact, of improving the morals and Christian practice of Great Britain—he focused on doctrine?

THE TRUE SOURCE OF MASSIVE ACTION FOR GOOD

It's because Wilberforce understood that massive practical action for good comes about not first as a result of moral exhortation or appeals to change but rather as a result of understanding and embracing doctrine—most centrally the doctrine of justification by faith alone.

In other words, embracing the truth that God accepts us apart from good works is the precise thing that causes us to excel in good works. Or, to put this in the context of productivity (which, as we have seen, is really about living a life of good works—like Wilberforce), the only way to be productive is to realize that you don't have to be.

So what is the doctrine of justification, and why does it lead to radical action for good?

WHAT IS JUSTIFICATION?

Justification is at the core of the gospel. Luther called it "the article by which the church stands or falls," and Calvin called it "the main hinge on which religion turns." Without the doctrine of justification, there is no salvation and there is no Christianity.[4]

To be justified means to be set right with God. It means to be accepted by him—to enter into a right relationship with him in which you are now at peace with him and have a title to eternal life. "Therefore, since we have been justified by faith, we have peace with God through our Lord Jesus Christ" (Rom. 5:1).

There are two components to justification. First, our sins are forgiven: "Blessed are those whose lawless deeds are forgiven, and whose sins are covered" (Rom. 4:7). Second, God credits to us the righteousness of Christ so that we have a record of perfect obedience before him: " ... just as David also speaks of the blessing of the one to whom God counts righteousness apart from works" (Rom. 4:6; see also Rom. 5:15–21).

Justification is received not through anything good we do but through faith alone: "And to the one who does not work but trusts him who justifies the ungodly, his faith is counted as righteousness" (Rom. 4:5).

CHRISTIANITY IS NOT FIRST ABOUT MORALITY

This truth of justification by faith alone is at the *essence* of Christianity and distinguishes it from all other religions and philosophies of life.

Many people have the misguided notion that the essence of Christianity is being a good person. It is not. Lots of religions and life philosophies exhort us to be good people. Our primary problem, though, is not that we don't know what to do. It's that even when we know what to do, we don't do it.

If Jesus simply came to tell us what to do and provide moral instruction so we could try harder to please God, then his life would have been an utter failure. For simply telling us how to live, without giving us the power to do it, would not solve our problem. This is what no other religion gets: we are lost in sin and unable to please God, even with our best efforts.

This is why the notion of justification by works—of being accepted by God through good behavior—is not only wrong but impossible. It is impossible because, prior to being forgiven, we have no good works to offer. "For by works of the law no human being will be justified in his sight, since through the law comes knowledge of sin" (Rom. 3:20).

Before we can live a life that is pleasing to God, we need deliverance from the guilt of sin and the power of sin.

THE GOSPEL IS NEWS, NOT ADVICE

That's why the essence of Christianity is not Jesus' moral instruction, as important as that is. It is the news of what he did for us: his death for

What Is the Gospel?

The gospel is very simple: Christ died for our sins, was buried, and was raised from the dead. Paul states it very clearly in 1 Corinthians 15:3–5: "I delivered to you as of first importance what I also received: that Christ died for our sins in accordance with the Scriptures, that he was buried, that he was raised on the third day in accordance with the Scriptures, and that he appeared to Cephas, then to the twelve."

It's not enough just to hear the gospel, or go to church, or have been baptized. We have to *believe* the gospel. Believing the gospel does not just mean assenting to it *intellectually; it means relying on Christ crucified and risen* for our acceptance with God and the gift of eternal life.

"If you confess with your mouth that Jesus is Lord and believe in your heart that God raised him from the dead, you will be saved.... Everyone who calls on the name of the Lord will be saved" (Rom. 10:9–10, 13).

We enter a right relationship with God through faith in the gospel alone, not as a result of any works we do before *or after* becoming a Christian. Good works are a result of having been accepted by God, not the means or basis of our being accepted by him.

Further, you never get beyond the gospel. Once you become a Christian, you don't "graduate" to more important realities. The gospel is always "of first importance," as Paul says (1 Cor. 15:3). Christ died for the sins of Christians, too — that is, the gospel is not just something we point unbelievers to, but is something we continue to rely on every day. As Christians, Jesus' death and resurrection continues to be the full and complete basis of our forgiveness and righteousness before God.

our sins and resurrection three days later. "I delivered to you as of *first importance* what I also received: that Christ died for our sins in accordance with the Scriptures, that he was buried, and that he was raised on the third day in accordance with the Scriptures" (1 Cor. 15:3–4, emphasis added).

We receive forgiveness of our sins and perfect righteousness—justification—by believing in him, and then our sin is forgiven so that we can begin following his moral teaching (and glorifying God through it).

Michael Horton gets at the heart of this: "The heart of most religions is good advice, good techniques, good programs, good ideas, and good support systems.... But the heart of Christianity is Good *News*. It comes not as a task for us to fulfill, a mission for us to accomplish, a game plan for us to follow with the help of life coaches, but as a report that someone else has already fulfilled, accomplished, followed, and achieved everything for us. Good advice may *help* us in daily direction; the Good News concerning Jesus Christ *saves* us from sin's guilt and tyranny over our lives and the fear of death. It's Good News because it does not depend on us. It is about God and his faithfulness to his own purposes and promises."[5]

That's it: the essence of the gospel—of Christianity—is that our acceptance by God does not depend on us. The gospel is about what *God* did for us in Christ, not about what we do for God.

Christianity is not merely an ethical system. We won't solve our problems by being better people. We have to first be forgiven for not being the type of people we ought to be, and *then* we are able, by the Spirit, to begin pleasing God from the heart.

THE DOCTRINE OF JUSTIFICATION CAUSES RADICAL ACTION FOR GOOD

Titus 3:4–8 is one of the chief (and most overlooked) places where we see that an emphasis on doctrine leads to a greater emphasis on practice, not less. Here's what it says: "But when the goodness and loving kindness of God our Savior appeared, he saved us, *not because of works done by us in righteousness*, but according to his own mercy, by the washing of regeneration and renewal of the Holy Spirit, whom he poured out on us richly through Jesus Christ our Savior, so that being justified by his grace we might become heirs according to the hope of eternal life. The saying is trustworthy, and I want you to insist on these things, *so that* those who have believed in God may be careful to devote themselves to good works. These things are excellent and profitable for people" (emphasis added).

The key to this passage is the "so that" in verse 8. Paul says, "I want you to insist on these things, *so that* those who have believed in God may be careful to devote themselves to good works." The "so that" indicates a connection between Titus' "insist[ing] on these things" and the believers in his congregation abounding in good works. "Insist on these things, *so that* ... [they] may be careful to devote themselves to good works." Insisting on those things results in good works in believers' lives.

But what are "those things?" What are the things Titus is to insist on, which will cause God's people to be devoted to good works?

The answer is not hard to see. When Paul says "these things," he is referring back to the core doctrinal truths of Christianity that he had just stated—namely that God has saved us apart from our works so that, being justified by grace, we would become heirs of eternal life. By insisting on *that* truth, a doctrinal truth, believers become engaged in good works.

We see here two very significant things. First, Paul sees a close and essential relationship between doctrine and practice. Specifically, understanding doctrine leads to and causes good works. Sound doctrine is not just the foundation for action. Sound doctrine causes effective action. Second, the primary doctrine in view here is justification by faith alone. The chief doctrine that leads to Christians' being devoted to good works is the doctrine that God saved us "not because of works done by us in righteousness" but that we are "justified by his grace." The practical is founded on the doctrinal, and the chief doctrine that founds the practical is the fact that God accepts us apart from our practice.[6]

This has huge implications for the way we do our work. It means that we cannot leave behind our doctrine and theology in an effort to be more pragmatic and productive. Rather, the way to become truly productive is to anchor our lives squarely and securely on the great truths of the Bible, especially the gospel of justification by faith alone.

WHY DOES THE DOCTRINE OF JUSTIFICATION LEAD TO RADICAL ACTION FOR GOOD?

But *why* does teaching that we are accepted apart from our good works cause us to abound in good works? And why does reducing Christianity to a mere system of ethics result in less ethical behavior rather than more? The chief reason is this: doctrine fuels the joy that empowers obedience.

Wilberforce argued that believing the core doctrines of Christianity gives rise to affections for God and spiritual things. These affections, in turn, break the power of sin and energize us in love to do good works for the glory of God and the good of others. Transformed affections, in other words, lead to transformed morals and a life in which we are abundant and enthusiastic about doing good.

Hence, if we want to be abundant in doing good for others and to the glory of God, then we can't treat doctrine as optional. Doctrine matters for *all* of us because sound doctrine is at the heart of a life fully committed to Jesus.

The Christians in Wilberforce's day, by reducing Christianity to a mere system of ethics, had obscured the greatness of Christ and thus cut themselves off from the joy that provides the true power to obey him and to be prolific in good works. Wilberforce observed that the nominal Christians in his day had low views of God's grace and Christ's work because they failed to grasp that, at its core, Christianity is about not what God requires of us but what he *does* for us — what he did for us by dying for us to provide the forgiveness and righteousness that we could not provide ourselves. Here is how Wilberforce puts it: "All these, their several errors, naturally result from the mistaken conception entertained of the fundamental principles of Christianity. They consider not that Christianity is a scheme 'for justifying the ungodly,' by Christ's dying for them 'when yet sinners,' a scheme for 'reconciling us to God — when enemies'; and for making the fruits of holiness the effects, not the cause, of our being justified and reconciled."[7]

Here's how John Piper summarizes the point Wilberforce is making: "The bulk of Christians in [Wilberforce's] day were nominal, he observed, and what was the root difference between the nominal and the real? It was this: The nominal pursued morality (holiness, sanctification) without first relying utterly on the free gift of justification and reconciliation by faith alone based on Christ's blood and righteousness."[8]

The notion that we must obey God in order to be accepted by him results in less moral action, not more, because it results in less love for God. Conversely, realizing that we are *wholly and completely* accepted by God apart from our works through faith in Christ results in massive and radical action for good because it results in great love and joy for God. As Jesus said, "He who is forgiven little, loves little" (Luke 7:47), whereas those who are forgiven much, love much (Luke 7:41–43).

THE CONNECTION BETWEEN DOCTRINE AND PRACTICE: JOY

Hence, the reason doctrine causes — not merely enables but *causes* — good works and moral reform is because doctrine creates joy. This joy

What Does It Mean to Live by the Gospel?

Here's what David Mathis, former executive pastoral assistant to John Piper, had to say when I asked him this question:

"To say that the Christian life is by faith, or by the gospel, or by the Spirit, is not to say that there are three different paths; rather, they are three different perspectives on the one reality of the Christian life.

"To be filled with the Spirit is to be someone in whom the gospel is dwelling richly.

"To say good works happen by the power of the gospel doesn't mean our will gets left out or that we don't have other motivations; it means that at the very bottom, the ultimate power source is God. The God who has revealed himself to us most deeply and richly and fully in Christ crucified."

makes us want to do good. It makes us *eager* to pursue holiness and the welfare of our neighbor and the world. Doctrine causes joy, which in turn is the fuel for good works.

Teaching morals alone will not result in morality. You cannot get moral and ethical behavior by urging people to try harder, for it is the *affections* that lead to transformed lives, and these affections are driven by the doctrines of Christianity. If you take the doctrine away, you destroy the foundation.

Thus, when doctrine goes, the ethical teachings of Christianity eventually go as well, because the ethical teachings grow out of Christian doctrine. Doctrine is the soil in which the ethical teaching of Christianity grows, and which gives it life and nourishment and energy. Thus, when emphasis on doctrine declines, emphasis on the practical eventually declines as well.

THE DOCTRINE OF JUSTIFICATION FREES YOU TO TRULY SERVE YOUR NEIGHBOR

One of the best ways of capturing this dynamic of how the joy we find in the gospel overflows into manifold good works for our neighbor comes from Martin Luther. In his classic tract *The Freedom of a Christian*, Luther writes:

Although I am an unworthy and condemned man, my God has given me in Christ all the riches of righteousness and salvation without any merit on my part, out of pure, free mercy, so that from now on I need nothing except faith which believes that it is true. Why should I not therefore freely, joyfully, with all my heart, and with an eager will do all things which I know are pleasing and acceptable to such a Father who has overwhelmed me with his inestimable riches? *I will therefore give myself as a Christ to my neighbor, just as Christ offered himself to me*; I will do nothing in this life except what I see is necessary, profitable,

C. S. Lewis on the Devotional Value of Theology

One of the side aims of this book is to show you the importance of caring about both the practical and the theological. Even those who aren't as inclined to theology probably do care a lot about the devotional side of the Christian life. This, in turn, is a great way to see the importance of theology: some of the best devotional books are often theological books.

C. S. Lewis makes this case very well, as this is exactly what he found in his life: "For my own part, I tend to find the doctrinal books often more helpful in devotion than the devotional books, and I rather suspect that the same experience may await many others. I believe that many who find that 'nothing happens' when they sit down, or kneel down, to a book of devotion, would find that the heart sings unbidden while they are working their way through a tough bit of theology with a pipe in their teeth and a pencil in their hand."*

So for those who are interested in the combination of head and heart that good theology brings together, here are three books I recommend:

- R. C. Sproul, *The Holiness of God*
- John Piper, *The Pleasures of God*
- J. I. Packer, *Knowing God*

---

* From his introduction to Athanasius' *On the Incarnation of the Word of God* (Kindle edition, Amazon Digital Services).

and salutary to my neighbor, since through faith I have an abundance of all good things in Christ.

The doctrine of justification frees us to serve our neighbor because we no longer have to worry about our own acceptance before God. The Christian does not have to worry about his right standing with God because that was taken care of at the cross; he is thus truly free. And how will he use this freedom? To serve, just as Jesus did.

This is what enables our good works to be truly good. If we had to do good works in order to become justified, we wouldn't truly be doing them for the sake of our neighbor. They would ultimately be for our own sakes. But since we don't have to do them in order to be accepted by God, we are able to do them truly for our neighbor.

This is also what enables us to be enthusiastic in doing good works. Legalism might get some people to do good works, but it will never get anyone excited about doing good works. The gospel, on the other hand, gets you excited about good works because it means you can obey freely, from the heart, rather than out of fear of what God might do to you if you don't.

In other words, we can not only say that the gospel makes us productive, but we can also go a step farther: the gospel makes us *eager to be productive*. The gospel not only causes us to engage in good works but also causes us to be "zealous for good works" (Titus 2:14) because grace is ten trillion times more motivational than law. Jesus died not simply so that we would do good works but so that we would be passionate about glorifying his name through them.

It is not that there is no place for the law (moral instruction). Rather, it's that "the law drives us to the gospel, and the gospel frees us to obey the law."[9] As a result, we can now obey freely and from the heart, rather than out of constraint.

Gospel-driven Christians are Christians who are enthusiastic in doing good not to gain acceptance with God but because they already have acceptance with God.

DOCTRINE AND THE TRANSFORMATION OF SOCIETY
One other implication of these things is that the way to change society—to change the nation and the world—is, interestingly, not primarily to

preach on politics or ethics or ten steps to a healthy marriage, but to preach on doctrine.

This is the exact effect that Wilberforce's book had. His biographers in *The Life of William Wilberforce* write that "the effect of this work can scarcely be overrated" and that "it may be affirmed beyond all question, that it gave the first general impulse to that warmer and more earnest spring of piety which ... has happily distinguished the last half century."[10]

And one of his recent biographers, John Pollock, writes:

> There is little doubt that Wilberforce changed the moral outlook of Great Britain, and this at a time when the British Empire was growing and Britain was the world's leading society. The reformation of manners grew into Victorian virtues and Wilberforce touched the world when he made goodness fashionable. Contrast the late eighteenth century (you must allow a broad brush in a brief essay like this) with its loose morals and corrupt public life, with the mid-nineteenth century. Whatever its faults, nineteenth-century British public life became famous for its emphasis on character, morals, and justice and the British business world famous for integrity. Most of those who ruled India and the colonies had a strong sense of mission, to do good for those they ruled—a far cry from the original colonizers.[11]

The gospel creates an affection for God that drives us to do good works that serve others and please God. In this way, the gospel is how we become truly productive, which ultimately affects not only us personally but all of society (as we will see in part 7).

But next we need to see that the gospel has massive implications not only for how we become productive (people who do good works for the glory of God) in the first place, but also for how we go about using any productivity approaches. In fact, even if we believe the gospel, we can easily end up falling into a law-based approach to our productivity and the Christian life. That's what the next chapter is about.

The Box

Core Point

Massive practical action for good comes about not first as a result of moral exhortation or appeals to change but rather as a result of understanding doctrine—and, most centrally, the doctrine of justification by faith alone.

Core Quote

There must be a reconciliation with God and an imputed righteousness from him before we can live holy and righteous lives in the world.

—John Piper, The Roots of Endurance

Core Passage

[Jesus] gave himself for us to redeem us from all lawlessness and to purify for himself a people for his own possession who are zealous for good works.

—Titus 2:14

Further Resources

On William Wilberforce

J. Douglas Holladay, "A Life of Significance" and John Pollock, "A Man Who Changed the Times," in *Character Counts: Leadership Qualities in Washington, Wilberforce, Lincoln, and Solzhenitsyn*

John Pollock, *Wilberforce*

Robert Isaac Wilberforce and Samuel Wilberforce, *The Life of William Wilberforce*

On Doctrine and Practice

John Piper, "William Wilberforce: 'Peculiar Doctrines,' Spiritual Delight, and the Politics of Slavery," in *The Roots of Endurance: Invincible Perseverance in the Lives of John Newton, Charles Simeon, and William Wilberforce*

Michael Wittmer, *Don't Stop Believing: Why Living Like Jesus Isn't Enough*

Keven DeYoung and Ted Kluck, *Why We're Not Emergent: By Two Guys Who Should Be*

John Piper, *The Pleasures of God* (see especially the introduction)

On the Doctrine of Justification

James Buchanan, *The Doctrine of Justification*

John Owen, *The Doctrine of Justification by Faith through the Imputation of the Righteousness of Christ Explained, Confirmed, and Vindicated*

Jonathan Edwards, "Justification by Faith Alone," in *The Works of Jonathan Edwards*

John Piper, *Counted Righteous in Christ*

CHAPTER 8

Peace of Mind without Having Everything under Control

Without a gospel-centered approach
to productivity, we can easily fall into
a law-based approach to the Christian
life that kills our joy and freedom

*We need to learn and remind ourselves every day that
God's favor—His blessings and answers to prayer—
comes to us not on the basis of our works, but on the
basis of the infinite merit of Jesus Christ.*
        —Jerry Bridges, The Gospel for Everyday Life

EVEN IF WE AVOID THE ERROR of seeking God's acceptance through
our productivity, there is another subtle and related trap that we easily can fall into—the trap of basing our day-to-day peace of mind on
whether we made it to the end of our to-do list, put "first things first,"
kept our action and project lists up to date, or got the results we wanted
from our day.

All of those things are important. But to base our peace of mind on
them is ultimately a law-based approach to the Christian life—a form of
living our daily Christian lives on the basis of what we do (works) rather

than what God has done (faith). This trap kills our joy and freedom because it makes our sense of peace and effectiveness dependent on our own efforts. And since we are all imperfect, this is never going to work.

Sometimes the way we use various productivity approaches leads us right into this trap.

MY EXPERIENCE

My own experience with *Getting Things Done* bears this out. After graduating from seminary (where what you need to do is mostly given to you) and transitioning to working full-time (where you mostly have to figure out for yourself what you need to do), discovering GTD was a big deal.

It helped me understand that the issue of defining my work was the primary challenge I faced. Most of all, it gave me a system for keeping track of my work—and a system that was flexible enough that I could refine it based on my own experience.

The big thing GTD promises is "mind like water." That means having your mind free from all distractions so that you can be focused on what you are doing at the moment. The way you do this is by keeping an inventory of all the things you have to do. When you have all those things outside of your mind in a trusted system that you review regularly, then your mind is able to relax without being distracted by dozens of "open loops" that have been left uncaptured and undefined.

I often tasted this mind like water. Most Fridays, for example, I'd get all my action lists caught up before leaving for the weekend, and I felt restful and focused on my family for the weekend. Those were great days.

But as my workload kept increasing, I found it increasingly difficult to keep my inventory of work and commitments up to date. And my ability to generate ideas far outstripped my ability to collect and process them in a meaningful way.

Consequently, keeping up became exhausting. There was a potential for "mind like water," but achieving that state consistently simply required too much effort. I knew how to do it but did not have the energy or time to keep doing it consistently.

"MIND LIKE WATER" AND PHILIPPIANS 4

I think a lot of people end up in that same boat. I don't think it has to be the necessary result of GTD, and David Allen likely has some good solutions. But I'd like to present another solution that is not often considered but comes straight from the gospel. Let's look at some interesting parallels between *Getting Things Done* and Philippians 4, and then flesh out some of the deeper foundations behind the principles David Allen is pointing to.

While it is helpful and important to capture our open loops, I suggest that the ultimate solution to the dilemma I faced is basing our ultimate peace of mind on something other than our own efforts. Making our peace of mind dependent on what we do (such as keeping up an inventory of our work) is ultimately a law-based approach to the *Christian life*, just as basing our acceptance by God on our good works is a law-based approach to *justification*.

According to the Scriptures, our ultimate peace of mind comes in the same way our justification does: through faith. That is, our ongoing peace of mind comes apart from works, just as our justification does. This is Paul's point in Philippians 4:6–7: "Do not be *anxious* about anything, but in everything by prayer and supplication with thanksgiving *let your requests be made known to God*. And the *peace of God*, which surpasses all understanding, will guard your hearts and minds in Christ Jesus" (emphasis added).

This passage has some striking similarities with GTD. First, notice that both concern peace of mind. David Allen speaks of "mind like water." This passage speaks of "the peace of God" and not being "anxious." I know David Allen isn't talking about peace with God, but the mention of anxiety in this passage hits exactly the same note that GTD is hitting. Paul is talking about how to handle the everyday lack of peace that we have from the stresses and complexities of daily life, just as GTD is.

Second, notice that both this passage and GTD deal with anxiety in similar ways. David Allen says to "get everything out of your mind into a trusted system that you review regularly." Likewise, this passage also speaks of objectifying your concerns—getting them out of your mind—when it says to "let your requests be made known to God."

So we see, right here in Philippians 4, the need to externalize our concerns. There is indeed something to "getting everything out of your mind." We shouldn't just let things run around in our head; we should externalize them.

Third, notice that both GTD and Philippians advocate being comprehensive about getting everything that is on your mind out of your mind. For the passage says "do not be anxious about *anything*, but in *everything* ... let your requests be made known to God." When David Allen speaks of getting things out of your head, and getting *every* incomplete out of your head rather than just some, he is echoing the same truth that the apostle Paul is calling attention to here.

But there is also a significant difference. GTD says to write everything down in a system that you trust and review regularly, whereas Paul tells us to "let your requests be made known to God."

I find it helpful to keep an inventory of all my actions and projects. But I can't always keep this up. What Paul teaches us here is that there is a way to have peace even when we can't keep everything under control: coming to God in prayer with our anxieties.

This approach is not based on our own efforts. We let all our requests be made known to God in prayer, and then God gives us peace. We don't have to keep a written inventory of our commitments, and we don't even have to go through the process of renegotiating the ones that are beyond us. We just lay them all out before God.

In other words, ongoing peace of mind comes through faith in Christ expressed in day-to-day life. This is the kind of peace that can endure even when everything is going haywire and we are simply unable to keep up with things. Why? Because it is not based on us. Just as we do good works *from* justification rather than *for* justification, we are also to do good works *from* peace rather than *for* peace.

With gospel-centered productivity, peace comes first, not second. The mistake we often make is to make peace of mind the result of things we do rather than the source. It is true that we can and should have a sense of satisfaction from our work, and even from having our work defined. That's part of how God made us. Further, being unsettled about what we have left to do is sometimes a way God uses to point us in the right direction (see 2 Cor. 2:13).

But as Christians, we are ultimately able to act from a sense of peace that comes independent of our ability to keep track of our work when circumstances (or energy levels) just make it impossible. And we are able to be more productive in this way because we are not tripped up by the anxiety of always having to get our system fully up to date through our own efforts.

FREE TO SERVE

There is an interesting result here: finding our peace of mind outside of ourselves frees us to serve more, not less.

The reason is that when our peace of mind comes from outside ourselves, it keeps us from finding our identity in our productivity. Living by

Michael Horton on Living a Gospel-Driven Life

I recently asked Mike Horton, professor at Westminster Theological Seminary and author of more than thirty books, including *The Gospel-Driven Life*, what it means to be gospel-driven in our daily lives:

Q: How would you describe what it means to be gospel-driven in our day-to-day actions?

A: It means to feed daily on Christ, which means feeding on the Bible, because the whole Bible is about him. That doesn't mean we squeeze Jesus into every task; it means that we see the Bible as an unfolding plot with Jesus as the central character. The central character can be off screen in some scenes, but we still need to think about how that highlights his central role.

Living life in the light of the gospel is really following Paul's invitation in Romans 12 to let our bodies be a living sacrifice in view of the mercies of God. We are always putting our eyes on Christ, the author and finisher of our faith. This doesn't mean that we're not running and working; as Hebrews 12 says, we're running the race set before us, but our attention is not on the track but on Christ.

Q: What does it mean to be driven by the gospel rather than by the law?

A: It's not a question of getting rid of the law. You can't get rid of the law; that's the heresy of antinomianism. The law is good and has never been the problem. I'm the problem, and the law just identifies that.

But the law can do only what the law can do. The law can only tell us what God requires and thereby explode our sin and misery, and when we find our righteousness in the gospel, the law can tell us what a life of gratitude looks like. The law has that important function to fulfill. But the law never becomes the gospel. The law is always an imperative, a command. The gospel is always an indicative, an announcement of a state of affairs, telling us what God has done.

We should not look to the law—either God's or a task list we have made up for ourselves—for our identity. I use the example of a sailboat. The law can tell us where we are and if we are in trouble. But only the gospel is the wind in our sails.

the gospel each day means that we find our ultimate identity in Christ and what he has done for us, not in anything we do. We will take satisfaction in and enjoy what we do, but it's not the ultimate source of our identity.

The result is that we are secure. Even if everything goes wrong, our identity remains, and this is what enables us to serve people more (which is the essence of productivity), not less. As Rick Warren points out, "Only secure people can serve. Insecure people are always worrying about how they appear to others. They fear exposure of their weaknesses and hide beneath layers of protective pride and pretensions. The more insecure you are, the more you will want people to serve you, and the more you will need their approval."[1]

The Box

Core Point

It is easy to unwittingly fall into the trap of basing our day-to-day peace of mind on our productivity or certain productivity practices. This is a law-based approach to the Christian life. Instead, we are to act *from* peace, not *for* peace. Ultimate peace of mind comes through faith, just as our justification does.

Core Quote

The gospel saves us, giving us a reason to walk through the wilderness to the promised land, and the law guides us, giving us directions for that journey. Christians are driven by God's promises, and directed by God's purposes.
> —Michael Horton, The Gospel-Driven Life

Core Passage

Do not be anxious about anything, but in everything by prayer and supplication with thanksgiving let your requests be made known to God. And the peace of God, which surpasses all understanding, will guard your hearts and your minds in Christ Jesus.
> —Philippians 4:6–7

CHAPTER 9

The Role of Prayer and Scripture in Our Productivity

How God-centered character is at
the foundation of our productivity;
and how we know what's best

*A Christian is something before he does anything; and
we have to be Christian before we can act as Christians.*
— *Martyn Lloyd-Jones,*
Studies in the Sermon on the Mount

EARLY IN HIS BOOK *The Seven Habits of Highly Effective People*, Stephen Covey makes an astute observation about a time when he was immersed in a study of the "success literature" published in the United States since it's founding.

As he read and scanned hundreds of books and articles, he noticed a pattern: most of the literature for the first 150 years of our nation saw character as foundational to success. But most of the literature since then focused on technique (often either human-relations techniques or positive thinking).

Os Guinness makes the same observation when it comes to leadership (and leadership is closely related to personal productivity): "Whereas a combination of faith, character, and virtue was the rock on which traditional leadership was founded, each of these components has crumbled in the twentieth century."[1]

THE CHARACTER ETHIC VERSUS THE PERSONALITY ETHIC

What Covey saw and Os Guinness points out represent two fundamentally different ways of viewing productivity and life: the personality ethic and the character ethic. The *personality ethic* looks mainly at externals as the way to be more productive and effective—how you relate to people, what tactics you use to get things done, and what techniques you follow to accomplish your goals. It might affirm the importance of character, but it is just one ingredient among many.

The *character ethic*, on the other hand, looks first at who you are. It says that true success is not first defined by externals, and the way to live an effective life does not come first from technique. True and lasting effectiveness comes from character, which is not simply an ingredient of an effective life but foundational to it. Techniques do have their place, but only as building blocks upon a foundation of genuine character.

The distinction between the character ethic and personality ethic has its roots right in the Scriptures. For example, Psalm 1 is all about the productive life, for it tells us of a person who is "blessed" (v. 1; "blessed" means "happy" and is a biblical term for the good life) and who prospers in all that he does (v. 3). The "blessedness" of this person is most fundamentally a matter of his character: "He is like a tree planted by streams of water that yields its fruit in its season, and its leaf does not wither" (v. 3; see also Jer. 17:7–8 and Prov. 11:28).

I like how Toby Mac captures this in his song "Lose My Soul," in which he bemoans the fact that so many in America preach prosperity whereas "the first thing to prosper should be inside of me." That's Psalm 1 (and the whole Bible). True productivity is first of all a flourishing of your character.

Notice that this person also bears fruit. I think the primary fruit in view here is character. But the fruit also includes our actions as a legitimate form of fruit, as verse three speaks of this person prospering "in all he does." They are always and ever *ultimately* productive. Nothing they do is in vain, and everything works for their good (cf. Rom. 8:28).

How's that for productivity? Even when things go wrong, everything works for your good.

Misunderstandings of Character

- That it is boring.
- That it claims perfection.
- That it is a substitute for competence. Good character is not an excuse for not knowing what you are doing. Trustworthiness is based not on character alone but on character *and* competence.
- That it always looks down on itself. True Christian character doesn't make the other mistake of going around always saying how horrible we are. That's actually a subtle form of pride. True Christian character is not chiefly self-deprecating, but self-forgetful.
- That it is judgmental. This is not Christian character, but the pharisaical counterfeit Jesus so often opposed through the Gospels.

Likewise, the apostle Peter speaks of God-centered virtue as the fundamental ingredient for a productive life. After listing an impressive number of character qualities (culminating in love), he then says, "For if these qualities are yours and are increasing, they keep you from being ineffective or unfruitful in the knowledge of our Lord Jesus Christ" (2 Peter 1:5–8). Virtue and character are at the root of what it means to live a productive and fruitful life before God, and we should seek to grow in them.

CHARACTER ENABLES US TO DISCERN WHAT'S BEST NEXT

How does character lead to productivity? First, as we have seen, character is itself at the heart of what God requires and is the essence of the productive life. The greatest success is to be a person of character—someone who walks with God, in Christ, and seeks to live this out every day by doing justice and loving mercy (Mic. 6:8). Second, character leads to making the most of our time in the decisions of everyday life because character is actually the *source* of our ability to determine what's best next.

This shouldn't be surprising, since the Golden Rule is the guiding principle for being productive. In order to put others first (love), you need to *be* a loving person. We also see this, for example, in Philippians 1:9–10, where Paul ties making effective decisions ("approve what is excellent") to love and wisdom: "It is my prayer that your love may abound more and more, with knowledge and all discernment, *so that* you may approve what is excellent." Wisdom and love—that is, character—are at the root of how we make good decisions.

Likewise, in Romans 12:2, Paul tells us not to be conformed to this world but to "be transformed by the renewal of your mind, that by testing you may discern what is the will of God, what is good and acceptable and perfect." Here is the character ethic again: Paul commands us to "be transformed" and then roots our ability to make good decisions ("discern what is the will of God") in that transformation of our character.

The core New Testament passage on time management also roots our ability to make good decisions and make the most of the time in wisdom and discernment (that is, character). As we saw, Paul tells us that we make the best use of the time by understanding and doing the will of the Lord (Eph. 5:15–17), and that his will is that we love others (Eph. 5:1–2).

But how do we know what is most loving in any particular situation? We've seen that the Golden Rule is at the heart of this. Obviously many situations are complex, and there are often many good options. But Paul tells us here how to go about this. When he says we are to "*understand what the will of the Lord is*" (Eph. 5:17), he is echoing verse 10, where he had said we are to "*try to discern* what is pleasing to the Lord."

The meaning here, as Peter O'Brien points out in his commentary on Ephesians, is that we are to make decisions by *using our critical judgment* to apply the Scriptures to our everyday situations.[2] God doesn't whisper in our ears what to do next—that would short-circuit the growth of wisdom and path to maturity. Instead, God works through our understanding to enable us to determine the best course of action. He has given us a clear body of ethical teaching in the Scriptures and then, within that framework, given us room to make our own decisions using our renewed thinking. Discernment based on love is the way to know what's best.

This means that the Scriptures are at the foundation of our productivity because the Scriptures are one of the chief ways God brings about

Theologian Wayne Grudem on Prayer, Scripture, and Productivity

Q: What is the most important principle for being productive?

A: Without question, Bible reading and prayer, before the day begins, every day.

Q: Why do you say that?

A: Because it's where I come into the Lord's presence. When you read his word, he speaks to your heart and mind.

Q: How do you keep track of what you pray for?

A: I pray about what I've read and I also have a little notebook with a page for various people in my life, such as my wife, my children, and my neighbors. Then early in the prayer book is a page for myself, where two of my main prayers are for the forgiveness of sins and helping me to grow in obedience to God.

Q: How do you do your Bible reading?

A: Right now I've generally been reading one chapter in the Old Testament (it was Lamentations 1 this morning) and then a chapter, or part of a chapter, in the New Testament (it was 1 Peter 5 this morning). I've been on 1 Peter 5 for about three days. I just read until I'm learning something from the Lord.

this transformation and builds our character. In Psalm 1, for example, the reason this person flourishes in his character and prospers in all he does (v. 3) is *because* "his delight is in the law of the Lord, and on his law he meditates day and night" (v. 2).[3] Related to this, prayer is also foundational to our productivity because in prayer we call on God for help and strength (notice also how Jesus connects prayer, the Scriptures, and productivity in John 14:7–8).

This is not moralism. The essence of character is walking with God.[4] The essence, the heart, and the basic dimension of the Christian life is living in fellowship with God, and central to that is prayer and the Scriptures.

The other component of character, which flows from love of God, is love of others. This manifests itself in a tendency to think of others, seek their welfare, and put them first. Rick Warren captures this well: "Thinking of others is at the heart of Christlikeness and the best evidence of spiritual growth. This kind of thinking is unnatural, counter-cultural, rare, and difficult."[5] That's why character issues in productivity: it is of the essence of Christlike character to always be thinking of others — which, as we have seen, is the guiding principle of our productivity.

If we want to get more specific and see how true character manifests itself in daily life, there are five primary passages that lay this out and get right to the core: The Beatitudes (Matt. 5:3–11), the Sermon on the Mount (Matt. 5:3–7:27), Paul's great chapter on love (1 Cor. 13), the fruit of the Spirit (Gal. 5:22–23), and the character qualities of 2 Peter 1:5–11.

SUMMING THINGS UP SO FAR

Here's what we've seen so far: We have an incredible opportunity to do good unlike any before, the doctrine of vocation and the radical call of the Christian life encourage and command us to maximize this, the doctrine of justification by faith alone empowers our productivity because it shows that God's action is always *first*, and prayer and Scripture build our character to equip us in this call. This is exciting.

As we've also seen, there is a villain in the midst of all this: It can be extremely difficult to capitalize on these opportunities because we have so many choices and often feel overloaded and pulled in too many directions. This tension makes it hard to navigate and be effective — and to do it all with joy.

That's why good intentions are not enough. We need a method for our productivity. That's where we now turn.

The Box

Core Point

The fundamental way to know what's best next—to make good decisions in an age of unlimited options—is to be a person of character. While lists and techniques have their place, none of them will bear the fruit we are called to bear if our productivity is not first founded on being the right kind of person.

Core Passage

Note the connection between prayer, love, and decision making in Philippians 1:9–10: "And it is my prayer that your love may abound more and more, with knowledge and all discernment, so that you may approve what is excellent."

Immediate Application

If you aren't already doing so, begin reading your Bible and praying every day.

Further Resources

> Martyn Lloyd-Jones, *Studies in the Sermon on the Mount*, especially chapters 3–12 on the Beatitudes and, in volume 2, chapters 2–6 on prayer
>
> D. A. Carson, *A Call to Spiritual Reformation: Priorities from Paul and His Prayers*
>
> Bill Hybels, *Too Busy Not to Pray*

CHAPTER 10

The Core Principle for Making Yourself Effective

We have to distinguish personal leadership and personal management; you have to be able to lead yourself before you can manage yourself

Leadership capability relates as much to how we lead ourselves as to how we lead others.

— *Scott Belsky*

THE BEST WAY TO UNDERSTAND A SUBJECT is not necessarily to learn everything there is to know about it. In fact, you can know all sorts of things about a subject and still be in the dark.

THE BEST WAY TO UNDERSTAND A SUBJECT

Instead, the best way to understand a subject is to understand the core idea—the governing concept that goes to the heart of the matter and holds everything else together.

For example, when we began the redesign of the website for Desiring God Ministries in 2004, we decided that our primary emphasis would be usability. So we learned everything we could about usability and built the site on that basis. When we finally released the site two years later, visits doubled within four months and page views nearly quadrupled. Audio listens quadrupled as well.

WEBSITES — AND ALMOST EVERYTHING — OPERATE THIS WAY

Everything that we learned in this process was helpful, but there was one integrating idea that went to the core and made everything else we learned useful. It's from Steve Krug, who pointed out that the definition of a usable site is that it doesn't make you think.[1]

There it was: the core idea of usability in a single sentence. This gave us the core principle for knowing what design choices made for a usable site and what didn't. A usable site minimizes question marks. You don't have to think hard about how to use it; the way to use the site is obvious, intuitive, and natural.

By knowing this core principle and some of the primary applications of it, we were able to think for ourselves about what makes a site usable. We could now evaluate any site using this framework.

This approach can be applied to just about anything: politics, government, communication, leadership, management, theology, everything. Seek to identify the core governing principle, and then everything else follows from that.

EVEN GOD'S COMMANDS CAN BE SUMMED UP IN A CORE IDEA

We even saw earlier that God's commandments can be summed up in a single idea. In the Old Testament Law, there are about 613 laws. But when asked which law was the greatest, Jesus said love God with all your heart and love your neighbor as yourself. Then he added, "On these two commandments depend all the Law and the Prophets" (Matt. 22:40). Likewise, earlier in Matthew 7:12 he had said, "So whatever you wish that others would do to you, do also to them, for this is the Law and the Prophets," summarizing the entire Old Testament law into a single principle.

Jesus was showing us that everything in the law flows from this core principle, and therefore everything we do should flow from that core principle as well. Paul (Rom. 13:9), James (James 2:8), and the other New Testament authors followed suit and said the same thing.

WHY FOCUSING ON TACTICS *PRIMARILY* IS A BAD IDEA

We need to approach productivity and time management in the same way.

We could seek to learn all sorts of tactics and principles for making the most of our time and our lives, and there would be some value in that. But the value would be limited if we didn't know the core idea that integrates everything and allows us to think for ourselves without having to be told all the tactics and principles.

The overarching, guiding principle for our lives is love. Putting the other person first equals maximum productivity. Now, when we come down a level, what's the core principle for translating that in to action every day — the core principle for making ourselves productive and effective, rather than continually being thrown off course by the busyness of life?

THE CORE PRINCIPLE OF PRODUCTIVITY

Here it is: Know what's most important and put it first.

There are lots of different ways to say this, but that's the core principle for how to be productive and effective. Like most core ideas, it makes the most sense when you see it fleshed out and see it applied, which we will do.

Here are some other ways to put it:

Rick Warren: "The secret of effectiveness is to know what really counts, then do what really counts, and not worry about the rest."[2]

Peter Drucker: "If there is any one 'secret' of effectiveness, it is concentration. Effective executives do first things first and they do one thing at a time."[3]

Stephen Covey: "The key ... is not to prioritize your schedule, but to schedule your priorities."[4]

WHAT'S DISTINCTIVE ABOUT THIS

This principle becomes especially clear when we contrast it with its opposite. A lot of times we simply seek to capture and organize all the things vying for our attention, thinking that if we can just get all those things under control, we will *then* have time to do the important things.

But that never works. The smaller tasks always multiply, so if you try to take a bottom-up approach to your productivity, you will be directed by the course of events rather than charting your own course and accomplishing the things you are called to do.

What you need to do is define what's most important first and *then* take a look at what's before you and identify what you are and are not going to do. This is a top-down, proactive approach to getting things done.

It doesn't mean that the little stuff doesn't matter or that it can be overlooked. Much of the little stuff does need to be done. But identifying the most important things and doing them first makes the smaller stuff fall into place. The reverse approach—focusing on the smaller things and trying to fit the larger stuff in where you can—does not work and is a recipe for frustration.

I think Stephen Covey has stated this the best: "Don't prioritize your schedule; schedule your priorities." That's the core principle in seven words. You can't do everything, so identify the most important things and make everything else work around them.

PUTTING THE MOST IMPORTANT THINGS IN FIRST

The illustration is fairly well known, but since it is so effective in illustrating this principle, it bears repeating.

In his book *First Things First*, Stephen Covey talks about an associate of his who attended a seminar on time management. At one point the instructor pulled out a large glass jar and set it on a table next to some large rocks. Then he asked the class, "How many of these rocks do you think will fit in the jar?"

The attendees made their guesses, and he proceeded to add one rock after another to the jar. Eventually, the jar was filled with the rocks. He then asked, "Is this jar full?"

The class said, "Yes," but he then pulled out a bucket of gravel. He dumped the gravel in, shook it around, and it filled up the spaces between the rocks. By this time, the class was on to him, so when he asked if the jar was full, they said, "Probably not."

He then pulled out a bucket of sand, and the sand filled in all the spaces between the rocks and the gravel. Then he pulled out a pitcher of water, and the water filled in the rest.

He then asked the class, "What's the point?"

One person spoke up, probably speaking for most of us when we first hear this: "There are always gaps, so if you work at it, you can always fit more into your life."

But the instructor said, "No, that's not the point." His point, rather, was this: If he hadn't put the big rocks in first, none of the big rocks would have ever been able to get in at all.

WE SEE THIS IN THE BIBLE

This is not simply a principle of common grace. The Lord also teaches us to operate this way with our lives. For example, he reprimands the Pharisees for tithing out of their spice racks while neglecting "the weightier matters of the law" (Matt. 23:23). Jesus' point is not that the smaller things don't matter; he immediately adds "these you ought to have done, without neglecting the others." His point is that we are to start with the most important things first (which, at an ultimate level, are justice, mercy, and walking with God); only then can everything else find its proper place.

Likewise, in the Sermon on the Mount Jesus tells us not to be anxious about food and clothing and things like that. His point is not that they don't matter; they do: "your heavenly Father knows you need them all" (Matt. 6:32). His point is that they aren't what's most important, and so if you put them first, everything goes haywire (and you are committing idolatry). Instead, Jesus says "seek first the kingdom of God and his righteousness, and all these things will be added to you" (Matt. 6:33).

Jesus is telling us to operate from priorities. And at the ultimate level, it is not up to us to determine our priorities. We have one ultimate priority, and it is given to us by God: Seek him and his kingdom first.

SETH GODIN ON THE CORE PRINCIPLE FOR PRODUCTIVITY

I had the chance to interview Seth Godin, one of the leading thinkers today on marketing and the world of work, when I was at the 2011 Global Leadership Summit at Willow Creek (which I highly recommend for all leaders, by the way).[5]

Godin was initially apprehensive about the concept of time management. He argued that when people talk of having too much to do, it often amounts to "productivity whining" (a term I think he coined during the interview). It's an excuse, he argued, to avoid having to make the hard decision of what's really important and thus what you should do next. Which is exactly, he argued, what the core principle of productivity really is: Decide what really matters *and do it*. "Once you decide, you don't need to worry about all this other stuff. You can just do the thing you've decided is important."

Decide what really matters, and then do it.

Seth Godin on the Essence of Productivity and Avoiding "Productivity Whining"

Here's what Seth Godin had to say when I interviewed him on personal productivity:

Q: What would you say is the fundamental idea for being productive? And by this I mean being effective, not mainly getting more done in less time.

A: You don't need more time. You just need to decide.

Q: You just decide? What do you do with the stuff that keeps bugging you and you don't know what to do with it?

A: Why is it bugging you?

Q: There's a lot of it.

A: There's a lot of other stuff in the world that's not bugging you. My neighbor down the street has a big pile of cans that need to go back to recycling, and that's not bugging me. The stuff that's bugging you is bugging you because it keeps you from deciding.

Q: What about when it seems like there will be consequences—such as when you're getting eighty emails a day?

A: Sure, there's consequences. Of course. That's why it's hard to decide. If you're on a boat and it's on fire and it's sinking, and your shoes are untied, you don't stop to tie your shoes. You just get off the boat. It's an easy decision. But if it's not that, but someone's bugging you, and someone's doing this, and you have to do this or that, you'll do those before you make the hard decision of deciding. But once you decide, you don't need to worry about all this other stuff. You can just do the thing you've decided is important.

Q: So you're saying decide what's most important, and actually do it.

A: I think "productivity whining" is largely an artifact for people who are looking for a way not to decide.

You can watch the full interview online: *http://www.whatsbestnext .com/2013/05/productivity-interview-with-seth-godin.*

CRAIG GROESCHEL ON THE CORE PRINCIPLE OF PRODUCTIVITY

While at the leadership summit, I also had the chance to interview Craig Groeschel, pastor of Life Church in Oklahoma City, one of the largest and fastest growing churches in the nation.

Here's the gist of what he said: "For me, one of the most important things is having the courage to say no to those things that are often good, but not dead-on mission.... I'm working on increasing my nos so that my yeses will stay on track with my primary mission, which is building the local church."

THE CORE PRINCIPLE IS ACTUALLY ... TWO PRINCIPLES

Coming back to how we've stated the core principle, you'll notice that, ironically, there are actually two core principles here. "Know what's most important" is the first one, and "put it first" is the second one.

Or, put differently, "know what you're trying to accomplish (know what comes first)" and "put first things first (actually put it first)."

Which means: Don't first ask, "What appointments and tasks are vying for my attention and how do I get them all done?" Rather, you need to ask whether you should be doing those things at all and, before that, know what's most important in your life—the "first things." Then you do those things—either right away, if you can, or by slotting them into your week if you can't.

And you need to do this constantly. When you are with your kids at night (or doing anything else), what's most important (what's best next) is different from when you are at the office. You need to make these shifts. Know what's most important right where you are and focus on that.

These two principles correspond to the two areas of effectiveness that we've encountered: personal leadership and personal management. "Know what's most important" is the arena of personal leadership; "put it first and actually do it" is the arena of personal management.

PERSONAL LEADERSHIP VERSUS PERSONAL MANAGEMENT

When most people hear the term *productivity*, they tend to think of finding ways to manage their time better, create shortcuts, become efficient, and get more things done in less time. The focus is on to-do lists, schedules, and cool tips and tricks. This is the realm of personal management.

It has to do with creating order and sanity out of complexity. It is the day-to-day management of our tasks, projects, and routines.

Personal leadership, on the other hand, has to do with the direction you are headed. Why are you on the planet? What is your ultimate objective in life? What are your roles and the primary things you are seeking to accomplish? What are your values and principles? What are your priorities?

If personal leadership is about *where* you are going, personal management is about *how* you get there. The saying goes "managers do things right; leaders do the right things." In our lives, as in our organizations, we need both. We need to determine what the right things are (personal leadership) and we need to put them into practice (personal management).[6]

HOW THE SIX HORIZONS OF WORK RELATE TO PERSONAL LEADERSHIP AND MANAGEMENT

This distinction between personal leadership and personal management is illustrated well by considering it in relation to the six horizons of work. The six horizons are:

Personal Leadership
- 50,000 feet: Mission and values
- 40,000 feet: Vision (or life goal)
- 30,000 feet: Long-term goals
- 20,000 feet: Roles

Personal Management
- 10,000 feet: Projects
- Runway: Next actions and calendar
- Supporting systems: Contacts, checklists, journals, and files

This provides a very helpful way of viewing all the different levels of commitments that we have.

Briefly, the levels of mission and values, vision, long-term goals, and roles are matters of personal leadership. The levels of projects and next actions are matters of personal management.

The six horizons of work, together with the supporting components, all translate into an overall framework, or system, for how to navigate your life and work.

The key is to determine your mission, roles, and goals on the basis of biblical principles, and then keep them "alive" in a way that allows for continual review and translation into action.

WHY PRODUCTIVITY SYSTEMS EXIST

We saw earlier that the purpose of productivity is doing good for others. A project list, for example, is not just a way of keeping track of what you have to do. It's a way of brainstorming, identifying, and managing initiatives that you are undertaking to make life better for others and build them up.

Further, our aim is not simply to do some good for others but, like John Wesley, to do all the good we can. This means we are going to have more ideas than we can act on right away, and we are going to undertake some initiatives that are not simple but complex—some of which are going to be long-term.

This leads to the need to be able to keep track of these things (personal management) and make good on them.

This is why productivity approaches and systems exist: as tools to equip you and enable you in the fight of doing good for others, to the glory of God.

AND THE ONE MAIN PITFALL

But there is one problem, of course, with any "system" for productivity: The system can end up strangling you.

When that happens, it's a sign that personal management has trumped personal leadership, that you've lost your direction and are now seeking solutions in how to manage your life rather than in how you lead it.

In other words, the same thing that is true of projects is true of us as individuals. Here's what Scott Berkun says about projects in *The Art of Project Management*: "More often than not, I've found that obsessing on process is a warning sign of leadership trouble: it can be an attempt to offload the natural challenges and responsibilities that managers face into a system of procedures and bureaucracies that cloud the need for *real thought and action* [emphasis added]. Perhaps even more devastating to a team is that methodology fixation can be a signal of what is truly important to the organization."[7]

So if you find yourself getting too bogged down in how you organize and keep up your next action lists and project lists, the problem is not your next action and project lists. Rather, these are simply symptoms of a leadership problem: you aren't leading yourself the way you ought. You don't have clarity on what you ought to be doing and the direction you should be taking. The result is confusion down in the lower levels.

Make your productivity systems streamlined, but don't spend time over-optimizing. *Act.* You are free to do this because knowing what's best does *not* depend on having your system all up to date; rather it depends on just stopping, reflecting, and asking, "What is the best thing to do *now*?"

KNOWING THE CORE QUESTION

Which is simply the core question of productivity: *What's best next?*

Even if you don't have your next action lists up to date, you don't have all your projects defined, and you don't even have all your appointments on your calendar, you can still do this.

You just need to have the *discernment* to answer it right and the *discipline* to do it. And you will have good answers for it only if (1) you know what truly is most important in life at the highest levels and (2) your character and mind are rightly informed by the Scriptures.

This means that you don't know what's best next simply by considering your immediate circumstances; you can know it only by also understanding why you are on the planet at all and what God has specifically called you to do.

GOSPEL-DRIVEN PRODUCTIVITY

There is a distinction we can make between productivity and the discipline of personal productivity. As we saw in previous chapters, to be *productive* is to be abundant in doing good for others, according to your gifts and abilities. But, as we also saw, productivity does not come automatically. We have to make ourselves effective. The discipline of *personal productivity*, then, is the *process* by which we do this — that is, the process of taking our talents, abilities, and opportunities and *making them useful* for the good of others, the glory of God, and our joy.

This brings us to the four steps of Gospel-Driven Productivity. We saw in this chapter that the core idea for making ourselves effective is to know what's most important and put it first. There are four steps to help us do this:

1. Define: Know your mission, vision, and roles.
2. Architect: Weave these things into your life through a flexible schedule.
3. Reduce: Get rid of the things that don't fit.
4. Execute: Make things happen every day.

Conveniently, these form the acronym DARE, which reminds us of the motive and guiding principle that is to lie behind all that we do: seek the benefit of others in all things, to the glory of God, and have a sense of adventure in doing this. Be creative, competent, and audacious in doing good for others, both where you are and around the world.

The first step for weaving this into the fabric of your life is to know why you are here at all and what is most important at the ultimate levels of life. That's what the next section, "Define," is about.

The Box

Core Point

The core principle of effectiveness is to know what's most important and put it first. Don't prioritize your schedule; schedule your priorities.

Immediate Application

If you are feeling overwhelmed and aren't getting done what you should, ask yourself, "Is this a personal leadership problem or a personal management problem?" That is, "Do I lack clarity on what I should be doing (personal leadership), or do I lack clarity in organizing and executing around those priorities (personal management)?"

PART 3

Define

KNOW WHAT'S MOST IMPORTANT

Our greatest fear as individuals and as a church should not be of failure but of succeeding at things in life that don't really matter.

— *Tim Kizziar*

IF THE CORE PRINCIPLE OF PRODUCTIVITY is to know what's most important and to do it next, it's essential to know what's most important. That's what "define," the first step in DARE, is about.

Unfortunately, most books on planning your life go wrong here and blow an incredible opportunity. What's most important is left to you to define for yourself. The notion is that this is about creating a life that matters *to you*, finding personal peace and affluence, and creating your perfect life effortlessly.

Certainly our desires and aims matter. But what most productivity books miss is that we need to set the ultimate trajectory of our lives based not on what we think but on what God says. We need to build our lives on Jesus' words, not our own (Matt. 7:24−27).

The direction we set for ourselves needs to be God-centered. John Piper captures this well: "Whatever you do, find the God-centered, Christ exalting, Bible-saturated passion of your life, and find your way to say it and live for it and die for it. And you will make a difference that lasts. You will not waste your life."[1]

The question, then, is, "How do I find this? And once I've found it, how do I live this way?" Numerous Christian books give an excellent call to living radical lives devoted to the glory of God and the good of others, but they typically don't go into much detail regarding how to weave this into the fabric of your life. This leaves us at a loss for how to apply these things consistently.

Define

Many secular books on productivity, on the other hand, have a great framework for capturing your overall priorities in life and making them happen, but they don't call you to set the right priorities based on what God says rather than on what you say.

We are going to solve that problem by showing how to find the God-centered, Christ-exalting passion of your life (this section), then showing how to keep this at the center of your life and weave it into everything you do (parts 4–6).

There are four components to the first step in this process, "define":

1. *Mission:* Develop a personal mission statement.
2. *Vision:* Know your overarching life calling, or life goal, and how it differs from your mission.
3. *Roles:* Know the specific everyday callings in your life.
4. *Goals:* Know how to create change at quarterly, yearly, and multiyear increments.[2]

CHAPTER 11

What's Your Mission? How Not to Waste Your Life

There is a purpose to life, and you can know it and center your life around it

Christianity requires that we should make God and Christ our main end; and all Christians, so far as they live like Christians, live so that "for them to live is Christ."

—Jonathan Edwards, Charity and Its Fruits

For none of us lives to himself, and none of us dies to himself. For if we live, we live to the Lord, and if we die, we die to the Lord. So then, whether we live or whether we die, we are the Lord's.

—Romans 14:7 8

IS IT BIBLICAL to have a mission statement, or is this just an idea borrowed from secular thinking?

Yes, mission statements are biblical. You can find them throughout the Bible (see the sidebar "Mission Statements in the Bible"), and God himself has one (see the sidebar "God's Mission").

In this chapter we will look at four things: what a mission statement is, why you need to have one, why most mission statements fail, and a simple way to get your mission statement right.

WHAT IS A MISSION STATEMENT?

Mission statements have a bad reputation for being lofty, wordy, and ambiguous statements that people don't really mean. That kind of mission statement doesn't help, and you don't need to fall into that trap—either with your personal mission statement or with your organization's mission statement. The focus of this chapter is your personal mission statement, but I will briefly apply the components to organizational mission statements at the end.

A good personal mission statement has three components:

1. Core purpose
2. Core principles
3. Core beliefs

You might add other components as well, but this is the essence of it. These three components address four main themes: (1) who you are, (2) why you are here, (3) where you are going to end up at the end of all this, and (4) what the main principles are by which you will guide your life.

Notice that I don't include *what* you are specifically doing with your life. That is for two reasons.

First, before you can even answer the question, "What am I going to do with my life?" you need to answer the question, "Who am I, what do I stand for, and why am I here at all?" Who you are and why you exist need to precede your specific aims in life.

Second, the purpose of your mission statement is to define the rock-bottom principles that define you even in times when you don't know what you are doing or where you are going. You want your mission statement to orient you even when your entire world seems to be giving way—when you've lost your job, lost your house, aren't sure what city to live in, and the wonderful plan you have for your life seems blown apart.

Think of the worst possible situation you could be in. Your mission statement is a good one if it is able to help you *then*, in those circumstances. Only then will it be able to guide you in the ordinary circumstances of life.

What you are going to do specifically with your life (your life goal or life vision) is thus a slightly distinct thing from your mission, and is at a slightly lower level. Think of the difference like this, using the great social reformer William Wilberforce as an example:

Mission: Glorify God and enjoy him forever.
Life Goal: Bring an end to the slave trade.

The key difference is that you can fail at your life goal and still succeed at your mission, and thus your life. Your mission is a matter of *principle*, and it is something you can do in failure as well as success. (Fortunately for us, Wilberforce accomplished both his mission and life goal — though not without great perseverance and much hardship along the way.)

We will talk about creating a good life vision in the next chapter.

Mission Statements in the Bible

He has told you, O man, what is good; and what does the Lord require of you but to do justice, and to love kindness, and to walk humbly with your God?

—*Micah 6:8*

"Let your light shine before others, so that they may see your good works and give glory to your Father who is in heaven."

—*Matthew 5:16*

And this is eternal life, that they know you the only true God, and Jesus Christ whom you have sent.

—*John 17:3*

It is my eager expectation and hope that I will not be at all ashamed, but that with full courage now as always Christ will be honored in my body, whether by life or by death. For to me to live is Christ, and to die is gain.

—*Philippians 1:20–21; cf. also 3:8–11 with 3:13–14*

Here's a way of summarizing: The purpose of life is to know God, enjoy God, reflect his glory back to him by pursuing justice and mercy in all things, and do this in community with others through Jesus Christ.

WHY YOU SHOULD HAVE A MISSION STATEMENT

First, having a clear mission is the essence of personal leadership. Without a clear mission, you are aimless and without direction. You cannot lead yourself if you don't know where you are headed. And note that I define "where you are headed" as first of all being a certain type of person. Not first as "do this" but "be this." Who we are precedes what we do.

Second, knowing your mission gives meaning to your life. If you are struggling with a sense of purpose and meaning, it may be because your mission is not clear—because you don't know why you are here. God doesn't intend for us to go through life without a sense of meaning and significance. The problem is not seeking significance; it's seeking it in the wrong things.

Third, you need to know your mission because the most effective Christians are not aimless; they know why they are here. Jonathan Edwards, for example, is famous for the seventy resolutions he created at the age of nineteen.

Jonathan Edwards' life was well lived. You can see that he had the right direction by just reading his resolutions, and when you learn about his life, you see that he lived by them.[1]

Edwards is an incredible example for us to follow here. He is an example to us of true productivity, showing us that true productivity is about a life well lived and that, even more, a life well lived is a God-centered life.

Edwards also shows us that a life well lived doesn't just happen; it requires intentionality. And intentionality manifests itself in certain "mechanisms" that help us maintain our intentionality. Edwards' resolutions are one example of such a mechanism.

Fourth, you need to give thought to your mission because, whether you know it or not, you already have one. Most time management books treat your mission statement as something you define for yourself. But in reality, defining your mission isn't in the arena of things you decide. There is an objective purpose to your life that you did not set. Your mission is discovered, not chosen.

This means that it's important not simply to have a mission statement but also to make sure you get it right. It is possible to have the wrong mission. If you don't think through your mission deliberately, you can easily default to the wrong mission in life.

WHY MOST MISSION STATEMENTS FAIL

It may be controversial for me to say that you can have the wrong mission in life. As I mentioned, most time management books treat your mission as something highly individual and personal. They talk in deliberately ambiguous terms, such as "what matters most," in order to leave room for each person to define what matters most for himself or herself.

I don't agree with that view for the simple reason that we did not create ourselves. Since we didn't create ourselves, we can't define our own purpose, either. God created you and defined your purpose. Your role is to *know* what that purpose is, *embrace it*, and *state it* in a way that captures your own individuality and uniqueness.

This explains why many of us who have tried to create a mission statement have found it frustrating. Most personal mission statements just don't work very well, if you can figure one out at all.

This is the experience I had when I first tried to write one. I got my first planner after seminary when I was launching the nationwide radio program. I went through the exercises they had in the back to define your mission, values, and goals, and found it very helpful—initially.

But as I continued to reflect on the mission statement portion, I simply could not figure it out. I wrote something down and went with it for a few months. But it didn't seem right or helpful (or motivating), so I came up with other ideas. Nothing really seemed to capture me.

In retrospect, the reason for my struggle is obvious, but at the time it was hard for me to see. The reason I had such a hard time figuring out my mission is because I was starting with myself. Sure, my thinking was biblically informed; I didn't just sit down and think about what I wanted, forgetting about God. The Bible shaped all of my thinking.

However, my mistake was in not realizing that the purpose of my life had already been defined. You don't get to choose your purpose. It has already been defined, and it's the same for everyone. There are a thousand different ways we can say it, and we all need to state it in a way that is unique to ourselves, but the essence is the same for everyone.

The reason most mission statements fail is because people are looking to themselves to figure out their purpose. Since we didn't create ourselves, simply looking to ourselves to find our purpose will never work. Rick Warren captures this very well: "The search for the purpose of life has puzzled people for thousands of years. That's because we typically begin at the wrong starting point—ourselves.... Contrary to what many popular books, movies, and seminars tell you, you won't discover your life's meaning by looking within yourself. You probably tried that already. You didn't create yourself, so there is no way you can tell yourself what you were created for."[2]

Since we were created by God and for God, we need to look to him to know our purpose. The purpose of life is attainable only by revelation, not speculation. "Trust in the Lord with all your heart, and do not lean

God's Mission

In his classic work *The End for Which God Created the World*, Jonathan Edwards looks at God's reason for creating the world and doing everything that he does to see if there is a single, integrating, ultimate goal behind everything that God does. He argues that there is: "Thus we see that the great end of God's works, which is so variously expressed in Scripture, is indeed but ONE; and this one end is most properly and comprehensively called, THE GLORY OF GOD."[*]

God is not arbitrary, or haphazard, or aimless. He has a purpose in everything that he does. There is even, if we may speak in this way, a purpose for his own existence—namely, to glorify himself. Or, as John Piper puts it, "The chief end of God is to glorify himself and enjoy himself forever."[‡]

We see this throughout the Bible. For example, God created his people for his glory (Isa. 42:6–7), commands us to do everything for his glory (1 Cor. 10:31), redeems us for his glory (Eph. 1:5–6), and is working so that one day his glory will fill the whole earth (Hab. 2:14).

For more on God's mission, see chapter 1 of John Piper's *Let the Nations Be Glad: The Supremacy of God in Missions*, or his book *God's Passion for His Glory: Living the Vision of Jonathan Edwards*.

[*] See John Piper, *God's Passion for His Glory* (Wheaton, IL: Crossway, 2006), 246.

[‡] John Piper, *Desiring God: Meditations of a Christian Hedonist*, 10th anniversary expanded edition (Sisters, OR: Multnomah, 1996), 33. Piper then spends the entire first chapter fleshing out the implications of this. See also chapter 1 of *Let the Nations be Glad* (Grand Rapids, MI: Baker, 2003) for the extensive biblical case for the glory of God being the ultimate purpose of God in all things.

on your own understanding. In all your ways acknowledge him, and he will make straight your paths" (Prov. 3:5–6).

This is a liberating truth because it means you don't have to "make" your life meaningful. It already is meaningful. God himself loves you and has a purpose for you. Ultimate significance is offered and available to you.

FOUR PRINCIPLES FOR CREATING MISSION STATEMENTS THAT WORK

Though we don't define our own purpose, it is our place to know what our purpose is and state it in a way that is unique to us. To do this, we need to know the four overarching principles for identifying our mission, and then we need to know how to flesh out our mission in a clear purpose statement and a set of core principles.

1. Don't start by envisioning your funeral. Often the advice is given to envision what you want people to say at your funeral. In sixth grade my social studies teacher gave us a similar task of writing our own obituaries. And, it actually was helpful. So I'm not saying there is no place for this sort of thing. But what matters first is what God says and what God commands. This means we start by looking explicitly at what the Bible says about the purpose of our lives first, and only then doing an exercise like writing our obituary.

Starting by reflecting on what you want others to say about you at the end of your life is just a species of a larger fallacy: starting with yourself. Rick Warren describes this problem well: "I once heard the suggestion that you develop your life purpose statement based on what you would like other people to say about you at your funeral. Imagine your perfect eulogy, then build your statement on that. Frankly, that's a bad plan. At the end of your life it isn't going to matter at all what other people say about you. The only thing that will matter is what God says about you."[3]

What do you want to say to God when you give an account? What do you want God to say to you? That would be a good place to start. Remember that we will all give an account of ourselves to God (Rom. 14:12). A successful life is a life you won't be ashamed to give an account of to God, a life to which he will say "well done" (Matt. 25:21).

Again, I don't think it's a bad idea to reflect on what you would want people to say at your funeral or to do the related exercise of writing your own obituary. Just don't do that first. First look at what God says and what account you will want to give to him,[4] and then consider your funeral or obituary, doing so in light of the biblical commands regarding how we are to be in the world.

2. Base your mission on the actual purpose of life. After Rick Warren came out with his book *The Purpose Driven Life*, Bill Maher accused him of arrogance for claiming to know what the purpose of life is. But it's not arrogant to say we can know the purpose of life for the simple reason that God himself has revealed the purpose of life. It is not prideful to believe and affirm what God himself has said; indeed, it would be arrogant *not* to.

God has stated the purpose of life throughout the Bible in dozens of different ways. The words God uses (and that you can use) to describe it can differ, but the essence is always the same. The purpose of life is to know God, enjoy God, reflect his glory back to him, and do this in community with others through Jesus Christ.

That's the ultimate purpose of life, both now and forever.

Note that Jesus is central to it all. The purpose of life is not simply to know God, or enjoy him, or reflect him, but to do so *through* Jesus: "And *this is eternal life*, that they know you the only true God, and Jesus Christ whom you have sent" (John 17:3, emphasis added). Thus, we can say that Jesus himself is the purpose of life. "I am the way, and the truth, *and the life*. No one comes to the Father except through me" (John 14:6, emphasis added).

One of the best statements of our mission in the Bible is when Paul says that his aim is always that "Christ will be honored in my body, whether by life or by death. For to me to live is Christ, and to die is gain" (Phil. 1:20–21). When Paul says "to me to live is Christ," he means, "Christ is my main end in life. I belong to him, and everything I do is for him. Nothing else matters without him" (cf. Phil. 3:8–14, where Paul states his purpose in more detail and then commends it to us all in v. 15).

Echoing this again in Romans 14:7–8, Paul states his and our purpose this way: "For none of us lives to himself, and none of us dies to himself. For if we live, we live to the Lord, and if we die, we die to the Lord. So then, whether we live or whether we die, we are the Lord's."

Outside the Bible, perhaps Jonathan Edwards has captured this best: "Christianity requires that we should make God and Christ our main end; and all Christians, so far as they live like Christians, live so that 'for them to live is Christ.' "[5]

Note that your mission is personal, not impersonal. It is not just principle-centered; it is God-centered. God—Jesus—is a person. Your mission is to live unto him—and die unto him. To serve him, love him, know him, reflect him—and do this in community with his people, with an outward focus that seeks to serve the world for its good.

In addition to Jesus being central to the purpose of life, our joy is central as well. The purpose of life is not to "worship Jesus whether you like it or not, so there." The purpose of life is to do so gladly and with joy, to find our ultimate satisfaction in God, to follow Jesus because we want to and can't imagine doing anything else, not because we are under obligation. This is why you exist, but you need to embrace it—with joy. There is no ultimate conflict between the pursuit of God's glory and the pursuit of your joy. The Westminster Confession captures this well: "The chief end of man is to glorify God and enjoy him forever."

But perhaps John Piper says it best: "The chief end of man is to glorify God *by* enjoying him forever." Piper rightly points out that glorifying God and enjoying God are not two separate things. Rather, we glorify God *by* enjoying him because it is by enjoying something that you show how great it is.

3. Be purpose directed, but gospel driven. Since a mission statement is, after all, a "mission," it's easy for the focus to be exclusively what *we* must do. But if your mission is all about what you have to do, it's all law and no gospel, which means that ultimately it cannot motivate or work.

As Michael Horton has said, "Knowing your purpose is a form of law."[6] Anytime we are in the realm of what we are to do, we are in the realm of law. The law is not bad; it's simply that the law's role is only to guide our lives and not ultimately empower them. The gospel—what God has done for us in Christ—is the ultimate motivation for what we do. We are to be purpose *directed* but gospel *driven*.

If you *only* capture your purpose, you are in the realm of law and will live a law-based rather than gospel-based life. That's why, in addition to our core purpose and core principles, a mission statement also includes the third component of core *beliefs*.

4. Include justice and mercy as part of your purpose. For some reason it's always tempting when we talk about glorifying God to think we need to retreat from life and go off into the woods to serve him. Resist this temptation. God is clear, as we have seen, that serving him implies a commitment to the good of others.

This is manifest in a commitment to justice and mercy in your life. Indeed, this is not just a good idea; it is required by God. For example, in stating the ultimate purpose of life, Micah 6:8 states, "He has told you, O man, what is good; and what does the Lord require of you but to do justice, and to love kindness, and to walk humbly with your God?"

The life of faith can be summarized as doing justice, loving mercy, and doing this in fellowship with God. Jesus also alluded to this passage in Matthew 23:23, referring to these three things as "the weightier matters of the law."

Doing justice means not just being fair and honest in all your dealings but using any influence and ability you have on behalf of those in need. That is the "right use of power," as Gary Haugen points out in *Good News about Injustice*. And it's what we see in Isaiah's statement on the nature of life as God intended it for his people in this world: "Cease to do evil, learn to do good; seek justice, correct oppression; bring justice to the fatherless, plead the widow's cause" (Isa. 1:16–17).

Likewise, to pursue mercy is to be diligent and proactive in seeking good for others. It means putting others before ourselves and sacrificing our own interests for their sakes. It also means being holistic and caring for the physical, social, and psychological needs of others as well as spiritual needs, as the parable of the Good Samaritan shows (Luke 10:25–37).

Our mission cannot be separated from the pursuit of justice. Gladly pursuing justice and mercy, in fellowship with God, is at the essence of our life purpose. It is the supreme display, you could say, of knowing God, and the chief means by which we glorify him. "He judged the cause of the poor and needy; then it was well. *Is not this to know me?*" (Jer. 22:16, emphasis added).

Given this as our mission, we should seek to walk with God continually through prayer and trust in his Word; be a part of a community of believers and a good church where we worship corporately; love people right where we are in all our vocations; seek to meet physical needs here and abroad; and pursue justice for the oppressed wherever we see it and around the world.

What would it be like if every Christian did this? Quite simply, the world would be transformed by the gospel. As Martyn Lloyd-Jones said,

"If only every Christian in the Church today were living the Sermon on the Mount, the great revival for which we are praying and longing would already have started."[7]

CREATING YOUR MISSION

How do you state your mission in a way that is specific to you and takes into account the specific things that God has most laid on your heart?

As we saw earlier, there are three main components to a good mission:

1. Core purpose
2. Core principles
3. Core beliefs

We will go through these three components of a mission statement using the Sermon on the Mount as our foundation. There are many places where we could go (including Philippians, like we saw earlier), but we are going to go here because the Sermon on the Mount was given by Jesus as a charter for the Christian life. The entire sermon is about the purpose of life. It *is* our mission statement.

We know this because Jesus makes this clear right off the bat by beginning the sermon with the beatitudes, which tell us whom we should regard as "blessed": "Blessed are the poor in spirit," "blessed are those who hunger and thirst for righteousness," and so forth (Matt. 5:3–11). "Blessed" is biblical terminology for what philosophers call "the good life" — life as it is meant to be lived; life that is lived in harmony with our ultimate purpose. As Martyn Lloyd-Jones notes, "The Sermon on the Mount says ... that if you really want to be happy, here is the way. This and this alone is the type of person who is truly happy, who is really blessed. This is the sort of person who is to be congratulated."[8]

Core Purpose

Your core purpose states your overall reason for existence.

This is where you state the biblical purpose of life in your own words, and in a way that reflects your uniqueness and that applies it to you. As we saw earlier, this gets at the *purpose* for everything you do more than *what specific course* you are to take in life. Here's how Jesus states your purpose: "Let your light shine before others, so that they may see your good works and give glory to your Father who is in heaven" (Matt. 5:16).

Define

There's the ultimate purpose of life: to glorify God. And, we are specifically to flesh that out by living in such a way that others glorify God (not us!) because of our good works.

Jesus' mention of good works here is helpful because it touches a bit on the what and not just the why. If we focus only on the why, it often becomes too abstract. We are left knowing our purpose for being here, but we aren't sure how that actually applies to the realities of daily life. So Jesus tells us what specifically glorifies God. His answer is: doing good works.

John Piper articulates it well when he states, "God created me—and you—to live with a single, all-embracing, all-transforming passion— namely, a passion to glorify God by enjoying and displaying his supreme excellence in all the spheres of life."[9]

I love how God-centered Piper is. And note that he hammers home the importance of understanding the purpose of your life in terms of a single, all-embracing purpose. This purpose is to glorify God (passionately!) by displaying his supreme excellence in all spheres of life.

The one thing that I don't think Piper makes clear enough, however, is how we display God's excellence in all spheres of life. But Jesus tells us the answer: we display God's excellence in all spheres of life by doing good for others to God's glory. And as we saw in chapter 5, these good works are not simply rare and special things we do, but anything we do in faith—even making dinner and going to meetings.

There are lots of different ways you can state your purpose, and it is important to state it in a way that captures your uniqueness. In reflecting on how you want to state your purpose, you might want to reflect not only on what Jesus says here but also on the passages in the sidebar earlier in this chapter. You can also look at how I've stated it or examples from Edwards, Piper, and the Westminster Confession. I also list some books at the end that are helpful for developing a biblical vision for life.

Core Principles

This is where we get more into the practical realm. We aren't yet at the level of what specific course you are seeking to take in life (that's the level of life goals, in the next chapter), but rather the guiding principles by which you will live your life.

The core principles section of your mission statement contains your answers to this question: What main principles am I going to use to guide my life?

Sometimes it is suggested that you list your values. Listing your core principles is basically a slightly adjusted form of doing this. I never found it helpful to list my values because there were always so many I wanted to list, and once you get beyond seven, it's just too many. For organizations, I find it easy to define values, but for myself, I never feel good limiting myself to seven.

You can try to list your core values (love, family, freedom, radical generosity, etc.) and keep it to seven if you want, but I find it more helpful just to list my top guiding principles and not worry about keeping it down to just a few.

Jonathan Edwards is a good model here. As I mentioned earlier, when he was nineteen he wrote his famous "Resolutions," which was essentially a list of principles taken from the Scriptures and applied in a way that was specific to his life. He ultimately had seventy resolutions. This is not a bad model at all; in many ways it is better than trying to distill seven core values.

Obviously we all have hundreds of principles by which we live. You don't need to state them all, or even state seventy like Edwards did. Just state the ones that stand out to you most and resonate with you most. Something passes muster as a core principle in your life if it is something you would hold to even if you were punished for it—even if it were not advantageous to you in an external sense.

For example, since the Sermon on the Mount is given to us by Jesus as a charter for our lives, and is given as a command and not a suggestion, the Sermon on the Mount should influence our principles significantly.

Jesus tells us, for example, that we are to put serving others and being reconciled to others above religious ceremony (Matt. 5:23–24); he says our default disposition is to practice radical generosity and *not* self-protection (Matt. 5:42; see also the parallel in Luke 6:32–36), and that this extends even to those who harm us (Matt. 5:38–41) and even our enemies (Matt. 5:43–48). In doing so, we are imitating God (Matt. 5:44, 48).

Jesus gives us many other commands by which we are to live, but he keeps it from being complicated because everything can be summed up in one statement: "So whatever you wish that others would do to you, do also to them, for this is the Law and the Prophets" (Matt. 7:12).

Define

As we've seen, that is to be our guiding principle for all of life. It is another statement of our mission, in a sense. And it is especially helpful because it states not only what we are to do (love our neighbor) but how (by doing unto them as we would have them do unto us). In everything we do, all day long, we are to be proactive to do unto others as we would have them do unto us. This tells us how to act in any and every situation, and every other principle is a manifestation of this one.

When listing your principles, you could list them in a straight list or in categories. If you put them in categories, the first grouping could be "overall life principles," which consists of things that apply to all categories—your life as a whole. Then you can have specific categories, such as good works, time management, relationships, suffering, and so forth.

If you just listed your top twenty guiding principles based on what God has revealed about our purpose and what glorifies him, you would be doing well.

Core Beliefs

This is essential for laying a gospel foundation underneath your mission. It answers the last two questions, which concern your identity (who you are) and ultimate destination (where you are going to end up at the end of all this).

Theologically Informed Values

Here's what Bubba Jennings, a pastor at Mars Hill Church in Seattle, had to say when I asked him about personal productivity and leadership:

"We emphasize what we value. What I value determines how I'm going to prioritize. So when I'm talking with people or trying to determine why I should or shouldn't do something, the paradigm I go through is identifying what God's Word says, then the theological convictions that are related to that, and then our values. Then we prioritize based on our values, and whatever is most important will determine what our activities are. There ought to be deep theological convictions that drive our values."

The gospel is the truth that God accepts us and gives us a title to heaven on the basis of the death and resurrection of Christ, which we receive through faith and not through our works (including living our mission).

The gospel is built into the Sermon on the Mount. Jesus is not saying "live this way and you will be my follower." All of us have already fallen short of the Sermon on the Mount, and you cannot live it in your own power. Jesus is saying, "You have to first acknowledge your sinfulness and come to me for life, and then this is how you are to live."

That is the meaning of the first thing Jesus says, the very first beatitude: "Blessed are the poor in spirit, for theirs is the kingdom of heaven" (Matt. 5:3). To be "poor in spirit" is to acknowledge our utter bankruptcy before God—that we have nothing to offer him on our own and must come to him for forgiveness and righteousness. To seek to live these principles without first coming to Jesus for salvation and a new heart completely overlooks the Beatitudes and is an abuse of the Sermon on the Mount.[10]

The ultimate foundation of your mission is not your character or even correct principles. It's what God has done for you in Christ and the fact that, if you believe in Christ, God is now your Father (Matt. 6:9; 6:26; 6:32; 7:11).

Further, knowing that heaven is secured for us and that we are going to end up there with Jesus forever motivates because it casts a vision for where we are going—and does so on the basis of what Jesus did, not on what we do.

Knowing where we are headed gives us the confidence and the direction to live as we ought to live. That vision helps us see that our purpose here is not to abandon the practical affairs of life and only seek to "save souls," nor is it to ignore spiritual realities and live as though only this life matters. Rather, it is to live in this world from the perspective of the next.[11] The joy that this hope produces, in turn, frees us up to spend our lives radically for the good of others and the glory of God.

AN EXAMPLE FROM THE BEST MISSION STATEMENT IN THE HISTORY OF THE WORLD

When creating your mission statement, it's helpful to see examples. Jonathan Edwards' seventy resolutions are one of the best examples of a biblically grounded, God-centered mission statement in the whole world.

Edwards didn't organize his resolutions into the three segments of mission sentence, core principles, and beliefs, but you see those strands running through them. (If you prefer to just state your mission as a set of core principles that includes your purpose and the gospel as well as your guiding principles, that works just fine.)

Here is Edwards' first resolution, which is essentially the purpose statement of his life (the core purpose part of the mission statement):

Resolved, that I will do whatsoever I think to be most to God's glory, and my own good, profit and pleasure, to the whole of my duration, without any consideration of the time, whether now, or never so many myriads of ages hence.

Resolved to do whatever I think to be my duty and most for the good and advantage of mankind in general. Resolved to do this, whatever difficulties I meet with, how many and how great soever.

Here are some of Edwards' most significant other resolutions that reflect the guiding principles component:

2. Resolved, to be continually endeavoring to find out some new invention and contrivance to promote the aforementioned things.

3. Resolved, if ever I shall fall and grow dull, so as to neglect to keep any part of these Resolutions, to repent of all I can remember, when I come to myself again.

6. Resolved, to live with all my might, while I do live.

22. Resolved, to endeavor to obtain for myself as much happiness, in the other world, as I possibly can, with all the power; might, vigor, and vehemence, yea violence, I am capable of, or can bring myself to exert, in any way that can be thought of.

62. Resolved, never to do anything but duty; and then according to Eph. 6:6–8, do it willingly and cheerfully as unto the Lord, and not to man; "knowing that whatever good thing any man doth, the same shall he receive of the Lord."

11. Resolved, when I think of any theorem in divinity to be solved, immediately to do what I can towards solving it, if circumstances don't hinder.

13. Resolved, to be endeavoring to find out fit objects of charity and liberality.

28. Resolved, to study the Scriptures so steadily, constantly and frequently, as that I may find, and plainly perceive myself to grow in the knowledge of the same.

You can find all of his resolutions online, and I have also created a version of them on my website that groups them into categories.[12]

WHERE TO PUT YOUR MISSION

One of the biggest traps people fall into when creating a mission statement or list of goals or any other such thing is that once they complete it, they never look at it again.

Now, in one sense, simply the act of creating a mission statement is helpful and will influence you. But it's actually not hard to avoid the trap of forgetting to look at it again.

Sample Mission Statement

Core Purpose

To do all the good I possibly can, for as many people as I possibly can, as often as I possibly can, in all spheres of life, regardless of whatever difficulties I meet with, and to do this to the glory of God through Jesus Christ.

Guiding Principles

1. Love my neighbor as myself, and love other believers as Christ has loved me.
2. To be proactive in doing good for others, and seek their welfare in everything I do, in any and every realm of life.
3. To be well organized, not simply for its own sake but to make the doing of good easier and more likely and friction free.

Core Beliefs

I am a child of God who has been forgiven and redeemed by Christ alone, through faith alone, to the glory of God alone.

Define

The reason people forget to review their mission statement, goal statements, and other such things comes down to two things: (1) They don't know how to create a routine for reviewing it, and (2) they don't make it easily accessible.

The routine side of things is simple: review your mission statement in your weekly review, which we will talk about in part 6, "Execute."

In terms of the second question, here's where to put your mission: Create it in a document, or in a mind map using Mind Manager or another program, or wherever feels natural to you and will be easy to access. I am also going to have you add a few other things to it in the next chapters as well to get it fleshed out a bit more.

Your mission is a way of "remembering" everything Jesus commanded (Matt. 28:20). That's the ultimate value in it. You can do it in whatever format you want, and you can call it whatever you want. Just be deliberate not only to *know* what Jesus commands for us but also to be intentional about *remembering it* to aid you in the most important (and nonnegotiable) thing of all: doing it.

INVOLVING OTHERS

There are two brief things to consider before we bring this chapter to a close.

Living with Purpose Together

Don't live your life alone or define your purpose in individualistic terms. We are to live on purpose together. This means having a group of like-minded Christian friends and being a part of a good local church. And if you really want to give feet to your mission, join up with other like-minded people in creating organizations and ministries and businesses to advance these purposes together.

Organizational Mission Statements

The focus of this chapter has been personal mission statements. But mission statements are also critical for organizations. They are, in fact, an essential tool for leadership—as long as the mission statement is something the organization actually means and is stated clearly and simply, rather than with fancy, wordy language.

Many of the principles for creating a personal mission statement carry over to creating organizational mission statements, but there are a few core differences:

1. If you are a ministry or faith-based nonprofit, your statement of faith or core doctrinal beliefs are the core beliefs component of your mission statement.
2. For businesses and nonprofits that are not faith-based, there are just two main parts to an organizational mission statement: core purpose and core values.
3. What I've termed core principles for your personal mission statement is best termed core values in organizational mission statements. When defining your core values as an organization, it is best to limit them to between five and nine. Any more than that will be unable to guide people's actions. Individuals can have dozens of core principles, but organizations need to keep their core values to a small number. This doesn't mean they don't value other things; it just means they need to focus on the things that are truly core.
4. In organizations, as with people, core values are discovered, not chosen. The way to know whether something is a core value is to ask, "Would we still hold to this even if we were punished for it?"

THE IMPACT OF HAVING THE RIGHT MISSION AND LIVING IT

Defining the core of your life on the basis of Jesus' teaching is what Jesus calls "building your life on the rock"—*if* you do what he says and obey him: "Everyone then who hears these words of mine and does them will be like a wise man who built his house on the rock. And the rain fell, and the floods came, and the winds blew and beat on that house, but it did not fall, because it had been founded on the rock" (Matt. 7:24–25).

To those who build on the rock by hearing Jesus' words and doing them—not *for* God's acceptance but *from* God's acceptance (Matt. 5:3)—Jesus will one day say: "Well done, good and faithful servant. You have been faithful over a little; I will set you over much. Enter into the joy of your master" (Matt. 25:21).

That's the ultimate aim of life.

The Box

Core Point

There is a purpose to life, and we can know it. The purpose of life is to know God, enjoy God, reflect his glory back to him in the pursuit of justice and mercy in all things, and do this in community with others through Jesus Christ.

Core Quote

Resolved to do whatever I think to be my duty and most for the good and advantage of mankind in general.
—Jonathan Edwards

Core Passage

Everyone then who hears these words of mine and does them will be like a wise man who built his house on the rock.
—Matthew 7:24

Immediate Application

Reflect on your core principles—the principles you would hold to even if it was to your disadvantage. Write down your top twenty, and you are halfway to completing your personal mission statement.

Questions and Answers

Should I use a verse as my mission statement?

You can, but you don't have to. The content of your mission is from the Scriptures, but it is best to state it in your own words. If you do use a passage, you need to have in your mind how it manifests itself in life.

Further Resources

Rick Warren, "Living with Purpose," chapter 40 of *The Purpose Driven Life*. Discusses how to create a life purpose statement.

Stephen Covey, "Habit 2, Begin with the End in Mind," in *The Seven Habits of Highly Effective People*. This is a secular book, but there are many ideas here that are universal and helpful.

John Piper, *Don't Waste Your Life*. See especially the first three chapters, in which Piper recounts his journey to find "a single passion to live by."

Keith Ferrazzi, "What's Your Mission?" chapter 3 in *Never Eat Alone*.

David Martyn Lloyd-Jones, *Studies in the Sermon on the Mount*.

The Resolutions of Jonathan Edwards[13]

CHAPTER 12

Finding Your Life Calling

Unleashing your dreams for serving others in radical ways and doing good for the world

To every person there comes in their lifetime that special moment when you are figuratively tapped on the shoulder and offered the chance to do a very special thing, unique to you and your talents. What a tragedy if that moment finds you unprepared or unqualified for work which could have been your finest hour.

— *Winston Churchill*

God almighty has set before me two great objects: The abolition of the slave trade, and the reformation of manners.

— *William Wilberforce,*
A Practical View of Christianity

SHOULD CHRISTIANS BE AMBITIOUS?

It's strange but sometimes there is an aversion in the church to thinking big. Perhaps this comes from the good tendency to realize that we ought to always value small things as well as big things, that caring only about big things and despising small things is not the Christian way.

But it is a fallacy to let our legitimate concern for small things lead to a despising of big things. We can—and must—value both. No one captures this better than Charles Bridges. In his commentary on Proverbs

3:18, he writes, "Do not despise the day of small things (Zech. 4:10). But do not be satisfied with it either. Aim high, and you will come closer to reaching the mark. Religion must be a shining and progressive light. We must not mistake the beginning for the end of the course. We must not sit down at the entrance and say to our soul, 'Take it easy now.' There is no point where we may rest in complacency, as if there were no loftier heights that it is our duty to climb."[1]

God is a big God (Jer. 32:27), he has given us a gigantic task (Matt. 28:18–20), and he is able to do abundantly more than we can even ask or imagine (Eph. 3:20). Thinking small, merely, is not the Christian thing to do.

As Dave Harvey shows in his excellent book *Rescuing Ambition*, God never intended true humility to be a fabric softener for our aspirations. We aren't to be ambitious for our own honor or glory. But we are to be ambitious for God's honor and glory, radically so. "Dreaming and doing things for God is the evidence, the effect, and the expectation of genuine faith."[2]

Thinking big and aiming high for the glory of God puts us in the realm of our life calling or vision.

WHAT IS A LIFE GOAL?

I used to think that the large objective I was seeking to accomplish with my life was my mission statement. For example, someone might say "Martin Luther King Jr.'s mission in life was to end discrimination and bring about a more just and fair society for all."

It is, of course, legitimate to talk that way. When we say something like, "His mission is to do this," we are stating the importance of the cause.

The Difference between Mission Statements and Life Goals

But the large objectives we have are not actually life mission statements. They are life goals, or visions.

The difference is this: as we saw in the previous chapter, your mission is more a matter of principles. It concerns the purpose for everything you do and the principles governing how you will go about your life. It defines what success is for a human life. And, having been justified by faith apart from works, everyone can succeed at it. You can fail at a major life goal (for example, bringing water to every village in Africa that lacks it) and still succeed in life, because the purpose of life is the same for all: do justice, love mercy, and walk humbly with God (Mic. 6:8). You can do this every day, in big and small ways, no matter what your circumstances.

A life goal, on the other hand, is a specific aim. Your mission is never completed (you will always be able to glorify God more), but a life goal can be completed. It has a finishing point.

Your mission is the ultimate reason for your existence—forever. It is your chief *why*. Your life goal is the concrete *what*. It is the chief way that you seek to fulfill your mission.

Hence, a life goal is also distinct from goals in general. We need to have all sorts of goals at different times and in different areas of our lives. But a life goal is an objective that is so big that it governs everything else you do, and it will likely take your entire life. And, it so resonates with you and so compels you that you take it up joyfully and willingly. Good life goals grab us, and we *want* to do them.

A life goal is what most people mean when they talk about finding your calling in life. It is the chief objective you are seeking to accomplish with your life. Life goals are analogous to what James Collins calls "Big, Hairy, Audacious Goals"[3] in businesses and nonprofits. A life goal is a large and almost overwhelming cause toward which everything else in your life is marshaled.

The Apostle Paul's Holy Ambition

The apostle Paul is a great example here. In the previous chapter, we saw many examples of mission statements from Paul's pen. When he talked about how, to him, "to live is Christ" (Phil. 1:21) and how everything was loss to him compared with "the surpassing worth of knowing Christ Jesus my Lord" (Phil. 3:8) and achieving "the resurrection from the dead" (3:11), he was stating his mission, his ultimate purpose and joy.

Paul also stands out for knowing concretely what he was here to do, and how he was to glorify Christ specifically on this earth. He talks about having a "course" to complete, a ministry "to testify to the gospel of the grace of God" (Acts 20:24). His aim is to build up the church and present everyone complete in Christ (Col. 1:28). Elsewhere, he talks of having an ambition to preach the gospel to those who had never heard it (Rom. 15:20–21). This ambition of spreading the gospel to the Gentiles who had never heard was so dominant that it was an all-consuming objective in Paul's life; it determined everything he did and was the basis on which he made decisions among other priorities, like when he would go to Rome (Rom. 15:22–25). John Piper rightly terms this Paul's "holy ambition," defining a holy ambition as something you really, really want to do that God also wants you to do.[4] That's what a life goal is.

Wilberforce's Two Great Objectives

William Wilberforce is another great, and inspiring, example of how to create life goals. He had two. Here's how Charles Colson describes Wilberforce's early realization and articulation of his life goals:

> Old Palace Yard, London, October 25, 1787: A slight young man sat at his oak desk in the second-floor library.
>
> As he adjusted the flame of his lamp, the warm light shone on his piercing blue eyes, oversized nose, and high wrinkled forehead. His eyes fell on the jumble of pamphlets on the cluttered desk. They were all on the same subject: the horrors of the slave trade, grisly accounts of human flesh being sold, like so much cattle, for the profit of his countrymen.
>
> The young man would begin this day as was his custom, with a time of personal prayer and Scripture reading. But his thoughts kept returning to those pamphlets. Something inside him—that insistent conviction he'd felt before—was telling him that all that had happened in his life had been for a purpose, preparing him to meet that barbaric evil head-on. . . .
>
> Wilberforce sat at his desk at that foggy Sunday morning in 1787 thinking about his conversion and his calling. Had God saved him only to rescue his own soul from hell? He could not accept that. If Christianity was true and meaningful, it must not only save but serve.
>
> Wilberforce dipped his pen into the inkwell: "Almighty God has set before me two great objectives," he wrote, his heart suddenly pumping with passion, "the abolition of the slave trade and the reformation of manners."[5]

Wilberforce did many things in his life, but these two objectives were his chief aims, and they governed everything else he did. Notice also that he was not afraid to think big. The story of his perseverance in accomplishing his chief goals is incredible and is told well in John Pollock's chapter in *Character Counts* (if you would like a brief treatment) and biographies such as *The Life of William Wilberforce* by Samuel Wilberforce, or *Amazing Grace: William Wilberforce and the Heroic Campaign to End Slavery* by Eric Metaxas.

Vision Statements in the Bible

"All authority in heaven and on earth has been given to me. Go therefore and make disciples of all nations, baptizing them in the name of the Father and of the Son and of the Holy Spirit, teaching them to observe all that I have commanded you. And behold, I am with you always, to the end of the age."

—Matthew 28:18–20

For I have appeared to you for this purpose, to appoint you as a servant and witness to the things in which you have seen me and to those in which I will appear to you, delivering you from your people and from the Gentiles—to whom I am sending you *to open their eyes* ... that they may receive forgiveness of sins and a place among those who are sanctified by faith in me.

—Acts 26:16–18

I do not account my life of any value nor as precious to myself, if only I may finish my course and the ministry that I received from the Lord Jesus, to testify to the gospel of the grace of God.

—Acts 20:24

I make it my ambition to preach the gospel, not where Christ has already been named, lest I build on someone else's foundation, but as it is written, "Those who have never been told of him will see, and those who have never heard will understand."

—Romans 15:20–21

Him we proclaim, warning everyone and teaching everyone with all wisdom, that we may present everyone mature in Christ.

—Colossians 1:28

HOW DO YOU IDENTIFY YOUR LIFE GOAL?

For identifying your life vision — the one or two overarching, major goals for your life — I find it most helpful to ask two questions:

1. What would I do if I had all the money I needed and could do whatever I wanted?
2. What would I do if I could do only one thing in the next three years?

The point of the first question is to allow you to think big, without logistical constraints, so that you can truly identify what fires you up. Many things will likely come to mind. The point of the second question, then, is to identify which of these things is truly most important to you by forcing yourself to choose just one thing.

If you could do only one thing on this planet (along with being a godly husband or wife and father or mother, if you have those callings), what would it be? That is your life goal.

Some people say that "there is no wrong answer, that it's all about what you want to do." But that's not true, because we are not our own (1 Cor. 6:19–20). On the other hand, nobody can tell you what your life goal is. You have to discover it. It's possible to get it wrong (i.e., sail around the world and have no responsibility), but there is no single right answer for everybody.

MAKING YOUR LIFE GOAL HAPPEN

Making your life goal happen comes down to three things:

1. Put it in a place where you will remember it and review it. Since a life goal is a step above even long-term goals, defining the trajectory of your whole life, it needs to be treated as the higher-level goal that it is. One of the best ways to do this is to include it in the same document as your mission statement. You do this just by adding a fourth section called "Life Goal" or "Life Vision."

If you are unsure what your life goal is, you can write down in that spot the main contenders you are thinking through, and whenever you review your mission statement, this will be a reminder to give some additional thought to your life goal.

2. Weave it into the structure of your life. When identifying your roles and architecting your prototype week, you need to give specific attention to weaving your life goal into the fabric of your life. If your life goal is to build up the church, for example, then you need to make sure that priority is reflected in concrete ways in the activities and roles of your life.

3. Utilize evolutionary progress rather than scripting everything out. When we have clear goals, it is tempting to create detailed plans to make them happen. Planning is a good thing. But for large goals, detailed plans will not work because circumstances change too quickly.

So instead of creating a detailed plan, create a more general plan and then advance your goal by keeping your eyes open to seize *unplanned* opportunities. Making progress by harnessing unplanned opportunities is the secret to accomplishing large goals in an environment of uncertainty and when you cannot know the future in detail (which, not being omniscient, you don't). This is called evolutionary progress.

WHAT IF YOU DON'T KNOW YOUR LIFE GOAL?

1. Do what's before you with excellence. When you don't know what your goals are or what your vision in life is, the last thing you should do is nothing. As Spurgeon has said, "If you stop and do nothing until you can do everything, you will remain useless."[6]

Instead, do what's before you with excellence. That is often the path to identifying what you should be doing, or at least opening up opportunities that will help you find greater clarity.

Related to this is doing what you most enjoy as well. You might say, "That's the problem; I don't know what I want to do." And, of course, you might not know on a macro scale. But you do know which activities are most enjoyable to you. As long as those are things that make a contribution, keep doing those (or start doing them) and see where it takes you.

As part of this, be willing to move forward imperfectly. You learn by trying things and making mistakes. This isn't contrary to the point about doing what you do with excellence. It means that, when making a decision about next steps, sometimes you might find you were wrong, and this can be an advantage in the long run because of the knowledge you will have gained from the experience. You sought to make that decision with excellence, but it turned out not to have been the best decision. You couldn't have known that before. As with everything, so with mistakes: make excellent mistakes. Make mistakes of forward motion, not mistakes of sloth. Try things, be bold, and see what happens.

2. Take steps for fundamental reasons, not instrumental reasons. Doing something for fundamental reasons means doing something because you love it in itself. Doing something for instrumental reasons means you are doing it because of where it might lead, even though you don't necessarily enjoy it in itself.

Don't take a step you are not going to enjoy simply because you think it will open up a door to something you do enjoy. It seldom works this way.

As Dan Pink, one of my favorite authors on the world of work, points out, the most effective people make choices for fundamental reasons rather than instrumental reasons, most of the time.[7] Keep choosing what you enjoy most and are best at, and let that guide your path.

3. Care about who as much as what. When there are several different types of activities you enjoy, pay special attention to what type of people you like to work with and be around. Some of my best decisions are decisions I made because they enabled me to join forces with quality people who love the Lord, whom I respect, and who make me a better person. When you aren't sure what to do, the next best thing is to navigate your course on account of who you want to be with.

Notice that my point here is not to follow the crowd or seek the approval of others. I'm talking about being integrated with people who make you a better person, not seeking popularity or trying to feel good about yourself. "Whoever walks with the wise becomes wise, but the companion of fools will suffer harm" (Prov. 13:20).

4. Increase your opportunity stream. Learn, network, and *do things*. The more you do these things, the more you increase your opportunity stream. And to make this work, you have to be open to surprise (point three above in "making your life goal happen"). Put yourself in the path of surprise and unplanned opportunities, and then seize them.

Scott Belsky captures this well in his article "Finding Your Work Sweet Spot":

> Unfortunately, this is often where we get stuck, discounting the potential opportunities that surround us as inadequate. There is no such thing as equal access to opportunity. Old boy networks and nepotism run rampant in all industries. And most opportunities are entirely circumstantial. As such, you must simply define "opportunity" as an action or experience that brings you a step closer to your genuine interest.

Opportunity is less about leaps forward and more about the slow advance. Most folks I meet recall their greatest opportunities as chance conversations. This is why personal introductions, conferences, and other networking efforts really pay off. Just surrounding yourself with more activity will inherently increase your "opportunity stream"—the chance happenings that lead to actions and experiences relevant to your genuine interests.[8]

5. Read inspiring books and biographies, and watch inspiring movies. Developing your vision is just as much a right-brain, creative, imaginative activity as it is a left-brain activity. To help tap into this, read biographies and books that encourage you to do hard things and dream big dreams for God and the good of the world. This is also one of the overlooked benefits of watching movies. God invented movies, in part, so that we can find inspiration in the visual presentation of stories with a hero who overcomes massive obstacles for the sake of a great cause.

6. Stay faithful in prayer! Don't just try to figure things out on your own. As with all planning, involve God and make him the center (Prov. 16:3). You are not the captain of your ship. God determines what happens to you and where your ship goes, and he is a good God who looks out for you and is eager to make your life count for his glory and his people's good. This is always true, but if you take it for granted by not involving him in thinking through your plans and pleading with him in prayer, the course you are on will suffer: "You do not have, because you do not ask" (James 4:2).

7. Take action and commit. You shouldn't be thirty years old and still trying to figure out what to do with your life. Don't live in your parents' basement playing video games all day while you "figure out your life's aim." Get involved in the world of work, get a job that is challenging and calls on the best of you, and live your life. Don't be aimless, even while seeking to discover your chief aim in life. Do *something*. Not something to bide the time, but something meaningful, and you will discover your life goal on *that* course.

The Box

Core Point

You need to have an overarching, passionate, God-centered aim to your life—an overarching goal and message that flows from your mission and directs the priorities of your life.

Core Quote

God almighty has set before me two great objects: The abolition of the slave trade, and the reformation of manners.
—William Wilberforce

Core Passage

I do not account my life of any value nor as precious to myself, if only I may finish my course and the ministry that I received from the Lord Jesus, to testify to the gospel of the grace of God.
—Acts 20:24

Help in Developing a Vision for Your Life

To develop a deeper sense of God's purposes for us, I recommend the following:

David Platt, *Radical*
John Piper, *Don't Waste Your Life*
Francis Chan, *Crazy Love*
Rick Warren, *The Purpose Driven Life*
John Bunyan, *Pilgrim's Progress*
Stephen Nichols, *Heaven on Earth: Capturing Jonathan Edwards's Vision of Living in Between*
Os Guinness, *The Call: Finding and Fulfilling the Central Purpose of Your Life*
Biographies of notable Christians like William Carey, George Whitfield, Jonathan Edwards, and others
Movies like *Amazing Grace* (on the life of William Wilberforce)

CHAPTER 13

Clarifying Your Roles

Orienting your life within the
Christian doctrine of vocation

*A cobbler, a smith, a farmer, each has the work and office
of his trade, and yet they are all alike consecrated priests
and bishops, and every one by means of his own work or
office must benefit and serve every other.*
— *Martin Luther,* An Open Letter
to the Christian Nobility

ROLES ARE A COMMON SUBJECT in most books on effectiveness, and
for good reason. But before looking at how to define and improve your
roles, I want to give you a new way to think about your roles altogether,
which most secular books are not able to do.

WHAT ROLES ACTUALLY ARE: ROLES AND THE DOCTRINE OF VOCATION

A role is often defined as an area of responsibility — that is, as your function in a family (parent, child), organization (marketing director, chief
happiness officer, etc.), or society (community member, etc.). This is
right. But we can say more.

Talking about roles puts us right at the heart of the Christian doctrine
of vocation. The Bible teaches that our roles are not just areas of responsibility, but *callings*. Our roles are each callings given to us by God and
through which we serve God and others.

This applies to all of us, and to every area of our lives, which means four things.

First, all Christians have a calling—not just pastors and missionaries. Whatever you are doing in life, you are not there by accident. *Jesus* has placed you there (1 Cor. 7:17–24), and you are able to carry out your role unto him and for his glory (Eph. 6:6–8). Here's how Luther puts it:

> A cobbler, a smith, a farmer, each has the work and office of his trade, and yet they are all alike consecrated priests and bishops, and every one by means of his own work or office must benefit and serve every other, that in this way many kinds of work may be done for the bodily and spiritual welfare of the community, even as all the members of the body serve one another.[1]

Second, it means not only that all Christians have a calling but also that *every area* of our lives is a calling. Our callings are not just limited to what we do as a job. *All* areas of our lives are a calling—husband, wife, child, friend, community member, parent, and so forth—and thus are to be lived before God and unto God.

Third, it means that *all* of our jobs and every area of our life has a dignity and meaning that gives great significance to it. Because of the priesthood of all believers, we can do all things unto the glory of God and there is no distinction between "first rate" Christians (i.e., those in ministry) and "second rate" Christians (i.e., everyone else). *Every* Christian is "first rate," and secular vocations are not only permissible, but *valuable*.

What makes a work good is the command of God. Therefore, it doesn't matter whether you are a pastor or a homemaker. If you are doing whatever you are doing in obedience to God's will, God values it and it matters.

Fourth, it means that each role is a stewardship for which we are ultimately responsible not to other people, but to God himself. The responsibilities of each of our roles derive not finally from our relationships to other people, but from God. This applies to the privileges of each of our roles as well—they are likewise not merely a human invention but gifts from God to equip us in our role. This gives not only significance to what we do, but great *weight* to what we are doing.

HOW TO DEFINE YOUR ROLES (THAT IS, VOCATIONS)

Since each area of our lives is a calling and stewardship from God, it is important for each of us to make sure we've clearly identified what our callings actually are.

Fortunately, this is simple. To get a clear grasp of what your vocations (callings, roles) are, take a few minutes just to reflect and then list what comes to mind.

For example, your roles might include Christian, husband, father, son, brother, friend, neighbor, citizen, blogger, and marketing executive. Perhaps you could also include small group leader, church member, and on and on. Which means that we immediately encounter a problem: we each have *a lot* of roles, and the list can easily become overwhelming.

One solution is to combine roles. For example, I could combine husband and father into a single role, called husband/father. I could also subsume son/brother underneath husband/father, so that I have less roles explicitly listed, while still remembering that role because it is now included every time I think of my role as a husband and father. I could also include "small group leader" and "church member" underneath "Christian," and so forth.

That option can work, but I've never been entirely satisfied with it. I tend to like having everything laid out so I can see the big picture as it really is. So there is another approach worth considering.

HOW TO ORGANIZE YOUR ROLES
Luther on "The Four Estates"
The Reformers (especially Luther) grouped the vocations of life into "estates." They saw four main estates: the family, the church, society, and "the common order of Christian love."

Luther included in the family, or household, the callings of marriage, raising children, and being a child. He also included here the way you make your living—your job. This makes sense (especially so in Luther's day), but I find it helpful to distinguish a job from the estate of the household, which you will see below.

In the estate of society, Luther included human government and society and culture in general. There is some overlap here, obviously, with our calling to the household, as Luther saw the work of judges and officials and clerks and servants and others in the workplace generally as falling into this estate as well.

By "the common order of Christian love" Luther meant our general, overall calling to serve *anyone in need*. The primary avenue of our service to others comes through our specific vocations. But as we see in Luke

Define

3:10–14, we are also to go beyond and, in Luther's words, "feed the hungry and give drink to the thirsty, forgive enemies, pray for all men on earth and do good to all people everywhere, as we have opportunity" (cf. also Gal. 6:10). This is what Luther calls the vocation of the common order of Christian love.

Grouping Your Roles into Categories

I take a variation on Luther's four estates to organize my roles. I group my callings into five areas: individual, family, church, social, and professional.

Each of these major groupings contains my specific callings, which I list more as responsibilities than the roles themselves.

Here is the list for my personal life:

Role Map for Life				
Individual	**Family**	**Church**	**Social**	**Professional**
• Spirituality and character • Planning and workflow • Learning • Health • Refreshment and adventure • Travel	• Marriage • Kids • Extended family • Household • Finances	• Bethlehem • Small group • Sunday school	• Friends • Neighbors • Community • State • Country • World	• Writing, publishing, and speaking • Blogging • Social good • Interesting endeavors • Consulting • Career management • Networking • Professional organizations • Formal education • Professional knowledge and skills • Work

As you can see, this amounts to a comprehensive picture of your life. If any new responsibilities are added, you can add them to the list and it will fit logically into one of the five overall categories.[2]

You can also do this for work. Though your work is typically just one role (for example, marketing manager), work roles typically break down into about five to seven areas, each with corresponding responsibilities.

Here is an example from my work life when I was director of internet strategies at Desiring God:

Role Map for Work (Director of Internet Strategies)				
Individual	Spreading	Departmental Management	Executive Leadership	Industry
• Planning and workflow • Learning • Travel • Technology	• Blogging and writing • Large-scale spreading initiatives	• Set website and department vision and strategy • Manage staffing, staff development, and department design • Direct functional operations • Direct site improvement	• Director team • Contribute to setting strategy, organizational design decisions, and systems design	• Keep up with ministry, web, and tech knowledge • Maintain and develop industry relationships • Serve, assist, and learn from other ministries and churches

Where to Keep Your List of Roles and Their Responsibilities

There are two main places you can keep your list of roles and responsibilities. First, it is not a bad idea to add it right into your mission document. In this case the list would go beneath your life goal, and the document would give you a full and complete picture of your life. This is an amazing thing to have.

Second, since it is helpful to add notes to each of your roles, it can be helpful to keep them in a program that allows you to create note fields for each item, such as a mind map in Mind Manager or an outline in Omni Outliner. Or, if your task manager program allows you to group things, you can do it in there. (OmniFocus works well for this; so does Outlook.)

Wherever you keep your list is fine, as long as it is easy to access and, conversely, not *annoying* to access. It is critical to minimize the annoyance factor in pulling out your list, or you will never want to look at it.

HOW TO MAKE YOUR ROLES HAPPEN

Listing your roles is super helpful in itself. There is some strange sense in which just clarifying them and writing them down leads us to naturally be more deliberate about them. But you can't leave it merely at that. In order to serve others and the Lord fully in your roles, you need to keep them at the forefront of your mind by reflecting on them regularly, weaving them into your life, and keeping them integrated so that they don't compete with one another.

1. Make it a routine to review your roles in your weekly review. Operating in our roles comes naturally, of course. The purpose of having them listed is not because you'll forget about them altogether, but to make it possible for you to give *deliberate* focus to them and to keep the most important roles from being short-changed in the busyness of life.

For example, if you have kids, your role as a parent is the most important after your roles as a Christian and as a spouse. Nonetheless, it is easy for us to fall into seasons in which work and life demands swallow up the time we want to give to our kids. Having your roles listed allows you to take stock *regularly* and ask, "How am I doing in each of these areas? Am I giving them the attention they deserve?" You can then make course corrections.

The best place to do this is in your weekly review. We will talk about this more when we discuss weekly planning, but the essence is that each week, you review your roles and ask three questions:

1. What things do I most need to do this week to serve my primary roles?
2. Is there any additional, out-of-my-way good I can do for someone in any of these areas?
3. Is there any critical role I'm *neglecting* and need to give more attention to?

I don't believe our lives can be—or are supposed to be—fully "balanced." I believe we are to seek to be *centered*, not balanced. Not every role can or should receive equal attention; that's a recipe for burnout and mediocrity. But some roles that should never be neglected can easily become crowded out in the busyness of life. Reflecting on your roles each week is one way to keep this from happening.

2. Weave them into the fabric of your life. Each role has a set of responsibilities that go along with it. For example, in my role as blogger, two of my responsibilities are to write blog posts and maintain my website. For each role, you need to identify the main responsibilities and slot the major ones into your week at specific times.

This is essential because if you just say to yourself, for example, "I need to write blog posts," you will almost always skip it. But if you determine exactly when you will write your posts, you have turned it from an intention into something you can actually do. (We will look more at how to weave your roles into your life in the next section, "Architect.")

Related to the issue of weaving your roles into your life, of course, is the issue of how your roles relate to your life goal.

3. How your life goal relates to your roles. Your life goal is the primary aim, underneath your mission, that you are seeking to accomplish. But there are lots of things you need to be doing in addition to your life goal. Your roles capture this.

Your roles are also the means through which you accomplish your life goal. For example, William Wilberforce's life goal of ending the slave trade was something he accomplished through his role as a member of parliament. He could have sought to do it through other means if he had to (though it would have been much harder), but this life goal gave additional purpose and force to his vocation as a parliament member.

4. Keep your roles from competing. It is easy for our roles to fight one another. The tension between demands at work and life at home is the primary instance of this.

In many ways, avoiding competition among roles comes down to how we look at them. While our roles are distinct, we should not see them as independent compartments. If we see them each as entirely separate, then giving more attention to one necessarily means giving less attention to another. But in reality, each one not only affects the others, but can *involve* the others.

Responsibilities and Productivity

A right view of your responsibilities will give you a right view of what productivity means in your life.
—*Mark Dever, Pastor of Capitol Hill Baptist Church*

> ## Avoid Splintering Yourself by Considering Leverage
>
> Here's what Bubba Jennings, a pastor at Mars Hill Church in Seattle, said when I asked him how he keeps from being pulled in so many directions by less important things:
>
> "For me, I try to look at things in terms of leverage. If I'm going to do something, I want to leverage it for as many outputs as possible. For example, we have an intern training program. So if I have a meeting to go to, I might invite not just the stakeholders who need to be there but also the people who just need to learn by observing. I always ask, 'How can I do what I'm doing in such a way as to get as many different outcomes from it?'"

You are not in competition with yourself. Your differing roles and responsibilities are not a juggling act, where you can deal with only one at a time, quickly having to touch it and then toss it up into the air so you can deal with the next role. That's a circus act, not life.

So how do we avoid becoming plate spinners and jugglers? We need to realize that many roles can be carried out in an interdependent way and create overlap. In other words, whenever you can, seek to do things in a way that involves *multiple* roles, not just a single role. This is one of the fundamental ways of avoiding the juggling mentality and keeping your roles from competing against one another.[3]

HOW TO IMPROVE ANY ROLE: ROLE PLANS

In addition to keeping our roles in motion, there are also times when we want to give more deliberate attention to thinking through and improving a specific role. One of the best ways to do this is to create a brief plan for fulfilling that calling in the best way you know how.

A role plan is not hard to create, and has just three simple parts (you can add more, but three is the basic framework): purpose, strategic principles, and activities.

To create a role plan, just create a checklist or document for the role, and then in that document create a heading for each of those parts. In the purpose area, state the overall purpose of the calling. In the strategic principles section, list any key overall strategies and tactics. In the activities section, list the ongoing activities that keep the role in motion and any other mindsets that are ongoing but not actionable *per se*.

This is a way that you can think through any role in a deliberate, intentional way. I'm not saying everyone should do this, but it's not hard and doesn't take very long. Here's an example of a plan for carrying out the role of being a learner:

Sample Role Plan

Objective

To have a complete, integrated, and thorough worldview and understanding of the world. To develop my skills and grow in wisdom for the benefit of society.

Strategic Principles

- Books are for insight, articles are for awareness. Give preference to books (70 percent) without neglecting articles (30 percent).
- When reading, use the SQ3R method to maximize understanding and speed.

Activities

- Read books.
- Listen to audio books and resources in the car.
- Review blogs daily.
- Keep up with subscriptions.

ROLES AND YOUR CAREER

Though our roles include much more than our careers, our careers are one of our most fundamental roles. We have talked a bit about how organizing and planning for our roles serves our work lives as well as our overall lives. But here are three other ways this relates to our careers. The third one is perhaps the question people ask most often.

1. Creating Job Profiles Right

I've listed the three main components of a role plan as purpose, strategy, and activities. Notice that good job profiles follow essentially this same structure: the purpose of the role, strategic principles, and primary activities.

Job profiles also ought to include the resources available, reporting relationships, and any other relevant information. But the main thing to point out is that these role plans represent how to think through any type of responsibility, at any level, and in any area of life.

2. Organizational Dashboard

If you are at a high level in your department or organization and are responsible for the work of many people or a team or a whole department or the whole organization, you can use the role-listing concept to keep the framework of the entire organization before you.

To do this, create a chart of your department or organization and review it weekly just like you review your roles weekly, giving intentional, proactive thought to whether everything is going along as it needs to, and identifying actions you can take to serve and improve your department.

3. Finding Your Career

Every discussion of vocation raises the question of how we find our primary calling in the world of work. I hope to go into more detail on this in a future book on the doctrine of vocation, but let me point you to three articles for now.

The first two articles are explicitly from a Christian perspective and are situated within the doctrine of vocation. The third is not from an explicitly Christian perspective but provides very helpful insight:

1. "Vocation: Discerning Your Calling" by Tim Keller: *http://redeemercitytocity.com/resources/library.jsp?Library_item_param=580*[4]
2. "How to Discover Your Calling" by Mike Horton: *http://wscal.edu/resource-center/resource/how-to-discover-your-calling*
3. "Finding Your Work Sweet Spot" by Scott Belsky: *http://the99percent.com/tips/7003/Finding-Your-Work-Sweet-Spot-Genuine-Interest-Skills-Opportunity*

The Box

Core Point

Your roles are all callings from God and thus avenues of worship. You can serve him just as fully in the "secular" areas of your life as you can in the spiritual areas.

Core Passage

Only let each person lead the life that the Lord has assigned to him, and to which God has called him. This is my rule in all the churches.... So, brothers, in whatever condition each was called, there let him remain with God.

—1 Corinthians 7:17, 24

Immediate Application

Which role do you need to give more attention to? Create a weekly focus goal to remember.

Further Resources

Gene Veith, *God at Work*

Stephen Covey, "The Balance of Roles," chapter 6 in *First Things First*

Andy Stanley, *Choosing to Cheat*

PART 4

Architect

CREATE A FLEXIBLE STRUCTURE

Living by your own creative tendencies, rationalizations, and emotional whims will not suffice. Sheer perspiration will come only from organizing your energy and holding yourself accountable with some sort of routine.
                    —*Scott Belsky,* Making Ideas Happen

THE FIRST STEP IN DARE, "define," had us in the realm of personal leadership — discovering and determining what the most important things are in our lives.

While this is a critical step in becoming productive, it's not enough, because systems trump intentions. You can have great intentions, but if your life is set up in a way that is not in alignment with them, you will be frustrated. The structure of your life will win out every time.

The key to effectiveness — putting the most important things first — is knowing what is most important and then *weaving it into your life* through simple structures and systems. This is the arena of personal management — that is, the practice of putting the most important things first in your life.

This brings us to the second step in DARE: "architect." This step is about creating a basic structure for your life by identifying the most important activities from your roles and then slotting them in to create a flexible framework for your week so that it is natural to do them.

As we will see, this is something I learned the hard way, because for a long time I suffered from what was probably a misunderstanding of *Getting Things Done*. The result was that my lists made my life worse! Instead of reducing stress, it felt like they were sucking the life out of me.

The architecture step is the solution to this problem. The essence of it can be summarized this way: Structure your life by living mainly from

Architect

a flexible routine, not a set of lists. To do this well, you need to know three things: (1) how to set up your week, (2) what routines to slot into your week and, because it's a special case, (3) how to get creative things done. That's what we will be looking at in this section.

CHAPTER 14

Setting Up Your Week

How to weave your priorities into your daily
life and decrease your dependency on lists;
plus, extreme measures for excellence

*You tame time through a routine—knowing what's
around the corner, and knowing how much time you have
to do it. Not all of your time is routine, but enough needs
to be to create a framework.*

— Bradley Blakeman

DAVID ALLEN PROVIDES some excellent, practical wisdom for productivity in his book *Getting Things Done*. But there is something I overlooked in applying GTD that eventually made my life feel more like "mind like tsunami" rather than the "mind like water" it promises.

I think other people have experienced this as well. While this problem was mostly a mistake in my own application, I think it's also because of something that is underemphasized in GTD itself. A (just about) missing component, if you will.

THE UNDEREMPHASIZED COMPONENT IN GTD

When I first started doing GTD, I felt a great sense of relief. The essence of GTD involves capturing all of your open loops and clarifying them into next actions that you keep on various lists. I had never done this before, and it was really good to finally have a complete inventory of all my work.

This greater efficiency enabled me to do more, which led to an increase in my workload, which led to the need to get even better at GTD. This should not be a surprise, of course. As David Allen points out, "the better you get, the better you better get."[1]

But as my workload continued to increase, I found that having a complete inventory of my work wasn't quite working. I was getting better at GTD, but it wasn't helping. In fact, it was making things worse.

I found that it took a lot of time to keep the full inventory of my workload up to date. But there was another, far more painful, effect: I felt I *always* had to work on my lists. There was so much to track that my mind just couldn't wrap itself around it all. I felt I had a massive inventory of actions to take with no time in which to do them. And so the lists, which were supposed to relieve my stress, were creating even more stress for me.

On top of this—and paradoxically—I would go for long periods without working on any of my lists. I would just ditch the lists and do what I knew needed to get done. What a strange reality this is: feeling like you always need to be working on your lists, but hardly ever actually having the time for them.

My solution for a while was to organize them in different ways. It wasn't a long-term solution.

That's when I realized that just having a catalog of the things I do is not enough. I also needed to have some sort of routine, or framework, into which everything fit. I needed time to work on my action lists. A basic but flexible schedule for the work provides this time.

And that's the missing component.

WHY YOU NEED A BASIC SCHEDULE

The issue is not that GTD gives no place to a schedule. The problem is that it doesn't show you how your lists and your schedule relate *specifically*. Without clarity on this, I found that my lists were always fighting against my schedule. The key insight for me was when I realized that my next action lists had to be *connected* to my schedule in some way. We will see this by looking at the four reasons you need to have a basic schedule.

1. People work best from routines, not lists (or, be like George Washington). This finally stood out to me one summer while I was listening to a biography of George Washington on a bike ride.[2] The author was describing Washington's routine after his presidency, and what stood out to me was that he didn't have any lists.

He would get up at 5:00 a.m. and give assignments to his workers. At 7:00 a.m. he would have breakfast, and then he would ride around his farms on horseback for about six hours, assigning tasks, inspecting things, visiting people, and doing other tasks to keep things running smoothly. He would have dinner with guests at 3:00 p.m., head into his office for two hours at 5:00 p.m. ("writing letters and reading one or more of the ten newspapers to which he subscribed"[3]), and come back out at 7:00 p.m. for tea with his guests. He and Martha would retire at 9:00 p.m.

Washington got an amazing amount of work done, but he didn't operate from a bunch of lists—just a simple routine.

And that is just as true today: people actually operate best from a routine, not a set of lists.

This principle can easily be obscured by how easy it is to rely on task and action lists as a means of tracking projects and deadlines. If you have all those lists—or hear that you should create them—it's easy to end up thinking that the lists should govern your actions and day. But they shouldn't. A basic routine, governed by your mission and roles, is the framework within which you should operate.

This is not to say that there is no place for creating lists. But the lists we make shouldn't operate on their own. They should support our routines, and the routines, in turn, can create the time we need to do the things we categorize in our lists.

2. A basic schedule helps keep you from massive overload (I speak from experience …). Another problem I had with GTD and relying chiefly on lists is that I always ended up trying to do far more than I had the capacity to do. Because I had this big mass of projects and actions, without a clear schedule that governed how much could fit, I just kept trying to do everything on my lists. There was no sense of proportionality. I'd do as much as I could each day and then I'd stop.

This can lead to overcommitting to projects and responsibilities. What I failed to realize is that time is like space. Imagine that you are organizing your closet. It's easy to see what you have and compare it with the amount of space available. If you have more stuff than will fit, you know you will have to get rid of some things or find a different closet for them.

Time is just like that, but we often miss this because it's not visible like the things we put in our closets. We do see this visually on our calendars. But project lists and action lists don't represent the quantifiable amount of time they will take. So we don't easily see when the tasks on our lists extend far beyond the time we have.

If you have a basic routine, however, it helps make your actions more tangible and forces you to consider where and when they will fit.

How Popular Blogger Tim Challies
Gets Things Done

I recently asked Tim Challies, popular blogger at *challies. com* and author of several books, how he organizes a typical day—when he blogs, reads, prays, spends time with his family, and gets his work done. Here's what he said:

"At present I have three different varieties of work days. Mondays I tend to take the morning off and spend it with my wife (all the kids are in school, giving us time to go on a date that doesn't require paying for babysitting). Then I spend the afternoon working and preparing a few blog posts.

"Tuesdays and Fridays I typically spend in the church office; I tend to leave early in the morning to avoid traffic, so I head home by midafternoon. Wednesdays and Thursdays I dedicate to my work with Ligonier Ministries, working roughly eight until five.

"Devotions come before the work day and family time comes after. I can't say that I always get the balance right, but I certainly do try. It's the rare day when my wife and I do not spend 8:00 p.m. until bedtime just hanging out and spending time together, even if that just means we're sprawled out on the couch together reading."

You can read the full interview at my blog: *http://www.whatsbestnext .com/2011/03/an-interview-with-tim-challies-on-productivity-part-one/*.

3. A basic schedule enables you to integrate all of your roles. Creating a basic schedule is not difficult. In line with our core principle of putting the big rocks in first, you simply identify the primary responsibilities from your roles that won't happen just by keeping them in mind but that need to be given concrete time.

One of the best examples is the responsibility of spending time with your family. It might be tempting to say, "That is so obvious; it comes naturally and will happen on its own." In generations past, this might have been so. But today, with our always-on society and our ability to work anywhere, anytime, it is easy for family routines to disappear. They are often crowded out by other demands despite our best intentions.

Hence, one important routine is to define specific, focused time in the week to be with your family. For me, this normally happens from

5:30 p.m. until bedtime every night. While I'm often with my family at other times as well, this gives me a mechanism to protect that time even when my action lists are spilling over.

Without a basic schedule in place, it is easy for certain roles and responsibilities to be crowded out of your week. Again, good intentions aren't enough. As you begin to schedule your time, you'll find that you can't schedule a specific time for everything. You'll also need to leave some room for spontaneity. But you will want to make sure your core responsibilities actually happen, and to do that you need to create time for them every week.

4. A basic schedule enables (rather than hinders) creative thinking. We might be tempted to think that creating a basic schedule will bring rigidity and crowd out or restrict our creative thinking. But it's actually the opposite that is the case.

Scott Belsky, founder of Behance and author of *Making Ideas Happen: Overcoming the Gap Between Vision and Reality*, rightly observes, "Structured time spent executing ideas is a best practice of admired creative leaders across industries. It is the only way to keep up with the continuous stream of action steps and allocate sufficient time for deep thought."[4]

Having a basic routine channels your ability to focus and protects time for creative work and work that requires sustained focus and concentration. If you leave yourself to the whims of inspiration, you will never get to your work. But when you have a routine in place, you will often find the inspiration you need to get your work done.[5]

By all means, harness your whims when they do come. But don't wait for them.

HOW TO SET UP YOUR WEEK

So how do you structure your week so that your most important responsibilities are woven into the fabric of your life? You create a prototype week—a time map.

A time map is another name for your weekly schedule. Instead of starting from scratch each week, you divide your week into time zones, each representing the main roles and responsibilities of your life.

You don't need to be too detailed here. In fact, getting too detailed might backfire. And you don't need to make every day the same either. You just need a basic template that represents your main roles at a high level, and provides zones for a few specific recurring routines. The chart on the next two pages provides one example.

Architect

	Sunday	Monday	Tuesday
Goal:	Family/Rest/Spiritual	Accomplish week/meetings	
6:00 AM			
6:30 AM			
7:00 AM		Prayer	Prayer
7:30 AM	Prayer	Breakfast/commute	Breakfast/commute
8:00 AM		Daily Workflow	Daily Workflow
8:30 AM		Projects	Projects
9:00 AM			
9:30 AM			
10:00 AM	Church/SS		
10:30 AM			
11:00 AM			
11:30 AM		Lunch/Free	Lunch/Free
12:00 PM			
12:30 PM		Meetings/Other	Meetings/Other
1:00 PM	People		
1:30 PM			
2:00 PM			
2:30 PM			
3:00 PM			
3:30 PM			
4:00 PM	Free		
4:30 PM		*Afternoon workflow*	*Afternoon workflow*
5:00 PM		Exercise	Exercise
5:30 PM			
6:00 PM	Family	Family	Family
6:30 PM		*Play with kids/homework*	*Play with kids/homework*
7:00 PM			
7:30 PM			
8:00 PM	*Bedtimes*		*Bedtimes*
8:30 PM		Blog	
9:00 PM			
9:30 PM	Free		Free
10:00 PM			
10:30 PM			
11:00 PM			
11:30 PM	Sleep	Sleep	Sleep
12:00 AM			

200

Wednesday	Thursday	Friday	Saturday
Accomplish week/meetings		Projects/development	Family
Prayer	Prayer	Prayer	
Breakfast/commute	Breakfast/commute		
Daily Workflow	Daily Workflow	Daily Workflow	Weekly Workflow
		Reading Pile	
Projects	Projects		
		Projects/Learning	
			Exercise
Lunch/Free	Lunch/Free		
Meetings/Other	Meetings/Other		Family Activity
Afternoon workflow	*Afternoon workflow*		Free
Exercise	Exercise	Free	
Family	Family		Family Night
Play with kids/homework	*Play with kids/homework*		
Bedtimes	*Bedtimes*	People	*Bedtimes*
Free	Free		Free
Sleep	Sleep	Sleep	Sleep

Notice that your zones are based on your roles, though you don't have to specify the role behind each zone. All of your roles should be represented in your typical week. But above all, keep it simple. For example, you might have a routine to check your email at noon and 3:00 p.m. Don't add these slots on your time map, or your time map will get too cumbersome. Those routines should just be on autopilot.

You can specify a theme for each day, which can be helpful, and specify the major area (individual, work, family/other) along the left, if desired. Michael Hyatt has an excellent example of a time map on his blog, including a template you can download if you need additional help with this.[6]

You won't follow your time map exactly each week. When planning the upcoming week, for example, you might decide that it will work best to take Wednesday afternoon, which you ordinarily leave open to respond to emails, for project time. That's fine. Again, the point is that you have a basic framework. You can adjust the specifics in any given week as needed.

One especially helpful benefit of a time map is that creating these activity zones will enable you to keep your related tasks together. Putting a basic schedule in place kept me from feeling like I had to *always* be doing something on my next actions list. I was able to keep the tasks on my lists off my mind because I now had scheduled times when I would actually do them. Julie Morgenstern captures this dynamic well: "Instead of feeling that you have to act on every request the minute it crosses your path, you can glance at your Time Map, determine when you have time for this unexpected task, and either schedule it or skip it."[7]

The secret, which I mentioned earlier, is thinking of your time a bit more like space. When many tasks come up all at once, you don't have to jam them into your week or add them all to your general actions list. Instead, you assign them to your various activity zones. Ideally, every task will have a general slot in your time map.

As we will see in the next chapter, the next step is to develop workflow routines for different time zones. Some of the major routines even have their own zone all to themselves: your daily workflow and your weekly workflow. And of course you will likely have other routines that fall into the broader work zones (like "work") but that aren't represented specifically on the time map.

In the end, the best thing you can do is create a time map that

How Does the President Schedule His Day?

I had the opportunity to interview Bradley Blakeman, professor of public policy and international affairs at Georgetown and a former scheduler for President Bush, on how he ran the president's schedule. Here are some highlights of the interview.

Q: What does the president's scheduler do?

A: The scheduler is basically in charge of the president's official schedule. Every minute of his day is the responsibility of the scheduler.

Q: How did you learn how to do this?

A: I had never been a scheduler before. I told him I'd never done this before, and he said, "You have two weeks to figure this out." When I came to the White House I studied what other presidents had done. Then I tried to figure out what I could do to manage the president's time in a way that is seamless, knowing that typically the scheduler is one of the first to get fired when you transfer from campaign mode to governing mode. I invented my own system and computerized things.

Q: How did something get on the president's schedule?

A: I determined that only an assistant to the president—there are fifteen of them—could ask for his time. So every moment of the president's time had a sponsor of that time. If someone wanted to get on his schedule, they had to find a sponsor for that time.

Q: How did you determine his schedule?

A: In addition to the routines and the requests people would make to get on his schedule, we would look at the year. There are certain things presidents must do—meet with certain other presidents, the UN general assembly, and so forth. So we first plugged in national events—the annual events—and then we would schedule around those fixed events.

Q: How far out did you schedule?

A: We made sure he always had a full schedule for at least twenty-one days. The reason being that if I'm the president and know what I'm doing for twenty-one days—many people don't think beyond a week—it made it easier for him to plan his life. If you go much beyond twenty-one days—other than for the major events—we found that it gets too iffy about what's going to happen.

Q: How did you make sure the schedule reflected the major goals of the administration?

A: We would have scheduler meetings with the senior staff, typically weekly, and also have major strategy meetings where we would map big goals and when to accomplish those goals. So if the president had to go to Ohio to push a bill, we would block out time in advance. We put onto the schedule what most needed to be on there.

Q: How did Bush do with his schedule?

A: Very good. He was highly disciplined and focused. This is important because a schedule is only as good as the person whom it is implemented for. If they don't honor it, time goes out the window, and you can't get anything done.

Q: How did the scheduling work during especially disruptive and volatile times, such as 9/11?

A: As disciplined as we were when 9/11 happened, we had to be flexible enough to throw everything out. We started scheduling hour by hour. It took three weeks to get back to normal. However, because we were so disciplined, we got there more quickly than most. We knew that during the aftermath of 9/11 it couldn't be business as usual, but as soon as we were able to regain control of our time, we got back into our routine.

Q: Any specific advice for the readers of the book?

A: You tame time through a routine—knowing what's around the corner, and knowing how much time you have to do it. Not all of your time is routine, but enough needs to be to create a framework.

is easy to remember so it becomes automatic and natural to the way you live. Not having to refer to it all the time will make things much easier.

When I recently interviewed Bradley Blakeman, a former scheduler for President Bush, I asked him how he went about scheduling the president's day. This is what he had to say:

> What I tried to do is craft a schedule by which the president didn't have to rely on a piece of paper—it became innate in his head. I said to myself, "How can I make the president comfortable so only pockets of time change every day?"
>
> So the president got a briefing at the same time every day—FBI at 7:00 a.m., for example. Then recurring meetings happened at the same time same day, such as the Secretary of State every Thursday at 10:00 a.m. There was also "use it or lose it" time, meaning that if someone didn't need a recurring meeting that week, they could give it back so it could be used for something else.
>
> Lunch was every day at the same time, and so was exercise. Thus, the president knew that only a few hours in the day changed, without even having to look at his schedule. The majority of his time he could therefore keep in his head, without relying on paper. The result is that the president is involved in a routine that he gets used to, and the presidency then becomes more normal. We tried to make an abnormal experience a normal experience.

Blakeman's goal was to create a routine for the president, a pattern for fulfilling his responsibilities that became natural to the way he lived.

FLEXIBILITY AND INNOVATION

Your time map is a rough guideline, and you need to be flexible with it throughout the day and week. Some things should be virtually inviolable—such as the daily workflow routine. (We will discuss this in the next chapter.) But if you are nailing it there, you will likely be highly flexible the rest of your day.

There's another reason that flexibility is important, beyond the fact that it just makes your life and day more interesting and engaging. Spontaneity is a necessary element for innovation. Steve Jobs made this point well in an interview in *BusinessWeek*:

> Apple is a very disciplined company, and we have great processes. But that's not what it's about. Process makes you more efficient.
>
> But innovation comes from people meeting up in the hallways or calling each other at 10:30 at night with a new idea, or because they realized something that shoots holes in how we've been

thinking about a problem. It's *ad hoc* meetings of six people called by someone who thinks he has figured out the coolest new thing ever and who wants to know what other people think of his idea.[8]

My point in suggesting a basic framework to your week is not to eliminate or reduce spontaneous interaction but rather to enable more of it. I find these spontaneous conversations and meetings among the most energizing parts of my day, and the point of a basic routine is to keep from letting them be crowded out by the sense that you always need to be plugging away on your projects list.

EXTREME MEASURES

There is one special challenge here: Creative tasks are often unpredictable and thus cannot always be kept within a routine.

For example, you can specify a four-hour block for writing, and then at the end realize that you have momentum to keep going for another four hours (contrary to your schedule) or that the task is twice as large as you anticipated.

If you are doing creative tasks week after week, this adds up. That's a problem.

Here are three measures that are helpful in extreme situations, which most people who are seeking to do good work that matters will find themselves in from time to time.

1. Sixteen-Hour Days

I prefer to work sixteen-hour days. Sixteen-hour days solve almost *everything*. And I find that it doesn't result in wasting much time. Longer blocks of work time allow me to dive deeply into things without worrying that I will neglect important meetings and appointments and emails. If you are inclined to work most effectively in long blocks like this, go for it.

But it doesn't work so well, at least for very long, if you have a family. Note that I'm not saying it doesn't work if you want to have a social life. It actually integrates well with a social life; for example, you might be at the office on a Tuesday until 8:00 p.m., then get together with some people for dinner, and then do more work from 11:00 p.m. to 2:00 a.m.

But kids and families have different schedules. I don't want to miss out on my kids' lives or time with my wife, so, for me, sixteen-hour days are a decent solution for limited, specific periods of time when necessary. But I don't use them as a general rule now.

So, for those of you who (like me) can't do the sixteen-hour days very often, yet still must deal with the significant unpredictability of many creative tasks, I have two main suggestions.

2. Be Insanely Good at What You Do

Being really good at something is a huge time saver. If you can't work sixteen-hour days, you will have to either do less work or shrink down your tasks. Being really good at something allows you to shrink your tasks *and* get them done quicker.

This will allow you to work with quality *and* quickness at the same time. The one downfall: learning how to be really good at something has a large start-up cost.

3. One-Month Sabbaticals

The other suggestion is to take a one-month project sabbatical every year. In this time, work on the large, beyond-the-boundaries projects that just don't fit into your typical schedule.

For example, the former preaching pastor at my church, John Piper, takes a one-month writing leave each year. In it, he usually completes at least one, and sometimes three, books. He wouldn't be able to give the necessary focused attention to writing if he tried to fit it into his ordinary schedule—even if he followed the practice of slotting four hours each morning for creative work.

This doesn't have to be limited to writers or pastors. Anyone who is involved in creative work should take at least one month per year to devote to long-term or extra-large projects. Think Bill Gates' annual think week extended to a month. The result would be, I believe, higher productivity and more experimentation while preserving, perhaps, a bit more sanity.

The key principle here is this: Extreme tasks often require extreme measures. Think creatively not just about your work, but also about *how you do it*. And if it really matters, you should be able to find the time to do it well.

The Box

Core Point

You need to create a structure for your week and have some basic routines in it.

Core Quote

Structured time spent executing ideas is a best practice of admired creative leaders across industries. It is the only way to keep up with the continuous stream of action steps and allocate sufficient time for deep thought.

—Scott Belsky

Immediate Application

Create a time map! (Or review and update yours if you already have one.)

Driving It Deeper

If you find that your creative work is relatively unpredictable, consider an extreme measure like an annual one-month creative sabbatical.

CHAPTER 15

Creating the Right Routines

The six routines you need to have

If you cram a new task in anywhere, hoping you will still get everything else done, you will soon find yourself running late again and feeling like you're not getting to the important things.

—*Julie Morgenstern,* Time Management from the Inside Out

IN THE LAST CHAPTER, WE NOTED that having a basic framework should not eliminate or reduce spontaneity. It should increase it.

We also noted that one of the perennial challenges of doing "creative" work (and remember, "creative" work doesn't mean just art, but anything you do that matters and requires sustained thought and focus) is that it can be unpredictable. You can do some things to keep tasks in their boundaries, but you can't always do this.

Regardless of the type of work we are engaged in, there is always the challenge of unpredictability. One important solution, as we saw, is keeping your weekly schedule flexible.

But there is another solution as well: having the right routines. If you establish the right routines, and execute them well, you'll gain a lot of flexibility. Here are six routines that can help you to retain balance, stay flexible, and get the right things done.

SIX CORE ROUTINES

1. Get Up Early!

This is the first practice because it makes each of the other core practices possible. If you don't get up early, you risk undermining your entire day.

In *Shopping for Time*, Carolyn Mahaney and her daughters recommend getting up at 5:00 a.m. They call it "The Five O'Clock Club," and it apparently has become fairly popular among the followers of their blog.[1]

If you can do it, 5:00 a.m. is the best. But I think for a lot of us, that's probably not going to work out! However you do it, a good rule of thumb is that you probably have to get up earlier than you think.

There is one exception to getting up early: The person who prefers to stay up *very* late, and is able to make it work. Al Mohler, president of Southern Seminary, is one such example. He is widely known for staying up until two or three every morning. In my interview (see the sidebar) I asked him how he does this.

Personally, I prefer staying up late. In college, I stayed up until 2:00 a.m. most nights reading theology and apologetics and writing articles to remember what I was learning and to post on my website. But unlike Mohler, I've found that staying up that late makes it too hard for me to get up when I need to consistently.

In the end, it doesn't matter whether you get up early or stay up super late. The key is that you need a long period of uninterrupted time to get your basic workflow and key projects done. That's the principle. However you make that happen is up to you. But without creating this uninterrupted, focused time, it will be hard to make substantial progress.

2. Daily Workflow

I've referred to something I've called a "daily workflow routine" several times already. This is the core routine you need to establish to keep on top of tasks, keep up with people, and make progress on your goals.

Basically, it boils down to one hour (or sometimes ninety minutes) of focused, uninterrupted work each day in which you can work through a set of four core tasks:

1. Plan your day.
2. Execute your workflow (including processing your email to zero).
3. Do your main daily activity.
4. Do some next actions or major project work.

Staying Up Super Late ...

Al Mohler on How He Does His Best Work between 11:00 P.M. and 3:00 A.M.

It has been widely rumored that Al Mohler, president of Southern Theological Seminary, stays up super late each night doing his core, independent work. Here's what he said when I asked him about that.

Q: Do you really do your best work between 11:00 p.m. and 3:00 a.m.?

A: Yes, absolutely. That's when I'm most mentally alert and when my mental faculties are most available to me. And it is my greatest opportunity for quiet, undistracted work. Leadership requires that.

I would not make that standard. I would not mandate any particular time. Everyone must find his or her own time. Speaking to pastors, you have to find the time in which you can actually get the work done.

I am hugely influenced in these things by Peter Drucker and his reminder that the effective executive maximizes his opportunities and knows himself. So we need to know whether we are more mentally active in morning or evening, and we need to maximize that.

... Or Getting Up Super Early

Mike Allen on How He Starts His Day at 2:00 A.M.

On the other hand, take Mike Allen of Politico. As of this writing, he produces the most read and most influential daily briefing in all of Washington, DC. It has more than one hundred thousand subscribers, and everybody of influence—including the White House staff—makes it a point to check it first thing every morning.

Mike Allen and Al Mohler work very differently. Mike Allen gets up early—*super* early.

Q: What is your general daily or weekly schedule like?

A: I usually get up around two or two thirty in the morning and get to work around three. I try to get the newsletter done by six, or sometimes seven. We have a TV hit at 6:15 every day. And then after that I'll often leave for a while, work out, go home; on Fridays I go to the Bible study I attend. I then come back at 8:00 a.m. for a call in which we talk about the day. To keep it short, we confine that call to what is happening new that morning. It's not long-term planning. It's just what is going to happen that day.

Then I'm usually around in the morning just to be helpful to my bosses or other people who work here. We work in suburban Arlington. Midday I go into DC to meet with people or wander around on the hill. Then I'm back to Politico by late afternoon. At 4:30 we have a standing meeting in which we talk about what will be in the print edition of the paper and the web the next morning. It's five minutes or less—a quick conversation. Then I usually go home after that. I usually see someone in the evening from church or work. I try to get to bed to get six hours of sleep, or as close to that as I can.

Plan Your Day

The first thing to do is plan your day. We will talk about this in more detail in the chapter on executing your day, but at root you need to identify the most important things for the day, list them, and sequence them.

Execute Your Workflow

Executing your workflow consists of processing all your sources of input to zero: your physical inbox, email inbox, voice mail, voice notes (if you use them), and physical notes. By processing your inboxes once a day, you stay up to date without having to worry that you are getting behind or out of date.

Some people might say: "Only once a day? I do email all day long and answer the phone whenever it rings." I'm not advocating checking email only once a day. I do advocate checking it in batches, rather than continually,[2] because otherwise you are essentially interrupting yourself all day. But I do recommend processing it to zero *at least* once a day. Keeping up with your RSS reader (if you use one) and the websites you visit also fits well into your daily workflow.

Do Your Main Daily Activity

Whatever your most important ongoing activity is, do it here. If you are seeking to devote some time each day to thinking about company strategy, do it here. If you are a blogger, blog here. Whatever your primary individual work is, do it here.

I've noticed that the things we do every day are things we tend to get very good at (if they line up with our strengths). If there is something you want to get good at, and which makes a difference for you and others and your organization, don't leave it to chance or good intentions (even the good intentions of your next action list). Do it as part of a routine every day. The best way to do this is to work it into your daily workflow routine.

Conversely, if you don't make it part of a routine, it's likely you will keep skipping it and never do it. The importance of working in your strengths has an especially significant application here. One way to know if you are working in your strengths is to ask yourself, "Do I have the opportunity to do what I do best every day?" That's what you want for your role: You want to be doing what you do best every day.

Now, this should pertain to all parts of your day, not just your morning workflow routine. But the main activity portion of this routine presents an easy way to stay on the path of your strengths. It's a way to make sure you are giving time *every day* to doing what you do best.

Don't just leave working in your strengths at the level of theory; you need to intentionally build time into your daily routine to do the activities that you do best and that energize you. The daily workflow routine provides an opportunity to do this.

Do Some Next Actions or Work on an Important Project

After you've been able to work on your main activity, look at your next actions list and knock some off. You might also want to put some time in on any major projects you have going on.

Obviously you will do some more next actions (probably!) and project work through the rest of the day as well. But this gives you a chance, especially if you won't have time to do any next actions that day, to make sure you can knock off anything that feels especially pressing. And it helps give you the confidence that when you add things to your next action list, they aren't dropping into a black hole.

After Your Workflow Routine

After your workflow routine, go on with your day, which means do whatever you have on your calendar or have planned for the rest of the day, whether that's specific project work or meetings or just being generally available for people.

Depending on your work and your schedule, this may include blocks of time dedicated to meetings or interacting with people. I've found that no matter what direction my day takes, as long as I reconfigure, touch base, and get up to date every morning, I have the flexibility to go with the flow.

A daily workflow routine like this is the only way that I know of to keep current, and it is highly efficient—if you do it in one uninterrupted block. And that's exactly why it's so important to get up early. If you try to start this at 9:00 in the morning, it will inevitably be derailed by the ordinary course of the day.

If you let yourself be interrupted, these tasks can end up taking all day. That's how inefficient it is not to group these together into a single block. But if you group them all together in an uninterrupted span of time, it goes quickly and you are able to keep an amazing amount of things going.

What do you do on days when things don't fit into the time you've allocated for your workflow routine? For example, when you have an extra large dose of email or lots of meetings back-to-back? That's when you have to reduce. This is the principle of *containing* your tasks: you have to size them in such a way that they fit in their slots.

Remember that it's okay if you can't do everything. Not realizing that is the mistake I always used to make. Then it finally occurred to me that in a world of so much opportunity, of course there will be more coming at us than we have time for. And that's a good thing.

3. Weekly Workflow

The weekly workflow routine is a variation on the daily workflow routine. Whereas the daily workflow routine is mostly for work tasks, the weekly workflow routine is for home tasks. I find that there are many home tasks that I cannot do during the week (such as mow the lawn). The weekly workflow routine (typically on Saturday mornings) is when I do these things.

Rhythms and Innovation
Get out of Your Routines Every Now and Then

Here's what Bubba Jennings, a pastor at Mars Hill in Seattle, said when I asked him about his routines:

"If you don't take time to get outside of your regular rhythms and dream, you'll never innovate. You need to reinvent your rhythms every so often and block out a day, like a dream day. Look at all the things weighing you down, look at how you can actually get them done or who you can delegate them to. Look at what rhythms are working and which aren't working. If you don't give yourself the flexibility and freedom to do that as needed, you'll burn yourself out."

4. Prayer and Scripture

Earlier, we talked about the necessity of maintaining a consistent time of prayer and meditation on Scripture. You can do this early in the morning before doing anything else. This is what works best for most people. Alternatively, you can do it later at night before heading to bed.

Either way, don't neglect it.

5. Reading and Development

A few things here. First, this is critical! For a great treatment of why this is so important, how to do it well, and an excellent four-step process for making what you learn work for you, see Tim Sander's chapter "Knowledge" in his excellent book *Love Is the Killer App*.

Second, an easy way to make productivity practices work for you here is to keep a reading list. That's obvious, but where do you keep it? If you are familiar with GTD, it falls into the category of checklists. Your reading list is a type of checklist. (Note: For more on checklists, see the extended "Managing Actions" chapter online.)

Third, remember that, as Mortimer Adler has said, "marking up a book is not an act of mutilation but of love."[3] Fourth, you can do more than just read for your learning and growth. The Teaching Company, for example, has many excellent courses on a full range of subjects. Most of these courses work great on audio and thus for your commute if you

Al Mohler on Reading

Al Mohler is legendary for how much he is able to read. He is known for reading a book a day—or more. So when I interviewed him, I asked him for his thoughts on reading.

Q: What is the most important advice you would give to others on reading?

A: I can't give just one word there. Two or three. Realize that when you read, you are putting investments in a bank from which to draw, even if it doesn't appear to have direct relevance. Second, use your books, don't just read them. Mark in them, keep a conversation in them. Third, don't build a book collection; build a library and make it work for you. Fourth, realize you're never going to read everything. We will die with things we wish we had read. But the fact is too many people do not read. The problem for most is not that they are learning too much, but that they aren't learning enough.

For more on reading, see also Tony Reinke's excellent book *Lit! A Christian Guide to Reading Literature* and chapter 2, "Knowledge," in Tim Sanders' excellent book *Love Is the Killer App*.

have one; but some of them work best on DVD, and you can get through those by integrating them into your reading time.

6. Rest

When I was in my twenties, I didn't always take this advice. I had the energy to do that, in part, because in our current era the line between work and rest is often blurred. But I think, long-term, I would have likely served myself better if I had given a higher place to rest.

So this one is simple: take at least one *full day* off each week.

OTHER ROUTINES WORTH CONSIDERING

- Daily exercise (running, weight lifting, or such)
- Weekly family night (movies or games every Friday or Saturday night)

- A day for things you don't like
- Having people over for lunch after church
- Camping with the kids in the back yard every summer

Basically, anything you want to not only do, but *keep doing,* turn into a routine. You'll get good at it and, if it involves other people, develop good memories as well.

WHEN TO CHUCK THE ROUTINE

These six routines are just suggestions. Your first thought when you see them might be, "That won't work for me." If so, that's okay. Start with one or two. The goal is to find routines that help you turn your mission statement, your life goals, and your weekly schedules into practices that reflect your priorities. Routines shouldn't invent new work for you. They should capture the work you already need to do and put it into a framework that lets you do it more efficiently.

Keeping up with your routines is not the point. Some days I skip my daily workflow because I am caught up and I know I can go a day without it. In fact, during a recent season, I skipped my daily workflow for an entire month. (Part of that was an experiment to confirm for my readers that it does indeed add more value than doing those things more *ad hoc* throughout the day—it does!—and part of it was because I simply had a huge project I was working on.) Do what works for you. The key is knowing how to get things done and to get the decks cleared in a regular way while doing what is most important, not simply doing everything that comes your way.

A WORD ON EXCELLENCE

Having a rough schedule, or just keeping up with your responsibilities and tasks in whatever way you do, represents the price of admission to keeping up in the knowledge economy and doing your job in a way that truly serves people.

But excellence happens when you go beyond your schedule. Competence is doing what you need to do. Excellence is knowing what you're supposed to do, getting it on autopilot, and going beyond. It means having that extra touch that goes beyond simply what you could write down in an article or in a manual. It's doing what not everyone can do, even if they know all the steps.

Seek to be excellent in what you do.

The Box

Core Point

There are six routines that are the most helpful for getting things done and staying up to date: getting up early, daily workflow, weekly workflow, prayer and Scripture, reading and development, and rest.

Core Quote

I am hugely influenced in these things by Peter Drucker and his reminder that the effective executive maximizes his opportunities and knows himself. So we need to know whether we are more mentally active in morning or evening, and we need to maximize that.

—Al Mohler

Immediate Application

If you aren't getting up as early as you need to, make that change right now.

Driving It Deeper

Maybe give the 10:00 p.m. to 2:00 a.m. schedule a try for one night and see how you feel!

PART 5

Reduce

FREE UP YOUR TIME FOR
WHAT'S MOST IMPORTANT

*Learning how to cope with not getting everything done is
just as important as getting more done.*
—*Stuart Levine*, Cut to the Chase

IT HAS HAPPENED TO EVERY ONE OF US. You have your prototype week in place and you feel clarity and excitement about your week. But then, as you get into your week, nothing goes according to plan, and everything falls apart.

Obviously your structure needs to be flexible so it can accommodate change in the moment. We need to create a *flexible* framework for our weeks, not a *rigid* framework.

However, if you find that it is almost impossible to make your structure work, it's likely because of a larger problem. The problem is that you are trying to do too much, and it doesn't fit.

This leads us to step 3 in our DARE process: the need to reduce.

The architecture you create for your life will never work if you try to force too much into it. It's like organizing a closet: only so much can fit. When things start getting packed, the solution is not mainly to find ways to pack things in more and more tightly. The solution is to get rid of some things.

So if your prototype week constantly fails and gets blown up, this is not a bad thing in itself. Rather, it tells you something very important: you simply have too much to do.

The way to make your flexible framework work, in other words, is to be ruthless in pruning and containing your tasks so that you are able to keep them within the time frames you've allotted. Without doing this, your structure will be blown and your life will easily descend into amorphous chaos (worst case) or frenetic rushing (best case).

Reduce

You won't get it all done. But don't just let balls drop either. The way to reduce is to eliminate the truly unnecessary, create systems to enable the rest to get done, and know how to contain your tasks when you are doing them (that is, how to keep them in their allotted time).

To reduce well, we need to know three things:

1. Why doing *less* actually enables you to do *more*.
2. How to free up time through delegating, automating, eliminating, and deferring.
3. How to handle the time killers—not by avoiding them but by actually *harnessing* them for greater effectiveness.

CHAPTER 16

The Problem with Full System Utilization

If your prototype week never works,
or constantly gets blown up, it's because
you simply have too much to do; and,
how chaos theory has implications
for how we get things done

*Chaos plays a very significant role in our lives. Lack of
planning for chaotic behavior can be a very costly oversight.*
— *Robert Monson*

THE REDUCE STEP is about getting rid of unnecessary things so that
the basic template you've created for your schedule can work. But it's also
about one other thing: avoiding the scary "ringing effect" by realizing
exactly why doing less enables you to do more.

THE RINGING EFFECT

When I was taking courses to get my Project Management Professional
certification, one of the teachers was especially helpful. He introduced us
to the importance of understanding projects in relation to chaos theory.

Researchers have found that whenever most systems—such as airports, freeways, and other such things—exceed about 90 percent capacity, efficiency drops *massively*. Not just slightly, but massively.

This is called the "ringing effect." The reason is that as a system nears its capacity, the effect of relatively small disturbances is magnified exponentially.

This is why traffic slows down at rush hour almost inexplicably. When you think about it, unless there is an accident, there's almost no reason that traffic should be going slow. And, here's the thing: you're right.

Or, in other words, there *is* a reason, but it's not what you'd expect. The reason traffic is slow is because of the relatively small and otherwise insignificant braking that some guy four miles ahead did—and the person a quarter mile behind him, and half a mile behind him. It's not that they are slamming on their brakes; under ordinary circumstances, what they are doing would have almost no effect on the flow of traffic.

The problem is that once capacity is past about 90 percent, small disturbances have a huge effect. And so traffic slows down, sometimes to a crawl.

That's the ringing effect.

The ringing effect doesn't just apply to traffic or airports. It applies to your projects and your organization as well. When all these small effects are cascading—"ringing"—through your life and the organization, work is not getting done. Or perhaps to put it better, useless work is being multiplied.

You see the ringing effect, for example, when you are trying to schedule a meeting for ten people, and they all have to be there. It's almost impossible to find a time that works for everyone, resulting in an untold number of emails going back and forth. And then, once everything is figured out, something unexpected comes up for someone and you need to reschedule the meeting again (and then reschedule the other stuff on your plate that is now interfering with the new time). That "rearranging" is the ringing effect. And it takes time away from the productive stuff that you have to do (in this case, times ten). And the effects continue cascading, for as you keep rescheduling, other people involved need to reschedule as well (even if they aren't part of the group for the original meeting). And on it goes.

Your projects themselves do this to you, even if no one else is involved. For when you are working on a lot of things simultaneously, they will often "bump into" one another, causing the same type of cascading effect.

This is why there is actually a relationship between chaos theory and managing your projects. The ringing effect is an expression of chaos theory. And, as my professor Robert Munson pointed out, since "all white-collar work is essentially project oriented," it follows that all knowledge workers "are faced with the likely occurrence of chaos within their daily activities."

OVERCOMING THE RINGING EFFECT

Here's what this means: In order to get *more* projects done (and do them better and faster), you need to *reduce* the number of projects you are actually working on at once. And for organizations and individuals, the ringing effect comes into play not at 90 percent capacity, but already at about 75 percent of capacity. Thus, as my professor said, "If you schedule projects for 75 percent capacity, you will get more work accomplished."

Our default mode is to think that in order to get as much as possible done, we need to cram as many projects as possible into a given time frame. Resist this temptation. Everything will take longer and you will discover death by the ringing effect. To get more done, do less, not more.

Now, if you are like many people, the "less" is probably more prominent in your head than the "more." "Do less in order to get more done" often translates in our minds to "Do less in order to ... (fade out into incoherent gibberish)."

So here's the thing: Really take the "more" seriously. Really go for the more. Just do it by means of doing less things at one time.

Don't just say "we're doing less now as an organization." That's a cop-out. There is *so much* to do and the needs of the world are *so great* that we need to be doing more, not less. Don't bail on us, please! Do less *truly* in order to do more.

The Box

Core Point

The way to get more projects done is to do less at once, not more, because when you approach capacity, the productivity-killing ringing effect kicks in.

Core Quote

All white-collar work is essentially project oriented. This would imply that all [knowledge workers] are faced with the likely occurrence of chaos within their daily activities.

—Robert Monson

CHAPTER 17

The Art of Making Time

How to delegate in the right way, and three other ways to create time

It's amazing how someone's IQ seems to double as soon as you give them responsibility and indicate you trust them.

— *Timothy Ferriss,* The Four-Hour Workweek

ONE OF THE BEST THINGS about David Allen's book, *Getting Things Done,* is that it gives you a way to keep track of everything you want to do, and every good idea people suggest to you. You never need to lose a good idea again.

And, this might also be its greatest weakness!

THE GTD DILEMMA

When I first started implementing principles from *Getting Things Done*, I began capturing every idea that seemed even potentially valuable. Many times on my twenty-five-minute commute home from work, I'd pull into my driveway with thirty new ideas in the voice notes on my phone.

Many of these were two-minute tasks that I could do right when I was processing the notes during my daily or weekly workflow. But other ideas were much larger things that couldn't be done right away, or even that week, and so I'd put them on my projects list or, at least, in "upcoming" or "someday-maybe."

At first, this was a lot of fun and I was able to keep up a pretty good pace for a while. But eventually I had accumulated *a lot* of ideas and things to do, and the size of it all was starting to weigh me down.

MY SEARCH FOR A SOLUTION

My solution? My friend Tim Challies, author of *The Next Story: Life and Faith after the Digital Explosion*, would flag this as a classic mistake: I turned to technology. I determined that I just needed to find a better way to organize my lists and maybe find a better program to do it with.

This worked for a while but, of course, it didn't work for the long run. There was just way too much to do for me to keep up with. And with a growing family, I needed to find a way to cut things down to size.

My next attempt at finding a solution was to comb through every productivity book I had to find a better way of doing things. So I stacked up thirty books and spent a Sunday afternoon and Monday skimming them as fast as I could for all the best ideas I could find. Then I created a document integrating these.

The ultimate solution still didn't come immediately, but through continued reflection on Peter Drucker's *The Effective Executive*, I came to see that I wasn't giving enough place to reducing. I was primarily relying on just one strategy for reducing my load: deferring (that is, putting items on a list to do later). Deferring is helpful, but ultimately all it does is delay things rather than reduce your overall load. I needed to do something that would reduce my load, not just space it out.

There are four main ways to reduce the amount of things you have to do:

1. Delegate
2. Eliminate
3. Automate
4. Defer

Interestingly, these four practices create the acronym DEAD. I don't really like that, and thought about changing the order just to avoid it. But I'm keeping it because it can help you remember it. After all, the point of these strategies is, in some sense, to *kill* from your schedule the things you don't need to be doing. Some things have to die, or you will never get anything done.

You need to know how to do each of these, but for space reasons I'm going to focus primarily on the most important: delegation.

STRATEGY 1: DELEGATION

Why God Does *Not* Give Us All the Time We Need

Freeing up your time for what is most important is not merely about eliminating things. If that was all you did, you wouldn't get very far. There are things that need to be done and ought to get done, even though they are beyond your individual capacity.

In other words, God has *not* given us all the time we need to accomplish what we have to do.

I say this because it reveals a faulty paradigm, one that views productivity as primarily an individual matter. God hasn't given us all the time we need because he wants us to rely on other people as well as our own resources and gifts. God has given us all we need, to be sure, but the mistake is thinking that all we need is time. What we need, more accurately, is time and other people (plus some knowledge!).

If you focus only on eliminating things, you miss the point. The first step in learning to reduce is rejecting the "solo mentality"—the notion that productivity is merely an individual matter. With this mentality you will end up isolating yourself, which is the opposite of what God wants for us.

God designed the world so that there will always be more things for us to do than we are able to do. This isn't just so we learn to prioritize; it's so that we learn to depend on one another.

And that's what delegation enables us to do.

I believe delegation is the single most important way to free up time. Enlisting others is essential because, when done well, delegation builds others up and deepens existing relationships. This means that before talking about how to delegate well, we have to clear up two common wrong views of delegation.

Delegation Is Not Simply a Way to Get Rid of Tasks You Don't Like

Delegation is often presented as something you do with your low-value tasks. We are often counseled to prioritize our tasks with the A, B, C, D, and E method. The A items are the most important, and the E items are the least important—which is highlighted by the fact that in this approach, E stands for "Erase."

Reduce

Right next to these lowly Es are the Ds—which stands for Delegate. In other words, the things you delegate are the things that don't even make the cut of being Cs, and are just barely above the status of the worthless Es.

The notion is that you delegate the things that are unimportant and lowly. That the point is simply to get these tasks *off* your plate rather than to build up others and give them meaningful tasks that build the organization and serve them.

Drucker gets at this well: "As usually presented, delegation makes little sense. If it means that somebody else ought to do part of '*my* work,' it is wrong. One is paid for doing one's own work. And if it implies, as the usual sermon does, that the laziest manager is the best manager, it is not only nonsense; it is immoral."[1]

Drucker is not against delegation. In fact, just a few sentences later he says "the only way he can get to the important things is by pushing on others anything that can be done by them at all."

Delegation Is a Way of Serving

But here is the point: Our aim in delegating is not simply to make our own lives better and free up our time. It is also to build up the other person. This is the aim we are to have in *everything* we do: "*Always* seek to do good to one another and to everyone" (1 Thess. 5:15). "Whether you eat or drink, or whatever you do [even delegating!], do all to the glory of God" (1 Cor. 10:31). And, as we saw earlier, doing something for the glory of God involves doing it for the good of others, not just yourself.

Yet most of the time, delegation is presented as a way to serve yourself, not a way to serve others. This is the second wrong view of delegation, and is out of sync with everything we saw about the nature of productivity in part 2 of this book. True productivity is about doing good for others and making others productive, not just yourself. And delegation is a key way to build up others and help them be more effective, not just you.

As other people are built up through delegation, the capacity of the entire organization increases. The organization will be able to do more, and do it more effectively, because of this type of delegation. So you are not only serving the other person, you are also serving your whole organization when you delegate.

This intent behind true delegation—that is, to build the other person up—implies something about how we delegate. It implies that most

What Do You Do When You Don't Have Anyone to Delegate To?

Technology offers some creative ways around the challenge of having nobody on deck to delegate to. Here are two:

1. Ask for volunteers on Twitter or Facebook. This is how I got my assistant. I received seven inquiries within an hour; my wife did the first round of interviews, then I interviewed the final candidates and made a choice.
2. Consider a virtual assistant. Tim Ferriss gives a good overview of virtual assistants and where to find them in *The Four-Hour Workweek.*[*] Michael Hyatt also has a good post.[‡]

Or consider a variation on delegation: partnership. Marcus Buckingham points out that partnership is "the quiet secret of the successful."[†]

The most important thing you can do is have an ongoing mindset of involving others in your work.

---

[*] See Timothy Ferriss, *The Four-Hour Workweek* (New York: Crown Publishers, 2007), 135–36.

[‡] See *http://michaelhyatt.com/should-you-consider-hiring-a-virtual-assistant.html*.

[†] Marcus Buckingham, *The One Thing You Need to Know* (New York: Free Press, 2005).

of the time we should practice *stewardship delegation* rather than *gopher delegation*.

Stewardship Delegation versus Gopher Delegation

The distinction between stewardship delegation and gopher delegation highlights the second wrong view of delegation we need to avoid. In gopher delegation, you hand people specific tasks as the need arises and are closely involved in supervising how they do them. The other person does not utilize much independent judgment and initiative, but is basically operating in a "wait until told" context. You have something for them to do, and you tell them to do it. Responsibility for the results and methods lies with you, not them. You have not handed off responsibility; the other person is simply doing what they are told. On and on this goes, as the basic underlying fabric of the relationship.

In this approach, the other person doesn't grow because this relationship doesn't require the other person to use their wisdom or judgment or insight. They are treated almost like a tool. I think our hamster is even able to handle this type of delegation. This approach is fitting for dogs, but not for people.

Further, managing people like this does not scale. How much time does it take to supervise people in detail and give them their every task? Quite a bit. There's no way you could delegate to more than a few people with this mode of operation.

One of the best ways to free up your time, let alone develop the other person, is to get rid of the tendency to use gopher delegation.

Gopher delegation can be efficient when your aim is just to get a bunch of tasks done. But it's not very effective because it doesn't increase the capacity of the other person and, hence, the organization. (And by not being very effective, it is thus also *inefficient* in the long run.)

Stewardship delegation, on the other hand, has the aim of not just getting tasks done, but of building others up through the accomplishment of tasks. It is concerned about tasks, but it is equally concerned about the other person. As with good management in general, the aim is not just to get things done, but to develop people in the process. The aim is the effective accomplishment of tasks *and* the good of the other person.

Stewardship delegation delegates the task—or, more often, an area of responsibility—and allows the individual to determine their own methods for accomplishing the tasks. The focus is on achieving the intended results, not on *how* they are done (as long as they are done in alignment with the overall guidelines and values). The one delegating hands over true responsibility for the accomplishment of the task to the one being delegated to.

Five Components of Effective Delegation

In their book *First Things First*, Stephen Covey, Rebecca Merrill, and Roger Merrill point out that there are five components of effective stewardship delegation: desired results, guidelines, resources, accountability, and consequences.

1. Desired Results

Desired results are the things that need to be accomplished. It is the *what*—not the how. For example, when I call up the local sandwich shop to order a sub, I ask for a #2 (roast beef) and tell them my address. I don't tell them how to make it, how to get to my house, or how fast they should drive.

It should also be noted that under stewardship delegation, the person you are delegating to can and should often be a participant in defining the desired results. They will have useful ideas that shape the intended outcome.

2. Guidelines

Stewardship delegation is not the same as *laissez faire* delegation. You don't simply tell others what is needed and give no other guidance. There are often parameters that are essential to accomplishing the task effectively—and sometimes these parameters might be mostly your preferences, which is fine.

So, give the guidelines and point out any wrong turns they should be aware of. But note that you are giving *guidelines*, not detailed rules. You aren't determining methods; you are showing the broad parameters that will help them be effective. Leave as much as possible for them to determine. They should be free to do whatever it takes to accomplish the desired results, within the guidelines.

3. Resources

This step is often skipped in delegation. Let the person know the budget available, if relevant, and the other people who might be helpful to consult or who are available to help if accomplishing the task is going to involve more than just one person.

4. Accountability

You don't need to define accountability for every task delegated; that would get tiresome. Accountability just needs to be in place for the overall context of the relationship. This means everyone knowing what the standards of performance are and when the regular reviews are.

5. Consequences

Again, this should be defined not for every specific task but simply as part of the framework of the relationship. This would include both the good outcomes if the delegated responsibility is fulfilled and what will happen if it isn't. Positive outcomes might include increased responsibility, promotions, financial rewards, natural consequences, and so forth.

The Manager Is a Source of Help, Not a Boss

Note that the manager here is no longer a detailed supervisor but instead becomes a source of help. In one sense, the person delegated to becomes the manager, because they are now enabled to *manage themselves* within the context of the agreement. This means, also, that the person is able to evaluate themselves. Rather than evaluation being something that comes from the outside in—a manager giving critique and recommendations—the person will primarily be evaluating themselves. The manager should of course provide feedback, and evaluation (every three months, or every year), but the primary responsibility for evaluation is on the person himself.

It is true that delegation means that some things will be done less effectively—at first. And, there is a higher up-front time investment. But it is worth it, because the aim is not just efficiency, but building people up, and because this increases capacity for the long term—which is always both more effective and efficient.

Is There Ever a Place for Gopher Delegation?

I've heard some people say that "some people can't handle stewardship delegation."

I think that sells people short. Tim Ferriss nails it when he says that "people are smarter than you think. Give them a chance to prove themselves." In fact, maybe people seem "incapable" of responsibility because they are just reflecting back to you the way you are viewing them. As Ferriss also points out, "It's amazing how someone's IQ seems to double as soon as you give them responsibility and indicate you trust them."

More Guidelines for the Less Mature; Fewer Guidelines for the More Mature

There are times when any of us may need more guidance and help. That help comes when someone is willing to help us grow and build us up to greater independence. Covey captures this well:

> The principles involved in stewardship delegation are correct and applicable to any kind of person or situation. With imma-

Volunteer Help: How to Get It

Here's what Bubba Jennings, a pastor at Mars Hill Church in Seattle, had to say when I asked him for advice on seeking out volunteers:

"I believe that a new generation is coming up that doesn't always know who they are or what they're good at and would love the opportunity to have someone invest in them and help them discover those things.

"So when an opportunity is created and made known, it will attract those who are interested in learning and growing and discovering. The value in volunteering—and you need to appeal to this, not money—is helping people discover who they are and experience the joy of living out the giftedness that God has given them. When we are worshiping God and serving God, we experience a great amount of joy as we minister by the Spirit.

"So for pastors who are overwhelmed and don't know what to do or where to start, I'd say to start with one or two people. If you have only enough time to invest in a couple of people, start there and slowly build.

"If you do that well, eventually what happens is it multiplies. When I started, I think I started with four guys and one became the natural leader, and two were able to invest in others, and then a second invested in a third and on and on. If you do this, before you know it you have ministries that have taken on a life of their own. You then spend your time casting vision and building into people, and the tasks are being taken care of."

ture people, you specify fewer desired results and more guidelines, identify more resources, conduct more frequent accountability interviews, and apply more immediate consequences. With more mature people, you have more challenging desired results, fewer guidelines, less frequent accountability, and less measurable but more discernable criteria.[2]

When we practice good delegation—stewardship delegation—we

are not simply enabling ourselves to get more done. We are serving others and building them up according to God's own purposes for his people. Treating people *not* as simple gophers who are to "do what they are told" and be at the beck and call of their manager (or other authority), but rather treating them as competent and capable individuals who will rise to the occasion when given responsibility, is a matter of loving our neighbor as ourselves.

STRATEGY 2: ELIMINATION

In addition to delegating tasks and responsibilities, we can utilize a second strategy for reducing our workload: elimination. Elimination has two components: getting rid of tasks that don't need to be done and, when doing a task, eliminating the parts of the task that aren't necessary.

The best strategy for elimination is to use the 80/20 Principle together with Parkinson's Law.

The 80/20 Principle states that 80 percent of your productivity comes from 20 percent of your tasks. Hence, identify the things that fall into the "trivial many" so you can devote more time to the "vital few."

Parkinson's Law states that a task will generally expand to fill the time allotted for it. This isn't always the case, but it often happens. Hence, to keep your tasks from taking longer than they need to, reduce the time you allow for doing them.

This doesn't work as well with innovative tasks, though. Parkinson's Law is a tactic for efficiency, but it doesn't always translate into long-term effectiveness. Still, it can be useful. Once you've identified the right tasks to be doing, harnessing Parkinson's Law is a good way to increase your efficiency on tasks where greater efficiency will not reduce quality.

Each of these principles is powerful on its own. But the magic happens when you combine them to harness the power of both together.[3] Here's how to do this: Decrease the number of tasks you have to do by eliminating what is not important (the 80/20 Principle), and then force yourself to focus only on the essential parts of those tasks by giving yourself tight deadlines (Parkinson's Law). This limits what you do to what is most essential, and then within that framework, you are forced to do your tasks in the most efficient way.

But use this wisely—you don't want to reduce the time you spend on the most energizing and enjoyable things you do!

How Information Overload Affects Decision Making

A recent article from Newsweek explains well how information overload affects decision making. Here's the summary:

The Twitterization of our culture has revolutionized our lives, but with an unintended consequence—our overloaded brains freeze when we have to make decisions ...

The booming science of decision making has shown that more information can lead to objectively poorer choices, and to choices that people come to regret. It has shown that an unconscious system guides many of our decisions, and that it can be sidelined by too much information. And it has shown that decisions requiring creativity benefit from letting the problem incubate below the level of awareness—something that becomes evermore difficult when information never stops arriving.[*]

[*] Sharon Begley, "I Can't Think!" *Newsweek* (February 27, 2011), *http://www.thedailybeast.com/newsweek/2011/02/27/i-can-t-think.html*.

Shrinking the time available to do a task is a subset of the principle of *containing* your tasks. Containing your tasks is essential to keep your framework in place. It means simply being on the lookout for ways to do your tasks that enable them to fit within the structure you have to do them. Usually by just giving our tasks a bit of forethought, we can identify some shortcuts that we might not have realized if we had just jumped in. The principle here is to preview your task before you actually do it.

STRATEGY 3: AUTOMATION

Automation means putting your tasks on autopilot so that they happen on their own without your having to even think about them (or, at least, without your having to think about them much). The easiest example is automatic bill payment: setting up your bills to be paid by electronic transfer automatically every time they are due.

More unconventionally, you can try to put your income on autopilot. One of the primary aims of Tim Ferriss' *The Four-Hour Workweek* is to show you how to do this. This isn't for everyone, and if you create a product that for some reason people buy but which adds no value to the world, you're wasting people's time.

But some people may find it useful to figure out how to generate their income in a short amount of time each week. (Tim's title suggests four hours. I think that if you can do it in ten you are doing very well.) You then have a whole bunch of extra time to devote to other pursuits.

Some people use this time to simply have more fun. But this approach can be used strategically to free up more time to devote to initiatives for the good of others and ministry. Again, it's not for everyone, but some should consider it.

STRATEGY 4: DEFERRING

The final strategy is to defer—which simply means putting things aside for later.

You might do this by putting the item on a list—your projects list or your next actions list or your someday/maybe lists. Then it's captured for when you are able to get to it.

But the best way to use deferring as a strategy for productivity is to *time-activate* the task. If a great idea comes to you, but it's not realistic for you to do it in the next week or two, put it in your calendar or tickler file and set a time down the road to come back to it. Then do it right then when it comes up again.

As I shared earlier, this used to be the only practice I used. Predictably, it overwhelmed me because I was collecting hundreds of good ideas that I couldn't possibly do. Remember that the goal is not to *collect* things but to *get things done*.

All four of these strategies—delegating, eliminating, automating, and deferring—will help you to "kill" the tasks and projects that threaten to overwhelm and defeat you, but each approach utilizes a different way of accomplishing this. As you engage in your work, you'll want to evaluate which strategies work best for different tasks. In some cases, you may want to work different strategies into your workflow routines.

While eliminating the things that take up your time can be helpful for most situations, there is also another approach: learning to harness these time killers to make you even more productive. That's what we'll look at in the next chapter.

The Box

Core Point

Put first things first, and *stop doing* second things. The fundamental ways to reduce are through delegating, eliminating, automating, and deferring (DEAD).

Core Passage

"Whether you eat or drink, or whatever you do [even delegating!], do all to the glory of God" (1 Cor. 10:31).

Immediate Application

Review the five components of stewardship delegation again and identify three ways you can begin delegating things to more people.

Driving It Deeper

If you start delegating more, it will take longer at first. But over the long term (and beginning very soon) it will save far more time—and you will find that the people you delegate to usually come up with better ideas than you!

CHAPTER 18

Harnessing the Time Killers

Turning the most challenging productivity
obstacles to your advantage

*Resolved, never to lose one moment of time; but improve
it the most profitable way I possibly can.*
— *Jonathan Edwards, Resolution #5*

THE SECOND COMPONENT of reducing is overcoming and eliminating the things that eat up our time and get in our way.

However, when we do this we encounter an immediate problem: a lot of the things that get in our way and might be classified as distractions are also highly beneficial in some ways.

Getting rid of everything in our lives that seems counterproductive may, in fact, be counterproductive. So we are going to look not simply at how to eliminate some of the most common time wasters but also at how to *harness* those time wasters and turn them into productivity machines.

MULTITASKING: KILLING IT (BUT UTILIZING SWITCHTASKING)

One of the most helpful books on multitasking is Dave Crenshaw's *The Myth of Multitasking*. He points out that we need to distinguish multitasking, switchtasking, and background tasking.

To multitask is to do two or more things at once that require mental focus. Multitasking seems like a way to save time but actually costs more time and is, in fact, impossible. It is inefficient because it makes *both* tasks take longer. Thus, the average worker loses 2.1 hours per day due

241

to unnecessary interruptions—costing the economy an estimated $650 billion per year.[1]

But it is also impossible because you cannot literally multitask. The consensus among experts is well represented by Rene Marois and David E. Meyer:

> Our research offers neurological evidence that the brain cannot effectively do two things at once.[2]

> [We] will never, ever be able to overcome the inherent limitations in the brain for processing information during multitasking. It just can't be, any more than the best of all humans will ever be able to run a one-minute mile.[3]

The human brain simply cannot focus on two things at once. God is the only multitasker.[4]

So what are we actually doing when we think we are multitasking? We are actually *switchtasking*. That is, we are switching back and forth between tasks. As a result, multitasking (or, better, switchtasking) incurs *switching costs*.

For example, if you answer email while talking on the phone, you are going back and forth in your attention between the phone call and the email—and, as a result, you miss a lot of both.

Likewise, when you switch back and forth between writing a report and checking your email every five minutes, your mind has to figure out where it left off each time. This incurs a cost. Some studies indicate it takes about five minutes to get back into things after being interrupted. And, you are less likely to gain momentum and get in the zone—which multiplies the cost.

With some tasks, the switching cost might be worth it. Switching costs aren't always bad; we just have to take them into account.

With multitasking, however, the issue is that the switching cost can almost always be avoided. You don't *have* to write that report while checking email every five minutes. It would be much more efficient and effective to spend an hour writing the report, then check email (or take a break, or whatever).

This helps us see when switchtasking can be beneficial, though: if an interruption comes, quickly assess whether the value of the interruption will be greater than the time and focus you will lose on your current task. If it's significantly greater, go ahead.

There are times when you are doing two things at once, such as jogging and listening to your iPod. But in these cases, you aren't multitasking, you are *background tasking*. The reason you can do this is because only one of the tasks (or neither!) requires mental focus. So you are *doing* two (or more) things at once, but you aren't *focusing* on two things at once.

Some might still say at this point, "Wait, I *know* that I multitask. You should see me making dinner. I'm tending to the pots on the stove, keeping the kids from tracking mud inside, and answering the phone. And I don't feel less effective. I love it."

In these cases, what you are really doing is a series of small tasks in rapid succession. You are engaging in *rapid refocusing*. Stirring the spaghetti doesn't take ongoing, detailed focus for five minutes. The spaghetti needs to be stirred for about ten seconds, then you can turn your attention to the kids, then you can answer the phone, then you stir the spaghetti again and put the garlic bread in the oven. You might have lots of things going on at once, but none of them requires significant, ongoing focus.

But try talking to your husband or wife about an in-depth subject during this time. It's not going to work very well!

Both background tasking and doing a series of small tasks in rapid succession have their place and should be utilized to increase your productivity. You just need to know which tasks are *not* compatible with switchtasking.

PROCRASTINATION: HARNESSING IT

A lot of productivity advice seems to center on giving you tips to stay focused on and get motivated to do things you don't want to do. I'm not into that sort of thing.

I think that if you are doing a lot of work that you have to force yourself to get done, you are probably in the wrong job. Plus, a lot of the detailed tactics for self-motivation don't work long term. It is far better to make procrastination a nonissue.

The best way to overcome procrastination, then, is to love what you do. It's far better to tackle the "problem" of motivation at the higher level so that you don't even need to deal with the more detailed and specific motivational tactics.

How to Read *Really* Fast

I don't know if speed reading is literally possible. But I do know that it's possible to read really fast.

There are three keys to reading really fast:

1. *Purpose.* Determine your purpose in reading the material. This allows your mind to focus on the most relevant information and filter out the less essential things.
2. *Preview.* Preview the material through a quick scan before you do your main read. This gives you a framework for understanding it, thus enabling you to comprehend the material more quickly the next time you go through it.
3. *Pointer.* Use your finger or a pen as a pacer to keep your speed up. I don't particularly enjoy this, and so I don't always do it; but if you notice your pace lagging, this helps you get it back up.

Some people say, "I want to savor what I'm reading." Not a problem. First, I find that reading fast and savoring what I'm learning are not mutually exclusive. Sometimes the most enjoyable thing to do is read fast. But, second, go ahead and slow down at the parts you want to savor. I wouldn't speed-read poetry, for example. Know when to read fast, and know when to read slow.

The three components of motivation are autonomy, mastery, and purpose.[5] If you find yourself needing to be motivated, rather than identifying tactics like "reward yourself after you get done with a hard task," take a look at whether you believe in the purpose of your tasks (which means that you have to actually *know* the purpose!), whether the tasks are too hard (or too easy), and whether you have the freedom to do them in your own way.

The best type of motivation is to *want* to do the things you have to do — to be *pulled* toward them by a desire to do them and make a difference and serve others — rather than to be pushed toward them through carrots and sticks (rewards and punishments). Intrinsic motivation trumps extrinsic motivation every time. When you *like* your work, procrastination typically becomes a nonissue.

If you love what you do but still find yourself procrastinating from time to time, there are three main tactics to help.

First, often the reason that we procrastinate is that we just aren't ready. We might need more information or there might be some precedent tasks we need to do first that we haven't identified. In these cases, identify that information or the precedent tasks and start there.

Second, if the task seems overwhelming or highly unpleasant, break it down into small chunks. You don't have to break the whole thing down into chunks; rather, identify a fifteen-minute chunk you can do and then *just get started*. Sometimes your momentum will get you in the zone and keep you going. And even if it doesn't, if you keep at it consistently every day, eventually the tree will start to fall.

Third, in cases in which you are most significantly tempted to procrastinate, the best thing to do is procrastinate positively: do nothing. Not something else, but nothing. This will help you avoid "procrastination in disguise," which is when you do other things that are less important and less necessary. To avoid this, do nothing. You will find that you often become uneasy and then get to the task. Plus, this break can be good thinking time.

So make procrastination a nonissue if you can, and know how to deal with it if you must. At the same time, recognize that procrastination can be used to make you more productive in certain circumstances, if used right.

Here's how Eugene Greissman puts it in *Time Tactics of Very Successful People*: "Energy is essential for good work. Highly creative people use various kinds of tactics to get their energy level up and keep it up. Delay is one such tactic. Coming face-to-face with a deadline you're not ready for can set the heart to pumping, the adrenalin flowing.... I have seen some students thrive on procrastination. Just be aware that those who live on the edge of a cliff can sometimes fall off."[6]

Likewise, procrastination can be a form of applying Parkinson's Law. By waiting to do the task, you shrink the time available and make it more efficient.

Now, I don't recommend procrastination. However, when it comes to creative tasks, sometimes what seems like procrastination is actually the incubation stage. If you find yourself procrastinating, it might be a sign

When Procrastination Makes Sense

1. Efficiency is the top priority.
2. You are dealing with *known territory*.
3. The consequences of falling over the edge are not great.

An alternative to procrastination: do everything super far in advance. It frees up even more time, and it's a lot less risky.

that you need more time to think. So *take that time*. Think proactively and hard so that you can then get on to the task sooner rather than later.

INTERRUPTIONS: MAKING THEM BENEFICIAL

Interruptions take the form of phone calls, unplanned stop-ins, emails, conversations, and so forth. They can be a huge time suck, and beyond that, they are bad for innovation and flow. In a recent interview with *Fast Company*, Gloria Mark, an informatics professor at the University of California, Irvine, talks about this:

> I argue that when people are switching contexts every ten and a half minutes they can't possibly be thinking deeply. There's no way people can achieve flow. When I write a research article, it takes me a couple of hours before I can even begin to think creatively. If I was switching every ten and a half minutes, there's just no way I'd be able to think deeply about what I'm doing. This is really bad for innovation. When you're on the treadmill like this, it's just not possible to achieve flow.[7]

The worst kind of interruptions are those that make you switch topics:

> It's generally counterproductive if you're working on one task and you're interrupted on a completely different topic. People have to shift their cognitive resources, or attentional resources, to a completely different topic. You have to completely shift your thinking, it takes you a while to get into it and it takes you a while to get back and remember where you were.[8]

The distraction that interruptions create is not the full story, however. Gloria goes on to point out that "if an interruption matches the topic of the current task at hand, then it's beneficial. If you're working on task A and somebody comes in and interrupts you about exactly that task people report that's very positive and helps them think about task A."[9]

In fact, I would argue that rather than trying to minimize interruptions, we should have an effective strategy for avoiding them and—alternatively—embracing them.

Here's what I mean. First, if you try to minimize interruptions throughout the day, you will likely just be setting yourself up for frustration. You can, and should, do this to a certain extent. But it's never going to be very effective, or if it is, it will likely cut you off from some fairly important interactions.

A better approach is to have an uninterrupted work zone during your day (I prefer mornings) or sometime in your week when you can do your focused, solo work. This can be as long as you need. Then, for the rest of the day (or the other times in the week), you are available for people and interruptions. Some may find that they need to take entire days away to get dialed in without interruptions. However you do it, the concept is to create chunks of time when you avoid, rather than just minimize, interruptions and then embrace them during defined periods.

Second, while we should seek to minimize interruptions, they can be opportunities to do good for others and be of use. You can't—and shouldn't—eliminate the possibility of all interruptions (at least as a constant way of life). Interruptions should be seen as a chance to do good.

I agree with C. S. Lewis, who says that interruptions often *are* our work. As he puts it, "The great thing, if one can, is to stop regarding all the unpleasant things as interruptions of one's 'own,' or 'real' life. The truth is of course that what one calls the interruptions are precisely one's real life—the life God is sending one day by day; what one calls one's 'real life' is a phantom of one's own imagination. This at least is what I see at moments of insight: but it's hard to remember it all the time."[10]

Imagine a surfer who regarded the waves as "interruptions." The waves are not interruptions—they are the reason he is out there in the first place! In a similar way, I don't think we should place as much priority on getting rid of interruptions as a lot of the time-management literature often does.

In fact, after two decades of interacting with a wide variety of senior executives, the author of the book *Organized for Success* has noted that "successful executives turn one key time management rule upside down: rather than closing the door on interruptions, they extract genuine value from them."[11]

Listen to this perspective of one senior executive: "What you are calling 'interruptions' *is* my work. From the beginning of my career, I have seen my job as being able to facilitate, troubleshoot, run ideas by, solve problems, and just be a presence. If I had an urgent deadline, I would go into a conference room and shut the door. But that rarely happens."[12]

Sounds a lot like C. S. Lewis' point.

Obviously, we do need uninterrupted, focused time. Much work just can't get done any other way, and some of us need a lot of that.

But we should not see people as the enemy, and we should be careful not to limit emails, phone calls, and discussions too much. There is much benefit in them — *even in the ones that wouldn't pass muster as "important."*

We need to both carve out time for focused work and then also weave into our days the flexibility to be freely available so that we can recognize interruptions as opportunities for productive interaction.

There is a both/and here: Minimize interruptions. *And* realize that there is a way to make use of interruptions for maximum effectiveness.

As we saw in the chapter on routines, the best way I know to do this is to start your day early so you can segment it into a period of focused work for a few hours, followed by a time when you are more freely available. I'm still working on this. But the most important thing to realize is that the biggest interruptions are those that we do to ourselves — like multitasking.[13]

"WASTING" TIME ON FACEBOOK AND SOCIAL NETWORKING

Many companies restrict employee access to social networks, personal email, and other sites, thinking that they are distractions that waste time.

This is a classic case of not trusting people and failing to treat them as adults. It also reflects an outdated notion of work. For knowledge workers, work is not just something you do nine to five. Email keeps coming long after you leave work, and good ideas come at 8:00 at night just as easily as 10:00 in the morning. Spending fifteen minutes on Facebook at

Why Surfing the Internet for Fun at Work Makes You More Productive, Not Less

Research shows that employees who are able to surf the internet at work are 9 percent more productive. Why is this? It's because of the way work is broken up. If you are writing a report, for example, it involves tasks such as formatting graphs, writing, gathering information, and a host of other such smaller components. To keep our energy up, we tend to reward ourselves with small breaks between each of these tasks. If we aren't allowed to do this, our concentration drops.

Allowing full internet access for people at work thus increases their overall net concentration for the day by enabling what are called "unobtrusive breaks."

The essence of an "unobtrusive break" is that you choose when to take it. That's why it's unobtrusive: you choose to do it when you realize a break will increase your concentration rather than distract you. (This is also why, on the contrary, unchosen interruptions, even if brief, typically don't help us: they come at the wrong time, typically when we don't need the break to refuel our concentration, and hence distract us and disengage us from the task.)

3:00 in the afternoon is not a big deal given the new nature of work as something that can happen anywhere, at any time, and when our most productive asset is now our minds rather than an ongoing willingness to create widgets.

But more than that, this attitude fails to realize that, when people are self-motivated (as the people you hire ought to be), you don't have to worry about their wasting time. They love what they do and are driven to do it. They don't want to sabotage themselves. They know the right time to take breaks—when it will actually benefit their overall energy and productivity rather than compromise it.

For self-motivated people, time spent on Facebook is actually productive. It is productive for building networks and spreading truth. Both of these build people up, and thus increase *productive capacity*.

Research bears this out by showing that employees with extensive online networks (such as through Facebook, LinkedIn, and so forth) are actually more productive than those without them. Scott Belsky notes:

> An article in the February 2009 issue of the *Harvard Business Review* cited a recent MIT study showing that employees with the most extensive personal online networks were 7 percent more productive than their colleagues, and those with the most cohesive face-to-face networks were 30 percent more productive. Clearly, our respective communities—both online and offline—play a critical role in helping us refine our ideas, stay focused, and execute to completion.[14]

Further, a recent article on *Slate* noted:

> There's no empirical evidence that unfettered access to the internet turns people into slackers at work. The research shows just the opposite. Brent Corker, a professor of marketing at the University of Melbourne, recently tested how two sets of workers—one group that was blocked from using the web and another that had free access—perform various tasks. Corker found that those who could use the web were 9 percent more productive than those who couldn't. Why? Because we aren't robots; people with web access took short breaks to look online while doing their work, and the distractions kept them sharper than the folks who had no choice but to keep on task.[15]

Facebook and other online networks and interaction help us refine, spread, and gain ideas. These are three core competencies in the era of knowledge work.

If you are worried that your employees are going to spend too much time on Facebook, you've hired the wrong people. Not because you've hired people who have the "audacity" to use Facebook on the job, but because you've hired people who don't know how to use Facebook rightly and incorporate it effectively into their overall lives.[16]

The Box

Core Point

Eliminate time killers such as multitasking, procrastination, perfectionism, and interruptions not simply by eliminating them but by harnessing them for good.

Core Quote

Our research offers neurological evidence that the brain cannot effectively do two things at once.

—Rene Marois

PART 6

Execute

DO WHAT'S MOST IMPORTANT

If there is any one "secret" of effectiveness, it is concentration. Effective executives do first things first and they do one thing at a time.
— Peter Drucker, The Effective Executive

NOW THAT WE'VE IDENTIFIED what's most important (step 1, define), woven it into the fabric of our lives through a flexible framework (step 2, architect), and eliminated the unnecessary (step 3, reduce), it's time for the last step: execute. Execution is about living out our priorities every day, on a moment-by-moment basis.

One of the major tools for the execution phase is the classic to-do list—a simple list of the things you need to get done. Yet to-do lists can become annoying. Many of the items we put on our lists can't actually be done because they are projects, not actions. And often, even if we do make this distinction, our lists easily become overloaded—making it hard to discern what's best next. On top of all this, we don't always know how to connect our lists with our schedules and our time maps.

As we've seen, to-do lists can't be our only—or even our primary—way of getting things done. On the other hand, we can't jettison them altogether. Things come our way, and things come to mind—continually. Not everything is worth doing, but some things are, and we can't do them all at once. This means we need to have *some* lists and know how to use them well without suffocating ourselves. We will see some ways to make to-do lists work better in this section.

Execution boils down to a three-part process that, in honor of the iPod, you'll notice spells the acronym POD:

Execute

1. *Plan*. Define your priorities for the week so your direction is clear and you aren't tossed to and fro by everything that comes your way.
2. *Organize*. As new input—reference material, action items, projects, steps to take on your projects, and so forth—comes your way, know how to slot what you can't do immediately into the right places so you can get it done at the right time.
3. *Do*. This is where the rubber meets the road. Execute your priorities and take action, doing this in accord with your overall mission, aims, roles, and goals so that you don't just get things done, but get the right things done.

The "plan" step, then, is about planning your week, the "organize" step is about managing workflow, and the "do" step is about making your projects and actions happen—along with just navigating your day in the moment. We will look at each of these in the following chapters. But if you can focus on only one of them, it's the first one: planning your week. To that we now turn.

CHAPTER 19

Weekly Planning

If you can do only one thing, this is it

The ideas that move industries forward are not the result of tremendous creative insight but rather of masterful stewardship.

—*Scott Belsky,* Making Ideas Happen

THERE IS ONE SIMPLE PRACTICE that, if you do nothing else, will keep you on track. That practice is weekly planning.

The "execution" step in DARE starts with creating a basic plan for your week because the core principle for getting the right things done is to determine what's most important and do it. Hence, we need to go into our weeks with a deliberate plan.

We shouldn't first ask, "What things are vying for my attention and how do I organize them?" Instead, we should first ask, "What things are most important for me to be doing and how do I make sure that I am able to move ahead on them?" Starting your week with a plan enables you to do this, navigating your life proactively and avoiding reactionary workflow.

THE BASIC PRINCIPLE: PUT THE BIG ROCKS IN FIRST

The basic principle for planning your week is this: identify what is most important for you this week, and slot those priorities into the design of your week. In other words, put the main things in first, not second.

Execute

If you put the sand and gravel—the small stuff—in first, you won't have room for the large, most important things. On the other hand, if you put the main things in first, there will typically be plenty of room for the smaller things to fall in between.

There are three steps to a solid, easy-to-do weekly review:

1. Pray and review your mission and vision.
2. Define your priorities for the week.
3. Organize your priorities in a way that makes them easy to do.

STEP 1: PRAY AND REVIEW

There are two components to this step: pray, and review your mission and vision.

1. Pray. We have an amazing privilege as Christians to integrate our planning with prayer. Prayer is essential for our planning, because God is the one who ultimately makes our plans effective. "Commit your work to the Lord, and your plans will be established" (Prov. 16:3).

But it's not just that prayer serves our planning; our planning also serves our prayer lives. The whole point of weekly planning is to identify the most important items to move on this week. Those items are, above all, items for prayer! Your weekly planning serves your prayer life by helping point you toward the most important items for prayer in your life at this moment.

Begin your weekly planning as a time of prayer, asking God to help you identify what's most important, and as you make your plans, ask God to work for his glory on your behalf in those things.

2. Review your mission and vision. You don't want to create your mission, vision, and long-term goals only to never look at them again. The weekly review is the perfect time to revisit these items without creating additional work. Further, this also helps you keep your weekly plans in line with the governing principles and overall objectives for your life.

STEP 2: DEFINE YOUR PRIORITIES FOR THE WEEK

To begin, get out a piece of paper, flip to a page in your journal, or open a document or whatever planning app you use. This is where you will record your priorities for the week. There are five parts to this step. The first three involve brainstorming an initial list, and then the last two involve pruning the list into your defined priorities for the week.

1. Reflect. The first step in identifying your priorities for the week is to stop, reflect, and ask yourself, "What are the most important things for me to do this week?" I know, it sounds too simple. But it is really the easiest place to start! Do this, and then write down what comes to mind.

Two questions are helpful here:

1. What do I *need* to do this week?
2. What would I *like* to do this week?

I made it through college and seminary without a calendar, let alone any lists (with one exception), by simply pausing and asking those two questions every few days. The power of these two questions is very significant.

2. Review your roles and goals. To make sure you don't miss anything, it's helpful to review some of the things we discussed earlier.

First, review your roles. These are the different callings and areas of responsibility that we discussed earlier. For each role, adapt the same two questions from the previous step: ask, "What do I *need* to do this week in relation to this role?" and, "What would I *like* to do this week in relation to this role?"

If something comes to mind that is important for keeping that role up to date and firing on all cylinders, write it down. You don't have to write something down for every role, however, lest you end up with far more than you can do. The point here is to reflect over the full scope of your life and identify what is *most* important—not everything that is conceivable.

Second, review your long-term goals and any shorter-term goals. Identify any steps you want to take directly on them this week (if relevant—many goals are best pursued indirectly, but oftentimes there are still concrete steps that can and should be taken), and any projects that might need to be created as a way of moving them forward.

3. Review your project and action lists. Stephen Covey lays out a helpful approach to weekly planning in *First Things First*. The best thing about his approach is that it focuses on identifying the most important things for your week. He has you review each of your roles and identify one or two small goals for the week for each of them, and then schedule them in.

That is a great process for putting first things first, and you'll see echoes of that here. However, the one difficulty I always had with Covey's approach is that you are basically identifying new goals for each week. My problem, then, was how to keep initiatives in play that last longer than one week.

The answer is that you need to have a list of those ongoing initiatives that last longer than a week. This is what your project list is. We haven't discussed project and action lists in detail yet, but we will shortly.

To keep initiatives that last longer than a week in motion, review your projects list at this point and write down any large steps or small and easy-to-do tasks that are important to move forward this week. After this, review your actions list for any actions that are critical to get done that week. Finally, review your someday/maybe lists for anything you would like to make active that week.

4. Review your calendar. Next, look at your calendar for the week to identify anything you might still need to prepare or do in advance of any meetings, travel, or other events coming up. Write these things down as well. Also review your calendar from the previous week to see if you missed following up on anything or if there are any events or meetings or tasks that need to be rescheduled.

5. Get creative about doing good. Being proactive in doing good for others should be implicit in the brainstorming you did based on just reflecting on your week and reviewing your roles, goals, and projects. But it is also important to give special focus to it by asking questions like these:

1. What actions can I take against injustice this week? Isaiah 1:17 says, "Learn to do good; seek justice, correct oppression; bring justice to the fatherless, plead the widow's cause." Don't just leave that at the level of good intentions. *Translate it into your life* by thinking concretely, on a regular basis, about things you can do to fight injustice and correct oppression.
2. Who is in need, and how might I be able to help?
3. What can I do proactively for the good of my family, my neighbors, my coworkers, and my community?
4. What action can I take, even if small, in the fight against large global problems like extreme poverty, lack of access to clean water, lack of shelter, communicable diseases, and obstacles to the advancement of the gospel?

Write down what comes to mind. Some will be small things you can do right away (see the next step). Others might be larger aims that will be among your highest priorities for the week.

Weekly Planning Reduced to One Step

No matter what type of productivity approach you use, it is not going to work if you don't identify your most important priorities for the week.

You don't have to go into a lot of detail. All you need to do is reflect on two questions:

1. What do I *need* to do this week?
2. What do I *want* to do this week?

That's really about all it takes. You might have some lists (goals, roles, projects, and actions) that can help you identify the core things, or you might not. Either way, you just need to ask those two questions and then write down the four to seven priorities that come to mind. There's more you can do, but that's the main thing.

Making a routine of giving thought to things you can do to fight injustice and advance the cause of the gospel can have massive power. One billion Christians doing one additional small thing each week would make a big difference. "He who is noble plans noble things, and *on noble things he stands*" (Isa. 32:8, emphasis added). In other words, making plans for good makes a difference.

This also helps unleash creativity in the cause of fighting large global problems, because you now have a consistent tool for brainstorming and prioritizing initiatives for the good of others.

STEP 3: ORGANIZE YOUR PRIORITIES IN A WAY THAT MAKES THEM EASY TO DO

Even though you've been focusing on the most important things, you now probably have a list of more things than you can do. Further, some items will be large and others, though essential, will be small. Now it's time to organize them and cut what you won't be able to do.

1. Separate the large items from the small items. Before you can prune, you need to separate the large items and small items into categories. This will allow you to have a more realistic picture of your load for the week. For example, having twenty actions may not be unrealistic if they are mostly five-minute items; alternatively, a list of three large things may be too much if they are all time consuming.

2. Prune and prioritize. You probably have a list of maybe seven to thirteen big things and maybe twenty or more smaller things. Now you need to ask yourself whether it is realistic to accomplish these things this week.

The key is to make sure you have a doable list. If your list is not doable, you will lose much of the flexibility that you need to have. Further, as we saw earlier, too much to do and not enough flexibility result in getting less done, because your projects will bump in to one another, causing the "ringing effect."

The main thing to do in this step is to look at the large items and reflect on what the time commitment might be for these items. If it seems like too big a load, you are going to need to eliminate some (using the DEAD formula that we saw earlier). When this is necessary, our intuition is usually pretty good at knowing what needs to stay. Identify the top three to five items that are most important and that you will actually be able to do, and keep those. The rest you can delete (or put somewhere else if you want to reconsider them next week). Then rank the remaining items in order of importance.

3. Schedule anything that needs to be scheduled. Some of the large items might be fuzzy, such as "spend time with my family" or "remember to eat less." Others might be specific tasks, such as "code home page for site redesign."

It's okay to have fuzzy things on your list, because that is a great way to keep them on your radar. By simply having them on your list, throughout the week you will be more likely to seize opportunities for acting on them.

Some of these fuzzy things can also be translated more concretely. For example, if one of your aims is to spend time with your family, you might want to put playing catch with your son on your schedule for Tuesday after work.

Among the concrete things, if you have a good sense of the basic structure of your week and the time they will take, some of them you may be able to schedule right into your week. Go ahead and do this now. Also take the tasks that involve people (meetings, events with others, etc.), and schedule them into your week. You may need to contact people to set up the meetings (or, your assistant will; add these actions to your list of "small tasks"), and so they might obviously be moved. But this begins to give you a preliminary idea of your load for the week.

Not all concrete things, however, will be able to be scheduled specifically. It just gets too hard to stick with our schedule if we make it too detailed. Schedule the concrete items that you can, but for the rest, simply having them on the list will keep them before you so that you can seek the best opportunities for doing them during the week.

4. Do the small actions right away. With whatever time you have available now that you have your week planned, it is helpful to knock out as many of the small actions that you identified as you can so that the number of small items that remains on your weekly list is very small or nothing. I don't find it super helpful to leave the small actions on the weekly plan to do when I can—I want my weekly list to be almost entirely my large priorities for the week. This allows me to keep my days most flexible.

You have now created your priority list for the week—as well as updated your calendar, goals, projects, and actions if desired. Simply having done this prepares you for the week. Now, keep this list before you through the week and review it in your daily planning to keep these priorities top of mind and make sure they happen.

TWO OTHER TIPS

1. Don't skip planning, even when you are super busy. The biggest reason that people skip planning is because they are busy. This is a trick. Feeling busy is the reason you *ought* to plan; it indicates that you need planning all the more, not less. Even spending a few minutes planning your week will bear fruit far beyond the time you invested.

2. Seize unplanned opportunities throughout the week. If you plan in too much detail, your plans will fall apart and you will be frustrated. We simply don't have enough knowledge or control to create highly detailed plans. Acknowledge this and submit to it, and you will get more done, not less.

One of the key purposes of a weekly plan is to enable you to seize unplanned opportunities. If you have identified what is most important for the week, you will be in a position to evaluate those opportunities when they come up and know whether it is better to take advantage of them or stick to your plan. But if you don't plan your week, you will be stuck without a rudder.

The Box

Core Point

Plan your week! The simplest way to do this is ask two questions of yourself: "What do I *need* to do this week?" and, "What do I *want* to do this week?"

Immediate Application

If you haven't begun doing so already, create a plan for the rest of this week. If you feel too busy to plan your week, do it anyway and use the method I suggest in the box for planning your week in one step.

Driving It Deeper

Plan your next three months as well. Just list the three to four primary things, in work and life, that you want to accomplish for the quarter. Then keep these before you when you do your weekly planning.

Further Resources

David Allen, "Reviewing: Keeping Your System Functional," chapter 8 in *Getting Things Done*

Stephen Covey, "Quadrant II Organizing: The Process of Putting First Things First" and "The Perspective of the Week," chapters 4 and 8 in *First Things First*

Yearly Planning: *http://www.whatsbestnext.com/2010/12/advice-for-entering-the-new-year-the-yearly-review/*

CHAPTER 20

Managing Email and Workflow

A good workflow system allows you to get
things done with less friction and frustration

*Creating smooth running silent systems is often the great-
est improvement opportunity for enhanced productivity.*
—*David Allen,* Ready for Anything

MANY OF US FEEL OVERWHELMED by the sheer amount of information we receive each day. Emails flood our inboxes and cry out for a
response, meetings generate notes and action items, phone calls need to
be returned, ideas occur to us ad hoc, and, yes, there is still some paper-
based input that comes our way. How do we *process* all of this stuff?

This is a fundamental skill of knowledge work. A good workflow
process enables you to clear the decks for greater engagement and get
things done with less friction and frustration.

Yet most of us haven't been taught how to do it well. For example,
most of us fall into the trap of using our email inboxes as small to-do lists
(bad), and sometimes we even end up using our inboxes as holding tanks
for major project items (far worse).

The result is that we go through the day with the sense of having a
thousand open loops continually before us. This mental distraction gets
in the way, limits our flow, and slows down the process of doing our
most important work. On the other hand, clearing the decks tends to

"foster new, productive thinking that happens almost by itself" and to "increase our ability to handle greater engagement with the world."[1]

The goal of this chapter is to outline some simple practices that will enable you to manage all of your daily inputs (especially email) in a simple, effective way that helps you maintain a sense of relaxed control. You should be able to use this chapter to go through any inbox and take it from whatever point it is—even if it's your email inbox with fifteen thousand emails—and get it down to zero.

And you'll be able to keep it there every day.

(Or if you don't, it won't be because you don't know how!)

The process for managing your workflow can be divided into three parts: (1) collect, (2) process, and (3) organize and act.

STEP 1: COLLECT

You can't process the input that is coming your way if you don't capture it. Lots of it comes our way automatically (like email), of course. But some of it comes through conversations, voice mail, and even our own ideas. That's why another fundamental principle of knowledge work is to always have a capture tool with you.

How to Get People to Send You Less Email

I don't believe in getting frustrated by email and complaining about how much email we receive (although on a bad day it can be tempting). Keeping on top of your email is a way of serving people.

But, except in some instances, email is not the primary task of your job. There are many other things you need to be doing, and email already takes up enough time. So it is smart to do what you can to reduce your email volume. Here are three ways to get people to send you less email:

1. Send less email yourself.
2. Send better emails.
3. Use meetings effectively.

For more on this subject, see my post: *http://www.whatsbestnext.com/2008/11/how-to-get-people-to-send-you-less-email/*.

Further, you will be less likely to give yourself the freedom to think about your projects and the best way to navigate your day when you don't have a way to capture the ideas you have. On the other hand, "give yourself a context for capturing thoughts and thoughts will occur that you don't yet know you have."[2]

When a good idea strikes you, or an action point for you arises in a meeting, or a coworker suggests a useful project in the hallway, *write it down*. You can do this electronically through your action manager on your mobile device, or physically by carrying a journal with you.

For years I preferred using a journal. I preferred writing things down physically because I found that faster and easier. But since my writing looks like Egyptian hieroglyphics and is super hard to read (even for me), the task of processing my notes came to feel too inefficient. So I recently transitioned to using OmniFocus (for tasks) and Evernote (for thoughts and everything else) as my main capture tools, and I like this approach a lot.

In addition to simply having a capture tool, the second principle here is to have one you like to use. This applies not just to capture tools, of course, but to any productivity tool you make use of, because if you have good tools, you'll *want* to use them. This in turn makes your work a bit more enjoyable, which pays dividends for your productivity. David Allen is right that "one of the best tricks for enhancing your personal productivity is having organizing tools that you love to use."[3]

But what do you do with all the items you capture? You don't just let them sit or assume that the key actions will just come back to mind when needed. You need to process the stuff you capture, which is the next step.

STEP 2: PROCESS
The Three Rules of Processing Stuff
David Allen gives the three cardinal rules of processing in *Getting Things Done*, which apply here:

1. Process in order.
2. Process one item at a time.
3. Never put anything back into your inbox.

1. Process in Order
This is crucial: don't jump around your inbox. That in itself simply feels disorganized, and on top of that, it creates more disorganization.

267

Execute

If you jump around, for example, to the emails that seem most fun or preferential to you, you end up looking at all the other emails several times before you get around to doing anything about them. This wastes your mental energy and is incredibly inefficient.

In the old days, productivity folks would say, "Handle a piece of paper only once." The essence of that advice is sound: you don't want to look at an item, say to yourself "not now," and then move on to another one. That just wastes time.

So go through your inbox in order and process each item to completion as it comes up. Don't worry, you won't get bogged down by a long action item in the midst of this if you follow the rest of the principles here.

2. Process One Item at a Time

This is really a corollary to going in order. Finish processing the email or item you are working on before going to the next. Don't do it halfway and then move on. Deal with it decisively, then move on.

3. Never Put Anything Back into Your Inbox

Your inbox is not for storing things. If there is an email that you will need to refer to later, your inbox is not the place for it. Likewise, if there is an email that seems hard to process, you can't skip it and leave it in your inbox for another time (see previous rule).

If you keep email in your inbox, you will have to mentally reprocess your inbox every time you look at it. "Okay, this email is new, so I need to look at that; that one is there to remind me of X, so I can ignore that for now ..." That's complicated and annoying. It creates drag on your life.

The Two Questions When Processing

When processing anything, there are two questions to ask:

1. What is this?
2. What's the next action?

"What is this?" comes first because before you can know what to do with something, you need to know what it is.

Once you know what it is, you can then determine how to handle it (that is, define the next action). And that's the essence of processing: With each email or other piece of input you are processing, define what needs to be done about it.

268

For example, if your mechanic left you a voice mail that your car is ready to pick up, the next action is to go pick up your car. You don't keep the voice mail as your reminder (that would break the rule of "never put anything back into in"). Rather, you either go get it immediately or put it on a list or on your calendar to trigger taking that action when you're ready.

Likewise, if a coworker emails you the time for the project meeting he's been trying to schedule, the next action is to review your calendar and accept or decline the meeting.

Other items might simply be information. In that case, you might just make a mental note of it and move on (in which case no action was required), or the action might be to read it more fully.

In sum, the key issue in processing any piece of input is to ask yourself what it is and then what needs to be done about it. Once you've identified those answers, you go on to the next step: organize and act.

STEP 3: ORGANIZE AND ACT

With any item that you are dealing with—whether an email, regular mail, voice mail, ideas you've jotted down, or anything else—there are only five possible things you can do with it:

1. Delete it.
2. File it.
3. Do it.
4. Delegate it.
5. Defer it.

Do Not Check Email Continually

If you continually handle your email in real time, right as it comes in, you will not be able to focus on your other tasks. As we have seen, multitasking is not effective. If you continually check your email, you are setting yourself up for eighty interruptions a day.

For more on this, see my post "What If the Post Office Delivered Mail the Way Most of Us Check Email?": *http://www.whatsbestnext.com/2009 /02/what-if-the-post-office-delivered-mail-the-way-most-of-us-check-email/.*

Execute

The first two apply when there is no action required; the last two apply when there is an action required (which you would have defined in the previous step).

When No Action Is Required

1. Delete it. With most stuff, this is easy and takes about a quarter of a second. Some things require no action. For example, junk mail gets trashed.

2. File it. When the item contains information you want to keep for the future, file it. Most people are frustrated by filing because they don't have a clear and simple way to do it. This doesn't have to be the case. While I can't go into it here, you can see my recommendations on filing in the "Supporting Systems" bonus chapter online.

Sometimes the item might contain information you just need to enter on your calendar. The best example here is an invitation. With an invitation, you create a calendar event and then put the details and info you want to refer to into the event note, and then toss or delete the original invitation. There is no need to file it.

When Action Is Required

1. Do it: the two-minute rule. When it comes to items that require action, the most useful tactic is the "two-minute rule" made famous by David Allen. This means that if you can do something in two minutes or less, do it right away. It's typically faster to do a brief action right away than to defer it or delegate it. So a newsletter from an organization I give to gets a quick look, for example, and then I toss it (or determine the larger action required by it and process it accordingly).

2. Delegate it. If something needs to be done, but doesn't have to be done by you, delegate it. By email, this can be done by forwarding the email with some background. When processing my physical inbox, I typically create a pile for things that I am going to delegate to take to my assistant or others.

3. Defer it. If something is going to take longer than two minutes and you cannot delegate it, defer it. There are two ways to defer. First, you can defer the item until you are done processing your email or inbox. I typically do this with actions that will take from two to five minutes, or with actions that are most easily done together in a batch. When I'm processing my physical inbox, I do this by creating piles for these items, and then I handle these piles once I'm done with the processing.[4]

How to Write Better Emails

Writing better emails is a big way that we can make other people's lives a little simpler and a little better. And it saves you time as well.

The essence of writing a good email is to make it possible for the reader to understand your point right away. The aim is for your email to have a big impact with a minimal time investment from your reader. Here are seven keys to do that:

1. Make the subject line specific so the person knows right away what the email is about.
2. State the purpose of the email or the required action first.
3. Give the background second.
4. Keep your paragraphs short.
5. Close by clarifying the next steps.
6. Don't forward emails without summarizing the point at the top.
7. Always be encouraging, and realize that being neutral sounds negative in email.

For more on this subject, see my post "How to Write Better Emails": *http://www.whatsbestnext.com/2008/11/how-to-write-better-emails/*.

The second way to defer an item is to put it on a list. If I need to do it in the next couple of days, I'll put it on my "this week" priority list. Otherwise I'll put it on my master actions list or my projects list, and the ball will be moved forward on it when I do my weekly review. (We will talk more about how to use these lists in the next chapter.)

THE PROBLEM WITH THE TWO-MINUTE RULE

As I mentioned, the two-minute rule is one of the most helpful productivity tactics. This means that, when processing any input like your email or physical inbox, if you can do the action in two minutes or less, do it right away. In these cases, doing it immediately saves more time than putting it on a list.

Execute

But there is one problem with this, which I've encountered myself and which one of my blog readers, Adriel Hollandsworth, captured very well:

I know everyone says they love it, but I actually hate the two-minute rule. The reason is that for me, especially during my years as an assistant, the rate of receiving two-minute tasks is greater or equal to the rate of completing them. I could spend all day working on two-minute emails, tasks, and so forth, and I would never get out of the trench to look at the bigger picture of what I am supposed to be doing. I feel like a slave responding, responding, and responding. I receive one hundred legitimate, nonspam, I-need-to-reply-to-this emails per day, and could send out a hundred more. If I followed the two-minute rule, I'd get nothing else done (such as special projects for my boss).

Hollandsworth also presents what I think is the best solution to this problem: "I do better blocking my time and turning off email to work on longer tasks. This is more crucial now than ever as I am having to do more creative tasks (write articles, design strategy for our blog, etc.). I can't do those things without a significant amount of focused, uninterrupted time."

The Box

Core Point

Implement basic principles of workflow management for processing and executing massive amounts of new material, action items, ideas, and requests.

Immediate Application

Get your email inbox to zero!

Driving It Deeper

Get it to zero every day this week.

Further Resources

For more detailed information on how to apply this process to email, see my article "How to Get Your Email Inbox to Zero Every Day": *http://www.whatsbestnext.com/2008/11/how-to-get-your-email-inbox-to-zero-every-day/.*

For an example of applying this process to physical input, see my post "How to Get the Mail": *http://www.whatsbestnext.com/2008/10/how-to-get-the-mail/.*

David Allen, "Getting Control of Your Life: The Five Stages of Mastering Workflow," chapter 2 in *Getting Things Done*

G. Lynne Snead and Joyce Wycoff, "Organizing Your Time and the Flood of Information," section 2 in *To Do, Doing, Done*

CHAPTER 21

Managing Projects and Actions

Keeping your next action lists from annoying you; the magic of project plans to help you organize your thoughts and get your projects done; and, how to time-activate tasks

Lots of people have been making lists for years but have never found the procedure particularly effective.
— *David Allen,* Getting Things Done

IN THE PROCESS FOR MANAGING WORKFLOW, we saw that actions that can't be done right away should be deferred to a *projects list* or an *actions list*.

What exactly are these lists, why do we need them, and how do we use them in a way that doesn't clobber us with unending lists of things that never get done?

Many of us just keep these lists in our head. The problem with this, as David Allen points out, is that our mental RAM can hold only so much before it "blows a fuse." Further, our mind doesn't tend to remind us of these things at the right time.

All of this is because our conscious mind is intended as a *focusing tool*, not a storage place. When we seek to keep all the things we have to do in our head, they constantly pull at our attention and become a large source of our stress.

This is what to-do lists are for. If we are able to off-load these tasks into a trusted system we review regularly, we get rid of the unconscious of having to track and remember so many things. We are then free to give our full attention to what we are doing in the moment. her, our mind is more free to focus on higher-level things, beyond ply trying to remember what we have to do.

However, there's a problem. It's easy to put things on our lists and hen never look at them again for months (if ever); it's easy to end up with *so many* things that we simply get overwhelmed by our lists; and it's easy to simply be frustrated by not being able to figure out how to *organize* these lists in a way that makes sense and minimizes our cognitive workload (a key principle for any good workflow system).

I think David Allen (the developer of GTD) is a genius, and he has developed one of the best approaches to managing actions so far. Nevertheless, I have always felt that there were some snags in the GTD approach at this point. I spent several years trying to figure out a better way. I finally found an approach that works well for me, with minimum snags.

CREATING PROJECT AND ACTION LISTS

The Difference between Projects and Actions

There are basically two types of tasks that come our way: large tasks and small tasks. If you keep both types of tasks on the same list, the small ones tend to crowd out the larger ones, making it hard to focus on what is most important.

Hence, I recommend keeping the large tasks and small tasks distinct. The large tasks are projects. The small tasks are actions. The large tasks, then, go on your projects list, and the smaller tasks go on your actions list.

How This Differs from GTD

Users of GTD will notice a significant difference here. GTD defines a project as anything that takes two or more steps to do. It then suggests keeping all the outcomes involving two or more steps on your projects list, and tasks with only one step on your actions list. Further, for each project, you identify the very next action and add that to your next actions list as well.

There are certainly some good principles involved in this approach, but I ultimately found it overwhelming. With projects defined in this way, most of us can easily have a hundred projects. This makes it hard for us to give the focus we need to the things that most of us think of as our "real" projects (large-scale initiatives). For example, with the GTD definition, "change printer ink" is a project (you have to order the ink [step 1] and then replace it [step 2]). I don't want that competing on my projects list with initiatives like "redesign website."

Further, having a next action for each project over on a distinct list (the action list) created too much redundancy for me and separated the actions from their projects—which I've never found natural.

How to Organize Your Projects and Actions

That's why I define *project* according to the more common definition of any large initiative that produces a unique result and has an end point. Projects certainly consist of multiple steps, but I don't put those steps on a distinct actions list. Instead, I reserve my actions list for smaller things— things that don't feel like actual projects.

Along with this, we need to be able to distinguish actions and pieces of projects that need to be done *this week*, and those that can be done in the future. Hence, I have four basic lists:

1. Weekly priority list (= this week)
2. Master projects list (= this quarter)
3. Master actions list (= this quarter)
4. Backburner (= someday/maybe)

Master Projects List

Large initiatives (projects, as I've defined them) that you need to complete or make progress on over the next three months go on your master projects list. It is helpful to divide this list into "personal" and "professional," but beyond that you don't need to group your projects into larger categories; just list them as a straight list.

The reason for this is that you want to keep your list down to about four to seven projects for work and four to seven projects for your personal life. Having many more than that makes it hard to stay focused on a few key priorities and is a sign that you need to reduce.[1]

Large ongoing areas of responsibility can also go on your projects list (for example: "client acquisition" or "blogging"); just don't overdo it or you will quickly overload.

Execute

Master Actions List

There are, of course, lots of smaller things that need to be done that fall outside of these four to seven initiatives. These things go on your actions list, which I recommend creating as the last project in your projects list. This keeps you from having dozens of categories, without having to ignore the legitimate stuff that doesn't fit into one of your main four to seven areas or projects.

Here's an example of what this might look like:

Website redesign (a project)
Marketing plan (a project)
Improve management knowledge (a project)
Build theological library in Haiti (a project)
Client acquisition (an area)
Small actions (everything else)

Whereas the main projects are simply listed as a flat list, within the "small actions" category I find it helpful to subgroup items by area of responsibility.[2]

Weekly Priority List

As we discussed in chapter 19, the weekly priority list is a list of your main priorities for the week—most of which are big items.

We've all had the experience of putting something on a list and never looking at it again. The weekly priority list, combined with weekly planning (from chapter 20) is the answer to that.

To keep your projects in motion, during your weekly review define a particular slice of the relevant projects on your master projects list that can be done this week, and put that chunk of the project on your weekly priority list.

Likewise, to keep your master actions list in motion, identify specific actions to bring up to your weekly list when doing your weekly planning. Additionally, this is a great list to review between meetings or when you just want to work ahead.

If a sizeable task comes up that can be done in less than a week, and you want to do it this week, then put that directly on your weekly priority list without putting it on your master projects list (thus avoiding having to double up). Some of these things may technically be miniprojects in that you have to work on them over several days, but the weekly priorities list handles them great. But again, if it can't be done this week, or if it is an initiative that lasts longer than a week and thus needs to be kept in motion over a period of time, then it goes on your master list.

Within your weekly list, you can list specific subtasks for each of the priority items, if desired. It's also helpful to have a category simply called "everything else" for small stuff that needs to be done that week but doesn't group into a larger category (nonproject actions). This keeps you from having a million categories and allows you to focus on what's most important.

Backburner

The backburner list is what David Allen calls the "someday/maybe" category, and it is an extremely helpful concept. Things you don't need to move on this week or within the next three months or so go here, along with any other interesting things you might want to do someday but don't have an essential commitment to.

The backburner is especially suited for free-for-all brainstorming. Since the result is that you can end up with a lot of items here, I recommend keeping these items outside of your normal task management system as checklists in text-based documents (like Evernote). I also recommend grouping them not necessarily by area but rather into categories like "books to read," "trips to take," and so forth.

Keeping This Functional

Again, no approach to organizing your lists will work if you do not regularly review those lists. Having a routine for reviewing your lists (the weekly review) and a place to put your immediate priorities (the weekly priority list) are the key ways to keep your projects and actions from dropping into the abyss.

MANAGING PROJECTS: THE PROJECT PLAN

Once you have your projects defined, how do you manage them well? How do you organize the flood of information that you want to keep before you start on the project, brainstorm and sequence the action steps, and keep track of where you are in the project?

This brings us to one of the most helpful, simplest, quickest things you can take away from this book (after weekly planning). It's the concept

How to Name Your Computer Files Well

1. Give the file a name that actually means something.
2. Don't abbreviate (it makes no sense and makes it harder to know what the file is at a glance!).
3. Make the file name the same as the title of the document in the file.

Good name: "Bookstore Procedure Manual." Bad name: "Bkstr_2305."

of creating simple, back-of-the-envelope project plans. I have found this to be almost as valuable as anything I've learned on productivity in the last ten years.

Creating Project Plans

A project plan is simply a text file where you can list all the actions involved in the project, along with any other information you want to keep in the front of your mind and any brainstorming you want to do. A project does not need to be complex to benefit from a project plan (though I use this same practice for very large projects, and it helps a lot). Even projects with just a few steps can benefit from project plans.

I started creating project plans because I noticed that, once I defined my projects, ideas about them kept coming to me. At first I wasn't sure where to put them. But then I started creating project plans for the projects with the most ideas and tossing the ideas into there.

Eventually I started to notice that all the ideas and information for a project could be grouped into a few simple categories. Not all projects will have all these categories, and some projects will have a few others, but here are the most common categories in my project plans:

- Purpose
- Principles
- Actions (which can be further grouped into stages or subcategories)
- Info

The purpose is what you aim to accomplish with the project. The principles are any high-level standards or values that you want to be embodied in the project and that govern how you will carry it out.

The actions section is where you list upcoming steps on the project. I find this to be the most helpful part. When I first started using GTD, I would put new project steps just on my next actions list whenever they occurred to me. I quickly found this to be annoying, because most of those I couldn't do yet. At the same time, I didn't want to forget about them. The project plan became a perfect place for those future actions. In fact, for medium and large projects, it is great to outline the whole project here, listing all the steps you can think of and adding more as you work on the project.

For many projects, in fact, I just work right from my project plan. My weekly priority list contains the reminder that I need to work on part of the particular project that week, and then I go over to the project plan to brainstorm the specific actions I need to take on the project. I then work down the list, and all of the actions on the project are nicely kept together so I can see the progress I've made and what's next. You can even create a section for things you are waiting on from others, if the project is complex.

Where should you keep your project plans? If you keep your project lists in a task management system such as OmniFocus or Outlook, you can create your project plan right in the notes field of the project. (That's what I do, and it's a piece of cake. I like how it integrates my project plans with my projects list.) Or if you don't want to do that, you can create your project plans in a document or text file.

Where should you keep support materials? In addition to a project plan, a project might have other support material, details, subplans, blueprints, and other things that might need to have their own documents. These just go in your file for the project so you can refer to them as needed.

For physical things that pertain to a project but don't fit in a file — such as books, huge binders, light fixtures (i.e., if the project is to replace a light fixture), model rockets (i.e., if you are building a model rocket with your son or daughter), and so forth — I suggest having a project shelf near your workspace.

MANAGING ACTIONS

We already saw how to keep our general next actions (the smaller tasks) in motion through the weekly review, weekly priority list, and ad hoc

Sample Project Plan for an Event You are Planning

Purpose

To carry out the national conference in a way that is God-centered and edifying, and with attendance of at least three thousand.

Principles

- *Radical generosity.* We are willing to make things harder on ourselves so they are easier on our people.
- *Excellence.* Everything needs to be done well, and half-done is not allowed.
- *Good design.* The conference is not merely utilitarian. Since God is a beautiful God, not just a functional God, the atmosphere and aesthetics matter and should combine to create a more enriching experience.
- *Community.* Our aim is not simply to share and spread truth but also to enable people to connect with one another around the truth.

Actions

Venue

- Determine auditorium to use this year
  [Can indent underneath any actions you want to define further]
- Pay remaining installment on contract

Speakers

- Send invitation letter to remaining speakers
- Book hotels for speakers

Info

Bookstore Location

Bookstore will be in 3B

Main Coordinators at Convention Center

Fred Smith
Bill Fred

review of the master actions list whenever we feel like it. The realm of managing our actions also brings us to some very powerful tactics for keeping things on track that would otherwise be hard to remember.

Repeating Tasks

How do you remember and keep track of things you have to do repeatedly? For example, how do you remember to renew your passport every ten years? Or, at a more basic level, to change your furnace filter every month?

This takes us to repeating tasks, which are my favorite type of next action, and I find this concept to work *extremely well*.

Here's how it works: if there is something you have to do on a regular basis, create it as a repeating task in your task management program. This is the way you keep responsibilities and routines in motion.

For example, since I want to keep up with my household responsibilities, I have slotted time in my time map to handle household stuff every Saturday morning. During that time, I perform a suite of repeating tasks to ensure that I cover all the bases I need to at home. Likewise, with my work there are some things I need to do on a regular basis, such as check web stats, write guest posts for certain blogs, and keep up with certain people. Rather than leaving these things to memory, I create repeating tasks for each of them. I have tasks that repeat weekly, monthly, and at other intervals as well. Anything that needs regular attention or action gets a repeating task.

There are a few tricks to making this work well. First, as with your general next actions, so also with your repeating tasks: you need a time to work on them. I find that the best way to do this is to make reviewing—and then doing—your repeating tasks part of your daily workflow routine.

Second, it works best to keep your repeating tasks grouped together. For example, for tasks that repeat weekly, don't have one repeat on Mondays, another on Tuesdays, and another on Fridays. This creates too much complexity, in my view. It is too likely that you'll miss one of those days and have to reschedule the task. Instead, have all your weekly tasks repeat on the same day. Knock them all out in a batch, and then move on.

The key to your repeating tasks, such as the daily workflow routine, is to get those tasks out of the way quickly and in their entirety. You

Making Your Memory Better with Two Simple Tactics

Here are two tactics for making your memory immediately better at remembering names, your seat number on the plane (so you don't have to look at your ticket fifty times), ideas, and other things that you need to keep in mind when it's not efficient to write them down:

1. *Association.* Take the item you need to remember and connect it to something else in your mind. For example, to remember my seat number on a plane, I associate the number with what it was like when I was that age, or when I will be that age. For some reason, this works.
2. *Chunking.* The fewer things you have to remember, the easier it is. If you have several items to remember, find a common characteristic that allows you to think of them in groups.

For more, see Kenneth Higbee, *Your Memory: How It Works and How to Improve It.*

don't want to have them hanging over your head all day. Knock them out quickly so you can move on to other things.

Time-Activated Tasks: The Electronic Tickler

What about single actions that you need to do down the road, at a certain time, and can't do right away?

Many productivity experts talk about having a tickler file. This consists of a set of forty-three folders that allow you essentially to mail something to yourself that you don't want to take care of today but need to attend to at a later time.

With the development of technology, it now makes sense to do this electronically. Instead of putting the item you want to consider in the future in a physical tickler file, just create a task for the item in your task management program and schedule the task to come up on the day you need to deal with it. If there is a physical item associated with the task—

for example, if you got a physical invitation to an event and have to return the RSVP, but you won't know if it will work with your schedule for another week—put the physical item in a physical pending file, and then create the task to consider the invitation in your electronic tickler, noting in parentheses after the task that you need to check your physical pending file for the invitation.

(You can file things like this if you receive them by email as well. Just put the invitation in an email folder called "pending" or "support," and do the same thing.)

This is a very easy and simple approach to follow up on and defer tasks that need to be done, but can't be done today. Just as repeating tasks use dates to have your ongoing tasks come back to you according to a schedule, an electronic tickler allows you to do the same with single tasks that need to come back to you at a certain point.

WHAT'S ON YOUR LISTS?

Regardless of how we go about making our projects and actions happen, the most important question is, What is on our project and action lists? Do we come up with projects and initiatives that only meet our own needs, or do we look for ways we can meet the needs of others and do good for them as well?

Project and actions lists are great ways to help us think proactively about the good of others. If we are to "plan noble things" (Isa. 32:8), as Isaiah says, what does that look like? If you have a project list, it's going to mean that a lot of the projects on your list are not about you but are about others. Our project lists are a tool to help us brainstorm and prioritize proactive initiatives for the good of others.

When you create and update your project list, don't just come up with things that meet your needs. Think about the needs of others (Phil. 2:4) and generate projects to do them good.

The Box

Core Point

Distinguish projects and actions, and have four main lists: weekly priority list, master projects list, master actions list, and a backburner list. Use project plans to keep track of project details, ideas, upcoming steps, and any other information you need to keep track of instead of letting it all float around in your head in the hope that you'll remember it at the right time.

Further Resources

Action Lists

David Allen, "Processing: Getting 'In' to Empty" and "Organizing: Setting Up the Right Buckets," chapters 6 and 7 in *Getting Things Done*

Gina Trapani, "Hack 22: Make Your To-Do List Doable," chapter 3 in *Upgrade Your Life: The Lifehacker Guide to Working Smarter, Faster, Better*

"Thoughts on Daily To-Do Lists": *http://www.whatsbest next.com/2009/08/thoughts-on-daily-to-do-lists/*

Project Lists

David Allen, "Organizing: Setting Up the Right Buckets," chapter 7 in *Getting Things Done*

Basic Project Management

Lynne Snead and Joyce Wycoff, *To Do, Doing, Done: A Creative Approach to Managing Projects and Effectively Finishing What Matters Most*. One of this book's best features is its discussion of how to tie managing projects to your daily planning.[3]

David Allen, "Getting Projects Creatively Underway: The Five Phases of Project Planning," chapter 3 in *Getting Things Done*

Industrial-Strength Project Management

Scott Berkun, *The Art of Project Management*. Fantastic, thorough, and unique. It covers much more than the process of how to manage projects, getting into the guts of strategy and tactics for in-the-trenches project managers. Even covers "middle-game strategy" and "end-game strategy."

Nancy Mingus, *Alpha Teach Yourself Project Management in 24 Hours*

Project Management for Websites

Kelly Goto and Emily Cotler, *Web ReDesign 2.0: Workflow That Works*

June Cohen, *The Unusually Useful Web Book*

CHAPTER 22

Daily Execution

Nine principles for making things
happen every day that you can put
into practice right now

*To have small dribs and drabs of time at [your] disposal
will not be sufficient even if the total is an impressive
number of hours.*
— *Peter Drucker,* The Effective Executive

THE OTHER DAY I was talking to my neighbor, who is starting a new
law practice. He said he sometimes wakes up early with a thousand different things going through his mind about what he could do that day.
There is always billable work he could be doing, clients he could be serving, and things he could be doing to grow his practice.

All of us experience this more than we'd like these days. How do you
decide what to do in the moment and get the most important things done
without unnecessary distraction and friction?

Beyond this, with your week planned and your projects and actions
organized, how do you make things happen in the moment, every day?
This chapter will give you nine principles for making each day as effective as it can be. These principles can be utilized whether or not you
keep project and action lists. I've mentioned some of these principles
elsewhere in the book, but this chapter is a good place to recall them
and realize how we can put them to use in our day-to-day lives.

LOOKING AHEAD TO YOUR DAY

Though GTD typically recommends working from your master next action list, I find it helpful to create a basic list for my day of the most important things I need to get done.

1. Plan your day. The most important planning you do is your weekly planning. But you can't make your weekly priority list and let it sit. You need to review it to make sure you get it done. Further, you need to look ahead to the other things you have going on in your day, since your priority list is a list of the core priorities you need to accomplish that week, not everything you have to do.

Planning your day is simple and can be done in four steps:

1. Write down the three *most important* tasks you can accomplish today, in light of your calendar and priorities.
2. Review your calendar and list any actions this generates.
3. Review your priority list for the week and actions list to ensure it is current and identify any other priorities you need to have.
4. Write down any other things you need to do in light of upcoming meetings, appointments, and just generally other stuff you want to get done.

Here's a quick way to summarize the process: Reflect on what has to be done, reflect on what you want to do, and consider your goals and projects to fill in the gaps.

There are two other helpful tips for making your daily list maximally effective. First, consider having two parts to it, as Scott Belsky suggests in *Making Ideas Happen*: "When it comes to organizing your Action Steps of the day—and how your energy will be allocated—create two lists: one for urgent items and another for important ones. Long-term goals and

Execution Made Simple

Ben Peays, executive director of the Gospel Coalition, gave a great summary when I asked him how he gets things done: "Here's how I roll. I have a clear understanding every week of what needs to be done for the organization. I get up, drink lots of coffee, and then do the things I think are most important. I'm not reacting to emails or calls, but doing what I think has to happen. Which means: the things that are important to the mission."

priorities deserve a list of their own and should not compete against the urgent items that can easily consume your day. Once you have two lists, you can preserve different periods of time to focus on each."[1]

Second, create your list in a place that is easy to access and update. Some find it most helpful to write their daily list out and keep it on paper. I did this for years, even after the rise of the iPhone, because every program I'd ever used for my daily list annoyed me. Finally, however, I figured out how to create a good daily list in an app.

I use OmniFocus, and what I do is create a project called "Today." My daily list goes right in there. It is easy to access and rearrange on my iPhone as well as my computer, and I'm not seeing my master next action lists at the same time and being annoyed and distracted by them.

2. Schedule your day at only 70 percent capacity or less. Don't fill your day to the brim with appointments and tasks. That is a recipe for failure and frustration, let alone missing out on some of the most important and interesting aspects of life. As Covey writes, "Bulldozing through a ton of scheduled appointments and to-dos sets you up for frustration; the nature of most days will violate that expectation, and you'll miss some of the richest, most meaningful dimensions of living. Chances are also good that for much of that time you won't be putting first things first."[2]

There is a second reason for not scheduling yourself at full capacity: you operate better when you have space to think. This is stated best in *The Next Level: What Insiders Know about Executive Success*: "When you think about it, absolutely everything anyone does starts with a thought. Because the quality of the thought has a large influence on the quality of the outcome, it makes sense to do what you can to think clearly. In a world in which technology provides the capacity to reach out and be reached anytime, anywhere, finding space to think clearly is more and more of a challenge. A lack of white space on one's calendar correlates with a lack of white space in one's brain."[3]

Don't get so enamored with your schedule or system that you aren't able to *think*.

GOING ABOUT YOUR DAY

3. Consolidate your time into large chunks. Peter Drucker is right that "to have small dribs and drabs of time at [your] disposal will not be sufficient even if the total is an impressive number of hours."[4]

Create Blocks of Time

Dave Kraft, author of *Leaders Who Last* and a leadership coach, pointed the following out to me when I recently interviewed him on productivity: "A major issue for most people is that they don't have blocks of working time. And so they have a large task, but because they haven't created boundaries, they aren't able to get it done. It is amazing what you can accomplish in ninety minutes if you can work for ninety minutes without interrupting yourself."

Important and creative tasks require concentration, and concentration requires time. If you simply seek to fit the work that requires high concentration in wherever you can throughout the day, you will be massively ineffective. You will never get into the zone and gain the momentum you need, and it will take an hour to do things that should take only fifteen minutes. This is a recipe not only for ineffectiveness but also for frustration.

As Drucker also writes, "Most of the tasks of the executive require, for minimum effectiveness, a fairly large quantum of time. To spend in one stretch less than this minimum is sheer waste. One accomplishes nothing and has to begin all over again.... To be effective, every knowledge worker, and especially every executive, therefore needs to be able to dispose of time in fairly large chunks."[5]

There are two ways to consolidate your time into large chunks. First, when you architect your week (as we discussed in part 3), you need to design your days with large stretches of uninterrupted time for important work.

Second, as you go about your day, think in terms of blocks of time, rather than small discrete actions. I get lost when I think in terms of small next actions. But when I think in terms of large chunks (work on book, play catch with my son), it works. My mind naturally seeks to place those things at the best spot in the day, and the smaller stuff falls in between and gets done as well.

4. Do the most important thing first. This is the fundamental principle when it comes to day-to-day execution: Do what's important first, not last.

One of the biggest obstacles to doing first things first is what I call "the trap of the small stuff." We easily fall prey to the idea that before we can get to the big things, we need to get these smaller things clamoring for our attention out of the way. *Resist this inclination*; it's a trick.

The small stuff inevitably multiplies. It's like running through a field full of locusts, like I did on a recent jog. When I started to run faster, the result wasn't that I got away from the locusts. Rather, more locusts came out. That's what happens when you do small stuff—you encounter more small stuff, and pretty soon you've spent your life perhaps feeling productive because you get a large quantity of things done, but in the wrong spot because you weren't doing the things that will take you where you want to go.

Do the most important things first, and let the smaller stuff fall in between.

5. Do one thing at a time. When you are extremely busy, it is especially tempting to work on too many fronts at once. Avoid this trap. Instead, identify what is most important and start there. Then build momentum by doing one thing at a time, bringing it to completion, and then moving on to the next thing. You might think this makes it take longer to do things, but it actually saves time. The scarcity of time is the reason we need to do one thing at a time. "If there is any one 'secret' of effectiveness, it is concentration. Effective executives do first things first and they do one thing at a time."[6] Concentration *saves time*.

As Drucker also says, "The more one can concentrate time, effort, and resources, the greater the number and diversity of tasks one can actually perform.... Effective executives know that they have to get many things done—and done effectively. Therefore, they concentrate—their own time and energy as well as that of their organization—on doing one thing at a time, and on doing first things first."[7]

As Drucker also says, "This is the 'secret' of those people who 'do so many things' and apparently so many difficult things. They do only one at a time. As a result, they need much less time in the end than the rest of us."[8]

Thus, once you've selected the most important task, it is crucial to stay focused and work it through to completion. This is the essence of discipline. As Brian Tracy has said, "Your ability to select your most important task at each moment, and then to get started on that task and to get it done both quickly and well, will probably have more of an impact on your success than any other quality or skill you can develop."[9]

Seth Godin on Carving Out Time for Work That Matters

At a Seth Godin Live event in DC, I asked Seth, "There are so many things to do that clamor for our attention and make it hard to focus on what we really want to do. How do we keep these things from setting the agenda and instead carve out the time to do work that matters?"

His answer was great. To slightly paraphrase, he said, "The issue is not 'How do I find time to work on projects?' Rather, a Linchpin says, 'I create projects that matter. How do I then carve out the time to work on the stuff they think is my real job?'"

That is great advice. You'll notice that this is simply another variation on the fundamental principle of time management: put first things first.

6. Focus on outcomes, not activities. If you define your work in terms of activities, it's too easy to invent work that doesn't need to be done at all. Worse, Parkinson's Law often comes into effect.

You need to keep your eyes focused on what you are here to contribute, not simply do. You need to direct yourself to effectiveness—the right outcomes—not mere activity.

Therefore, don't ask yourself, "What tasks need to be done?" Ask yourself, "What outcomes need to be accomplished?" *Then* determine the activities that will get you there.

GENERAL MINDSETS

7. See your day in terms of people and relationships first, not tasks. Creating connections and interacting with people make up the most important parts of your work. Tasks matter and are important and fun, but tasks have to take a back seat to people.

8. Ask in everything: How can I build others up? This brings us back to the fundamental principle behind everything: You are here to do good for others, to the glory of God. All productivity practices, all of our work, everything is given to us by God for the purpose of serving others. Therefore, we need to be deliberate about this in all of our work—both the work we get paid for and the work of running our households. This means not simply doing the things we do for the sake of others; it means building others up *in the very act of doing what we do.* The aim needs to be not simply to get our tasks done but to build people up in the accomplishing of our tasks.

9. Utilize the key question in the moment: What's best next? That's the key question in the moment: What's the best use of my time, right now? Asking this question helps you overcome the temptation to distraction that often happens after an interruption. After an unexpected visitor or interruption, recalibrate by asking yourself, "What's the best use of my time *now?*"

The Box

Core Point

Throughout your day, do first things first and one thing at a time.

Core Quote

This is the "secret" of those people who "do so many things" and apparently so many difficult things. They do only one at a time. As a result, they need much less time in the end than the rest of us.

—Peter Drucker

PART 7

Living This Out

Christian love ... disposes a person to be public-spirited.
A man of a right spirit is not a man of narrow and private
views, but is greatly interested and concerned for the good
of the community to which he belongs, and particularly
of the city or village in which he resides, and for the true
welfare of the society of which he is a member.
                    —*Jonathan Edwards,* Charity and Its Fruits

WHAT WILL THE RESULTS BE of being productive in a God-centered, gospel-driven way? That's what this section is about.

We will see that a concern for personal productivity leads not simply to greater peace of mind and fulfillment, but to a wider concern for the productivity of our organizations and even society.

Beyond this, a biblical concern for productivity leads us to care about something surprising: world missions. Instead of diminishing the importance of our work, however, this actually shows how our work and everyday lives play a key part in the spread of the gospel and transformation of the world.

CHAPTER 23

Productivity in Organizations and Society

Why we need to broaden our view of productivity, and what this looks like

Modern society depends for its functioning, if not for its survival, on the effectiveness of large-scale organizations, on their performance and results, and on their values, standards, and self-demands.

— *Peter Drucker,* The Effective Executive

WHEN MOST OF US THINK OF PRODUCTIVITY, we think of increasing our own effectiveness. That is, we think of our own personal productivity.

I've argued that our aim in increasing our own productivity should be to increase our ability to do good for others — that we should care about personal productivity not simply for our own sakes but also for the sake of others.

But we need to go farther than this. Thinking about productivity in relation to the biblical command to seek the good of others means that we need to broaden the concept of productivity altogether.

BROADENING OUR VIEW OF PRODUCTIVITY

There are actually four components of productivity: productivity in life, work, organizations, and society. As Christians, we will care about

> ## The Four Dimensions of Productivity
>
> 1. Personal life
> 2. Work life
> 3. Organizations
> 4. Society

increasing our own—and others'—effectiveness in all of these areas. We should seek to make our organizations more productive as well as our own personal workflow habits. And even beyond that, we should seek to make our *society* more effective so that everyone's lives can be improved on a large scale.

A CHRISTIAN SPIRIT DISPOSES US TO SEEK THE EFFECTIVENESS OF OUR ORGANIZATIONS AND SOCIETY, NOT JUST OURSELVES

Jonathan Edwards understood this well, arguing that caring about the good of society is not simply necessary for being a good human, but it is essential to the character of a true Christian.

Here's the way he puts it in his excellent book *Charity and Its Fruits*, which is an extended discussion on love: "Christian love ... *disposes a person to be public-spirited.* A man of a right spirit is not a man of narrow and private views, but is greatly interested and concerned for the good of the community to which he belongs, and particularly of the city or village in which he resides, and for the true welfare of the society of which he is a member."[1]

Edwards gets it. A rightly oriented Christianity causes us to care not only about ourselves and our families but also about our communities, cities, and society generally.

Edwards is simply expressing the truth of Jeremiah 29:7, where God commands his people to "seek the welfare of the city where I have sent you into exile, and pray to the Lord on its behalf, for in its welfare you will find your welfare."

This is a restatement of the creation mandate for Israel's time in exile. It shows that, even in exile, the creation mandate is not suspended. But neither does the creation mandate mean taking over culture; rather, it means serving the culture.[2]

As Christians today, we are sojourners and exiles on the earth (1 Peter 1:1, 17; Heb. 11:13). Jeremiah 29:7 is intended to be instruction for us: even though we have no lasting city here, we are to seek the good of our cities and communities and society.

Further, a true spirit of Christian love disposes us not only to be concerned for the good of society but also to exert ourselves on behalf of society at sacrifice to ourselves: "And a man of truly Christian spirit will be earnest for the good of his country, and of the place of his residence, and will be disposed to *lay himself out for its improvement.*"[3]

The role of Christians in praying for and seeking the good of their societies is essential to the long-term prospering of their societies. That's why William Wilberforce wrote, "I must confess equally boldly that my own solid hopes for the well-being of my country depend, not so much on her navies and armies, nor on the wisdom of her rulers, nor on the spirit of her people, as on the persuasion that she still contains many who love and obey the Gospel of Christ. I believe that their prayers may yet prevail."[4]

"SO THAT THE WORLD WOULD BE BETTER FOR OUR LIVING IN IT"

It is common for people today to speak in terms of "making life better for others" and "making the world a better place." Sometimes, these statements are criticized because they don't seem gospel-centric enough. While the point of Christianity is not first to make society a better place, the call to do that *is* an implication of the gospel simply because the gospel sends us into the world to serve in love.

Even Jonathan Edwards talked this way. In *Charity and Its Fruits,* he spoke explicitly of how Christians are to seek to make the world a better place: "Whatever the post of honor or influence we may be placed in, we should show that, in it, we are solicitous for the good of the public, *so that the world may be better for our living in it,* and that, when we are gone, it may be said of us, as it was so nobly said of David (Acts 13:36), that we 'served our generation by the will of God.' "[5]

WHAT DOES THIS LOOK LIKE TODAY?

Edwards wrote his words more than 250 years ago. What does it mean today for a "truly Christian spirit" to lay itself out for the good of its community and society in our current context of mass affluence and mass technology?

MODERN SOCIETY DEPENDS FOR ITS FUNCTIONING ON THE EFFECTIVENESS OF LARGE-SCALE ORGANIZATIONS

One thing it implies is that we need to be more concerned than ever about seeking the good of our organizations because large-scale organizations play a much more critical role in society today than they did in Edwards' day. This connection is spelled out well by Peter Drucker: "Modern society depends for its functioning, if not for its survival, on the effectiveness of large-scale organizations, on their performance and results, and on their values, standards, and self-demands."[6] Which means that individual effectiveness is also essential for the proper functioning of society, since individual effectiveness is a building block of organizational effectiveness.

EFFECTIVE INDIVIDUALS HELP ORGANIZATIONS BECOME MORE EFFECTIVE

How does individual effectiveness lead to the greater effectiveness of the organization? It's not simply that by doing your work better everyone around you gets more done and thus the organization gets more done (though that is true).

It is also because personal effectiveness has an impact on the spirit and culture of an organization, creating an environment that calls forth the best from everyone. This raises the sights of everybody and creates an environment that calls forth their best. This is good for everyone individually and for the organization. As Drucker puts it, "As executives work toward becoming effective, they raise the performance level of the whole organization. They raise the sights of people—their own as well as others. As a result, the organization not only becomes capable of doing better. It becomes capable of doing different things and of aspiring to different goals."[7]

Thus, "executive effectiveness is our one best hope to make modern society productive economically and viable socially."[8]

TO TRULY SERVE OUR ORGANIZATIONS, WE NEED TO UNDERSTAND MANAGEMENT AND LEADERSHIP

So how do we help make our organizations more effective? First, we need to become more effective ourselves. By being more effective, we aren't simply serving our bosses and coworkers better, as important as that is. We are serving our entire organizations and enabling them to become better as well, and thus serving everyone they influence.

Second, we need to run departments, divisions, and organizations themselves more effectively. For the effectiveness of an organization is more than just an aggregate of each person's individual effectiveness. Organizations are entities of themselves, and as such there are principles that make each of them more or less effective, independently of our own individual effectiveness.

This means that we need to understand effective management and leadership if we are going to serve our organizations as effectively as we can. Our organizations cannot flourish without a good understanding of what it means to run an organization well.

Beyond that, this is simply a matter of loving others. Bad management hurts people, and bad leadership hurts people; in fact, doing *anything* badly hurts people. Doing anything poorly that pertains to the practical arena is unloving because it brings harm to others.

This applies to *everyone*, at all levels of the organization, and to all organizations, large and small. Everyone needs to gain a better understanding of leadership and management. Those who are in positions of leadership and management need to do it so they can lead and manage better (as well as initiate and support good training programs). And even those who are not in positions of leadership and management need to learn these things so that they can support the practices of good management and leadership.

We cannot simply wing it. Many times when we go by what just seems right, apart from any reflection on and understanding of the area, we get things wrong and do more harm than good.

So we need to not simply aim to do good in all areas of life, but be diligent in seeking to learn what actually will do good. We need to be smart about doing good. Good intentions are not enough. We need to do good that actually helps.

HOW PETER DRUCKER, A MANAGEMENT THINKER, CONTRIBUTED MORE TO THE TRIUMPH OF FREE SOCIETY THAN ALMOST ANYONE ELSE

The importance of understanding management is underscored by a point Jim Collins, the business thinker who is famous for his books *Built to Last* and *Good to Great*, makes in his introduction to Drucker's classic text *Management*. He writes:

> Business and social entrepreneur Bob Buford once observed that
> Drucker contributed as much to the triumph of free society as any

other individual. I agree. For free society to function we must have high-performing, self-governed institutions in every sector, not just in business, but equally in the social sectors. Without that, as Drucker himself pointed out, the only workable alternative is totalitarian tyranny. Strong institutions, in turn, depend directly on excellent management ... and no individual had a greater impact on the practice of management and no single book captures its essence better than his seminal text, *Management*.[9]

In other words, management matters immensely for the health of society. Free society is not ultimately sustainable without effective organizations and, therefore, effective management.

Thus, knowing how to build and run organizations does even more than serving our organizations themselves. It serves all of society and everyone in it.

One of the best ways to grow in our understanding of leadership and management is to do some reading; hence, some of the best books on these subjects are listed in the box at the end.

But this alone is not enough. We must also be concerned for the environment in which our organizations exist within society. For a poorly run society will undermine and strangle its institutions, no matter how effectively managed and led they are. Which means, above all, that we must understand economics.

TO MAKE SOCIETY PRODUCTIVE, WE NEED TO UNDERSTAND ECONOMICS

One of the most important things for making society more effective is to understand economics because one of the biggest impacts on our organizations, for good and ill, comes from the economic policies instituted by the government. As citizens, we need to understand sound principles of economics so that we can implement them if we are in positions of leadership, and support them even if we are not.

CARING ABOUT ECONOMICS IS A FORM OF LOVE

Just as caring about effective management and leadership is a form of love because it pertains to how we treat people, so also caring about economics is a form of love because it pertains to the structural context that enables people and organizations to be better or worse off.

Productivity as the Only Long-Term Solution to World Poverty

Here's what leading evangelical theologian Wayne Grudem had to say when I asked him about the relationship between economic productivity and world poverty:

Q: What is the most important thing we need to know about helping our society and the world be more productive? How do we address large, global problems like poverty?

A: Well I'm working on a book now on a sustainable solution to poverty in poor nations. It lists fifty or sixty factors within individual nations, saying that all of those factors can contribute to or hinder economic productivity. The only way nations ever come out of poverty is by becoming more productive economically—by producing more goods and services of value. It's not contributions from other nations; it's not debt forgiveness; it's not blaming international trade relations; it's not any of those things. It's becoming more productive. It's increasing gross domestic product which is increasing per capita income. Now I'm saying, "What principles from the Bible can contribute to that?" Because that's the true solution to poverty.

Q: How did you get interested in this issue?

A: What got me on that topic was what Paul says in Galatians, that we should remember the poor (Gal. 2:10). I had been going with my wife a few times to this inner-city ministry to the poor in a poor area of Phoenix. But after three or four weeks I thought, This is a wonderful ministry, but I wonder if there's some better way to use my gifts than primarily handing out food and clothing. I thought maybe if I could write on the causes and solutions to poverty, I would be using my gifts more effectively. And so it was a concern for being obedient to the biblical teachings to care for the poor.

> **Q: That's interesting, because a lot of people see tension between business, productivity, and the poor.**
> **A:** Greater economic productivity is the only way any nation has ever come out of poverty.
>
> **Q: So your concern for economics comes from a concern for the poor?**
> **A:** Yes, absolutely.
>
> ---
>
> For more on this subject, see Grudem's book with Barry Asmus, *The Poverty of Nations: A Sustainable Solution* (Wheaton, IL: Crossway, 2013).

To see this, consider the comparison between the bad effects of disease and the bad effects of bad economic policies.

We would all agree that it is good and right and important for people to study medicine to develop cures for diseases that take lives and decrease our quality of life. Equally important is for all of us to take whatever steps we can to help those who are suffering from sickness whenever we have an opportunity.

Bad economic policies can wreak as much havoc as disease. In fact, bad economic policies often have far more victims. Guy Sorman points out in his book *Economics Does Not Lie* that "during the course of the twentieth century alone, bad economic policies ravaged entire nations, producing more victims than any epidemic."[10]

For example, in Russia in the thirties, in China in the fifties, and in Tanzania in the sixties, the collectivization of land "starved hundreds of millions of peasants." This bad economic policy didn't simply make life harder for people; it actually cost hundreds of millions of lives through the starvation to which it led.[11]

If a disease was ravaging the globe and taking the lives of hundreds of millions of people, we would all be concerned about finding the cure. More than that, if the cure was already available, we would be concerned about making sure it was distributed.

And that's the case with economics. It's not that these things happen and no one knows why. Rather, many economists do understand why. But the principles are often opposed or rejected. The cure is available, but no one is distributing it.

As with leadership, so also with economics: one of the best ways to grow in our understanding is simply by doing some reading. Thomas Sowell's book *Basic Economics: A Citizens Guide to the Economy* is the best place to start.

The Box

Core Point

Productivity is not just about personal productivity. There are four dimensions of productivity: life, work, organizations, and society. In order to be effective in making our organizations more effective, we need to understand the basics of management and leadership; in order to make society more effective, we need to understand economics and government.

Core Quote

For free society to function we must have high-performing, self-governed institutions in every sector, not just in business, but equally in the social sectors.

—Peter Drucker

Core Passage

But seek the welfare of the city where I have sent you into exile, and pray to the Lord on its behalf, for in its welfare you will find your welfare.

—Jeremiah 29:7

Immediate Application

Manage well in your organizations, and support good management practices! And be personally effective. This not only enables you to be more effective and serve others better, but also strengthens your organization.

Driving It Deeper

Pick one of the books on leadership or management in the recommended resources below, get it, and read it.

Further Resources

On Management

Marcus Buckingham and Curt Coffman, *First, Break All the Rules: What the World's Greatest Managers Do Differently*
Peter Drucker, *Managing the Nonprofit Organization*
Peter Drucker, *The Practice of Management*

On Leadership

Marcus Buckingham, *The One Thing You Need to Know*
John Kotter, "What Leaders Really Do" (*Harvard Business Review*, December 2001, reprint), *http://hbr .org/2001/12/what-leaders-really-do/ar/1*
Rudy Giuliani, *Leadership*
Stephen Covey, *Principle-Centered Leadership*

On Economics

Thomas Sowell, *Basic Economics*
Milton Friedman, *Free to Choose*
F. A. Hayek, *The Road to Serfdom*
Doug Bandow, *Beyond Good Intentions: A Biblical View of Politics*

CHAPTER 24

The Greatest Cause in the World

Productivity, world missions, and how
our faith relates to our work

For its own soul the church needs to be involved in missions. We will not know God in his full majesty until we know him moving triumphantly among the nations.
— *John Piper,* Don't Waste Your Life

THE CONCERN OF THE CHRISTIAN does not end with the good of our organizations and society, as important as those aims are. After pointing out how Christian love is "public spirited," and therefore concerned for the community and nation, Jonathan Edwards takes this idea to its culmination: "And those that are possessed of the spirit of Christian charity are of a more enlarged spirit still, for they are concerned, not only for the thrift of the community, but for the welfare of the church of God, and of all the people of God individually."[1]

A concern for the church implies a concern for missions. First, because, as Piper writes, "for its own soul the church needs to be involved in missions. We will not know God in his full majesty until we know him moving triumphantly among the nations."[2] And second, because a truly Christian spirit has a heart for all those who are among Christ's sheep but are not yet in the fold because they have not yet heard the gospel. As Paul states, "I endure everything for the sake of the elect, that they also may obtain the salvation that is in Christ Jesus with eternal glory" (2 Tim. 2:10).

Love itself demands this concern. Because productivity is concerned about making life better for others, it will be concerned about getting the gospel of salvation to the 2.87 billion people who still have no access to it[3] and taking action on behalf of large global problems that are keeping millions in poverty around the world.

GOD'S GLOBAL CALL

God has given us a *global* call. We are commanded to make disciples of all nations (Matt. 28:18–20) and to take the gospel to the ends of the earth (Acts 1:8). Pastor David Platt puts this well: "The message of biblical Christianity is not 'God loves me, period' … the message of biblical Christianity is 'God loves me so that I might make him—his ways, his salvation, his glory, his greatness—known among all nations.'"[4]

Sometimes it is thought that the call to missions means that only preaching the gospel matters. But God's global call is holistic. We are not only to preach the gospel (though that is most foundational)[5] but also to meet physical needs. We know this for several reasons. First, this is the example Jesus himself gives. He went about teaching *and* healing (Matt. 4:23) and was mighty in word *and* deed (Luke 24:19).

Second, the command to love our neighbor as ourselves, which is at the heart of the Christian ethic, teaches us to care about the full range of human needs because that is how each of us loves ourselves. When I am thirsty, for example, I don't say to myself, "Well, I'd better read the Bible first." I go get a drink. Every day, all day, we meet our own physical and emotional needs as they come up, and even make plans to meet them; we are to love others the same way.

Third, the Scriptures teach us that meeting the full range of people's needs is part of the righteousness God requires. Micah 6:8 tells us that showing mercy to those in need is one of the three chief things at the heart of what it means to know God. Jesus lists mercy as one of the weightier matters of the law (Matt. 23:23, likely echoing Mic. 6:8) and regards it as far more important than outward ordinances (Matt. 9:13; 12:7, echoing Hos. 6:6).

James 1:27 shows us that compassion for those in need is one of the things in which "pure and undefiled" religion consists. Jeremiah 22:15–17 tells us that upholding the cause of the poor and needy is part of what it means to know God. John tells us that the Christian who has the ability to help and comes across a brother in need, but who does not help, is likely not a Christian (1 John 3:16–17). And Jesus tells us that on the last day, the righteous will be evident because they attended to the full range of the needs of the poor (Matt. 25:33–46; in this case, most specifically, the believing poor).

Further, we are not only to bring relief to those in need, but also work against the unjust social structures that have led to their oppression. Psalm 82:3–4 tells us to "*give justice* to the weak and the fatherless," to "*maintain the right* of the afflicted and the destitute," to "*rescue* the weak and the needy" and "*deliver them* from the hand of the wicked." Isaiah commands us to seek justice and "*correct* oppression" (1:17) and to "break every yoke" (58:6), and Job regarded the righteousness God requires as not only providing food, shelter, and clothing to the needy (Job 24:1–21; 31:16–23) but also going after those who perpetrated injustice and took advantage of the poor as part of that righteousness (Job 29:17). As Chuck Colson has noted about the great evangelical reformers of the nineteenth century, "Wilberforce and the band of abolitionists knew that a private faith that did not act in the face of oppression was no faith at all."[6]

The call to meet the full range of needs is based on both creation and redemption. From creation we see that God created us as multidimensional creatures. We are not merely spiritual but also social, psychological, and physical beings. And from redemption we see that sin brought its destruction to all realms of our existence, but the salvation Christ won for us is just as pervasive and all-encompassing as the destruction wrought by sin. Hence, Christianity teaches that we are to be concerned for the whole person, not just the spiritual dimension. As agents of the kingdom, we are to bring healing to all realms of life, not just the spiritual realm.[7]

Further, God's call is that we make a large dent, not a small dent, in helping the poor, because the needs are large, not small. We live in a world where 26 percent of the population lives in extreme poverty. In addition to malnutrition and hunger, other giant problems like disease, lack of access to clean water, illiteracy, poor education, and corrupt leadership affect billions. As Christians, we are to attack these problems head-on. God's call is that we bring the gospel to all nations *and* engage in the fight against large global problems. Anything else misrepresents the pervasive concern of God, who cares about all suffering and distortions of his handiwork.

How does what we've learned about productivity practices and technology relate to this?

PRODUCTIVITY AND GOD'S GLOBAL CALL

Since Gospel-Driven Productivity is about putting our productivity practices—and all that we have—in the service of God's purposes, that means we will put our productivity practices in the service of fighting large global problems and bringing the gospel to all nations. This is at the heart of Gospel-Driven Productivity, whose essence is the recognition that we glorify God by loving others as Christ loved us, and that we are to go to extremes to do this because Jesus went to extremes to help us. In fact, the call to use productivity practices to engage in fighting large global problems is an especially interesting aspect of the biblical teaching on productivity.

God calls us to use productivity practices for the sake of the poor. We saw earlier that we are to not only seek the good of others but also to make plans for their good: "He who is noble plans noble things" (Isa. 32:8). The wider context of this passage is that chief among the plans we are to make for people's good are plans specifically to help lift the poor out of poverty, for Isaiah here is contrasting the plans the noble make with the plans the wicked make, which are to harm the poor.

That is also the teaching of Psalm 41:1, where we read, "Blessed is the one who considers the poor!" The term "considers" here means giving deliberate thought to something (in this case, how to help the poor).[8] Hence, we are not simply to give money to help those in need (though that matters), but we are also to think hard about how to take the best actions on behalf of the poor and then create plans to make them happen.

This is rooted ultimately in the character of God, for God proactively identified our need for salvation and engineered a plan to save us when we were helpless, poor, and needy before him. Likewise, if we are to be truly gospel-centered, we must use what we have to take action on behalf of the poor, even to the point of proactively identifying their needs and generating plans to help them, for that is how Jesus treated us (2 Cor. 8:9; cf. Gal. 2:10).[9]

Knowing how to make plans and overcome the gap between vision and reality helps us to take action for the poor, and conceiving wise initiatives to help lift the poor out of poverty and advance the gospel among the nations ought to be one of the chief uses to which we put our increased skills in productivity.

We saw in part 2 that we don't have to run to the hills or even become missionaries to Africa in order to serve God. The chief arena in which we serve God is the vocation of our everyday lives. At the same time, as we see here, God *also* calls us to go beyond and meet needs wherever they are as we have opportunity to do so. The call of God is to serve right where we are *and* to go beyond. One of the chief ways we can go beyond is by using some of the time our improved productivity frees up to engage in the fight against large global problems. In fact, we have a greater opportunity to do this now than ever before because of technology and mass affluence.

Technology provides the opportunity to do this on a greater scale than ever before. Clay Shirky brings this out very well in his book *Cognitive Surplus*. He points out that the massive prosperity of the West since World War II created unprecedented amounts of free time. However, up until recently, most of that time was wasted on TV.

But now, because of technology, people are turning more and more from TV to being involved in collaborative projects for good. Rather than settling for the one-way interaction of television programs, it's much more engaging and interesting to be involved in the two-way interactions that the internet now enables.

In other words, though many of us feel a time crunch, the rise of mass affluence since World War II has given us much more freedom over our time. Technology now enables us to use some of this time and these resources to take large-scale action to address large global problems because it amplifies our ability to connect with others and do good on a larger scale —in many cases without even having to leave our homes. This is one of the reasons technology exists, and using it this way is part of God's call for us to be deliberate in taking strategic action on behalf of the poor (Isa. 32:8; Ps. 41:1) and to use our affluence on behalf of those in need (1 Tim. 6:17–19).

For example, we can loan to entrepreneurs in the developing world from our living rooms through Kiva; we can encourage missionaries halfway around the world within seconds through a quick email; we can purchase wells, medicine, and crops for those in need at the website of Food for the Hungry; we can let hundreds of people know about ways to serve global needs through a quick retweet on Twitter; we can expose hundreds of others to a biblical truth through a simple (and tactful) Facebook post or a link to an article.

And simply through Facebook or just plain email, we can collaborate with our friends from all around the world to organize initiatives for good. These uses of technology are not only high impact, but also fun. They connect with the call to have a sense of adventure in doing good.

The solution to large global problems is in sight. Along with the means to take action on a larger scale than ever before, there is also greater hope of success than ever before because, for the first time in history, perhaps the solution to many large global problems is in sight.

Bjorn Lomborg has done some excellent work on this issue. His books *How to Spend $50 Billion to Make the World a Better Place* and *Global Crises, Global Solutions* lay out some innovative ways to make a major dent in the most pressing problems for a relatively low cost. We can all participate in these innovations, in one way or another, because the collective efforts of massive numbers of people can now be harnessed through technology.

How to take action. So what can we do to take action? To begin, we need to remember that serving the poor is about more than just dropping off material goods. We need to understand economics and sound principles of poverty relief so that we can serve in a way that actually helps (see the previous chapter on the importance of understanding leadership, management, and economics).[10] We also need to ditch the superiority complex and see ourselves as partners who listen and come alongside, rather than people who think they have all the answers and come in and do all the work.

With those things in mind, I suggest a simple starting point: First, use your increased productivity skills to carve out some time once a week, or perhaps each night, to take a few steps in the fight against large global problems. Learning more about missions, fighting poverty, and the role of new technologies in solving large problems (such as innovative approaches in using ebooks to eliminate global illiteracy)[11] would be one good thing to do. Certainly prayer would be as well. Another would be to get directly involved through some of the means listed earlier, such as loaning to entrepreneurs in the developing world through Kiva or connecting with organizations that are seeking to advance the gospel and address large global problems.[12] Even small actions, done consistently over a period of time, will make a difference and will be amplified by technology as we collaborate together.

Second, for any who are involved vocationally more directly in the fight against large global problems (whether through working or volunteering at a nonprofit, ministry, church, or even business), use the skills you've learned in this book (planning, defining, architecting, reducing, and executing) to increase your effectiveness in your work. By improving our individual productivity, we can greatly increase the impact of our organizations in fighting large global problems.

There is one other way to take action in the service of God's global call, and that way has been at the heart of this book: See everything you do, in all areas of your life, as means of serving God and others. Your ability to change the world is not limited to your cognitive surplus and the amount of free time you have to devote to large global problems. Perhaps the chief way God transforms our communities and the world is through our everyday vocations. It's time to see how this works and why it's so important.

HOW MAKING THE MOST OF THE TIME RIGHT WHERE WE ARE TRANSFORMS THE WORLD

We saw in part one that there are two types of wisdom the Scriptures call us to have. The first kind is the wisdom that helps us live in this world. It is the wisdom of how to do our work well, how to be a virtuous person, and how to be effective. This wisdom is good (Eccl. 2:13), but it is unable to take us beyond this life and show us the way to God (Eccl. 3:16–17).

The second kind of wisdom is the wisdom that leads to eternal life. That is the wisdom Proverbs has in view when it says things like "blessed is the one who finds wisdom" (3:13) and "she is a tree of life to those who lay hold of her" (3:18). This is the wisdom that consists in how to know God and live a life that is pleasing to him in a spiritual, eternal sense.

Often we downplay the first type of wisdom in light of the second type, but the Scriptures do not do this. As we saw earlier, when Paul commands us to "make the best use of the time" and walk as wise people (Eph. 5:15–17), the first kind of wisdom is an essential part of his meaning. His command that we "walk as *wise*" is hooking up with Proverbs 6:6–8, which commands to be *wise* in the skill of living in this world.

Now it's time to see that this is not the only type of wisdom Paul has in mind. Interestingly, Paul's command that we be wise also hooks up with Proverbs 11:30, which says "the fruit of the righteous is a tree of life, and *whoever captures souls is wise.*" So both types of wisdom—knowing how to live well in this world and pointing people to Christ—are the way we "make the most of the time."

How, then, do these two types of wisdom relate?

Both are commanded, but even deeper than this, we can say there is a critical relationship between the two (which is what we would expect since Paul is alluding to both as involved in "making the most of the time"—our productivity).

This relationship goes to the heart of the apostle Paul's vision of the Christian life. Paul's vision of the Christian life is not, as D. L. Moody allegedly said, about "getting everybody in lifeboats," with everything else amounting to rearranging the deck chairs on the *Titanic*.

Rather, Paul sees an essential and profound connection between the arena of our everyday lives and the advancement of the gospel. This is evident in Ephesians 5:7–17, which provides the fuller context in which Paul commands us to "walk as wise" people who are "making the most of the time."

It would take too long to go into the exegesis, but Peter O'Brien nails it in his commentary on Ephesians when he shows that Paul is essentially saying that through living in a Christ-honoring way among unbelievers in the world—in the context of our jobs, communities, trips to the grocery store, and everything else we do in everyday life—the light of the gospel shines through our behavior, with the result that some people come to faith.

That's what Paul means when he says "take no part in the unfruitful [unproductive] works of darkness, but instead expose them" (5:11). The meaning of "expose" here is not "rebuke unbelievers when you see them sin." Rather, the meaning is that by living a gospel-driven life, you are walking as "light in the Lord" (5:8) and exhibiting the "fruit of light" (5:9), and that this light illuminates some unbelievers by causing them to see the futility of their ways and the glory of Christ.

The result of living our Christian lives—wise in all respects, in terms of how we manage our time and our jobs, as well as making sure to speak up about the gospel—is that many people around us will come to faith. That's what Paul means when he goes on to say that "when anything is exposed by the light, it becomes visible" (5:13). When anyone is illuminated by the light of your Christian walk, they become "light in the Lord" (cf. 5:8), *just as you did.* J. B. Phillips gives a good paraphrase of this passage: "It is even possible (after all, it happened to you!) for light to turn the thing it shines upon into light also."

Paul's point is that the light has a transforming effect, and in Ephesians 5:13–17 he has described for us the *process* by which darkness is transformed into light.[13] It is among the chief ways that "whoever captures souls is wise" (Prov. 11:30).

This is the same thing Jesus is saying in Matthew 5:16 when he says, "Let your light shine before others, so that they may see your good works and give glory to your Father who is in heaven." How do they glorify God? There are only two possible ways. First, and I think the way in view by Jesus here, is that some will glorify God by becoming believers because of the example of your good works (that's part of the "light" that shines). The second way some will glorify God is by, on the day of judgment, being put to shame by seeing they had no basis on which to reject the Christian message (which Peter is probably alluding to in his allusion to Matt. 5:16 in 1 Peter 2:12).

Either way, it's not boring to be around Christians, and it will always have some type of impact. Otherwise, as Jesus said, you are sort of missing the point of your life. "You are the salt of the earth, but if salt has lost its taste, how shall its saltiness be restored? It is no longer good for anything" (Matt. 5:13).

Four Reasons the Doctrine of Vocation Is Essential to Missions

1. It shows how everyone can be involved in more ways than just giving and sending.
2. It shows that the gospel has social implications, not just personal implications.
3. It shows us how to use our faith in a tactful way in the public arena.
4. It is in our vocations that we take our faith into the world and the gospel spreads most fully.

Whatever your job is, wherever you are, it is both meaningful in itself *and* a means of advancing the gospel. It is through your work that God changes the world.

In other words, the Scriptures make a connection between making the most of our time (productivity) and the advance of the gospel. Hence, the true effect of being productive and "making the most of the time" as Christians will be the transformation of our communities, cities, societies, and nations for the sake of the gospel. Being productive in our lives is not separate from our task to transform the world through the light of the gospel; it is an integral part of it.

THE ESSENTIAL ROLE OF THE DOCTRINE OF VOCATION IN REACHING THE NATIONS

We can go even farther and say that nonministry vocations are the key to the spread of the gospel globally, because our vocations are the chief way we bring our faith into the world. The gospel spreads through our vocations.

But if we don't know how to serve others by doing our work well and getting things done, we will undermine our testimony to the gospel (Titus 2:7–10; 1 Tim. 6:1). Hence, we must have a robust doctrine of work if we are going to reach the nations with the gospel.

It is essential that some Christians cross cultures and go to other nations and live among those who have never heard. I am not downplaying that in the slightest. The point is that our vocations here also have an impact on the spread of the gospel, and that we need to give greater emphasis to the place of our vocations in the way we approach cross-cultural missions as well.

Let's finish the mission. To do this, we need to start thinking about how to complete the Great Commission. At the center of our thinking needs to be the recognition that productivity is one of the chief means through which we transform society and the gospel spreads—both here and abroad.

CHANGING THE WORLD WITHOUT LEAVING YOUR JOB

In one sense, this brings us back to the individual level. The world changes especially when institutions change, and institutions change when the people within them change.

Which, in turn, brings us back to the doctrine of vocation. Scott Belsky talks about how you enter your "sweet spot" in your job when you work at the intersection of your interests, skills, and opportunities. It is this kind of "work with intention" that moves industries forward—and, I would add, changes them for good.

Thus, Belsky captures perfectly what the doctrine of vocation has to say about changing the world: "Want to change the world? Push everyone you know to work within their intersection. Mentor people to realize their genuine interests, skills, and to capitalize on even the smallest opportunities that surround them. When it comes to your own career, make every decision with a constant eye for work in the intersection. A career of 'work with intention' is the kind that moves industries forward. Do it for yourself and for the rest of us."[14]

Belsky also nails it when he says, "Please take yourself and your creative pursuits seriously. Your ideas must be treated with respect because their importance truly does extend beyond your own interests. Every living person benefits from a world that is enriched with ideas made whole—ideas that are made to happen through your passion, commitment, self-awareness, and informed pursuit."[15]

HOW THE EARLIER SECTIONS OF THIS BOOK RELATE TO THIS SECTION

That's why the earlier sections of this book, on improving your personal productivity, are not separate from this later section on improving the productivity of the entire world. By being effective right where we are and working within our strengths and interests, we are not only effective ourselves, but we also move our industries forward.

Tens of thousands of Christians doing this in all sectors of society, and within key culture-shaping institutions, would change the world. And in the right, non-spiritually-weird way that cannot be accomplished by boycotts and campaigns that illustrate what we are against rather than what we are for.

To change the world, first change your world. Be a positive influence for good in your family, your workplace, your community, and the nation. If thousands of people are intentional about changing their world by living out biblical and common grace principles in each of their vocations, the whole world will be changed.

The Box

Core Point

A concern for the good of others leads inevitably to a concern for missions. Our vocations are how we carry our faith into the world, and as Christians one by one, and together, seek to serve others in their vocations to the glory of God, the light of the gospel shines and the world changes.

Core Quote

The message of biblical Christianity is not "God loves me, period ..." the message of biblical Christianity is "God loves me so that I might make him—his ways, his salvation, his glory, his greatness—known among all nations."

—David Platt

Core Passage

When anything is exposed by the light, it becomes visible, for anything that becomes visible is light.... Look carefully then how you walk, not as unwise but as wise, making the best use of the time, because the days are evil.

—Ephesians 5:13–16

Further Resources

On Missions

John Piper, *The Supremacy of God in Missions*

David Platt, *Radical: Taking Your Faith Back from the American Dream*

Vishal Mangalwadi and Ruth Mangalwadi, *The Legacy of William Carey: A Model for the Transformation of a Culture.* (This book is especially helpful on the relationship between missions and social good.)

On Social Good

Tim Keller, *Ministries of Mercy*

Steve Corbett and Brian Fikkert, *When Helping Hurts*

Peter Greer and Phil Smith, *The Poor Will Be Glad: Joining the Revolution to Lift the World out of Poverty*

Bjorn Lomborg, *How to Spend $50 Billion to Make the World a Better Place*

Gary Haugen, *Good News about Injustice: A Witness of Courage in a Hurting World*

On the Intrinsic Significance of Our Work

Timothy Keller, *Every Good Endeavor: Connecting Your Work to God's Work*

Paul Rude, *Significant Work: Discover the Extraordinary Worth of What You Do Every Day*

Tom Nelson, *Work Matters: Connecting Sunday Worship to Monday Work*

CHAPTER 25

Productivity in a Fallen World

We need to get a larger view of suffering, minimizing our own suffering when we can, but embracing it with joy when it is necessary for the good of others.

The cross is not the terrible end to an otherwise God-fearing and happy life, but it meets us at the beginning of our communion with Christ. When Christ calls a man, he bids him come and die.
　　　—Dietrich Bonhoeffer, The Cost of Discipleship

To all eternity we shall live and reign with Christ, but shall we ever be able to make sacrifices for him again? When sin and pain and death are no more, and all tears are wiped away, shall we ever have again the privilege that is ours now of sharing the fellowship of His sufferings "to seek and to save that which was lost"?
　　　—Mrs. Howard Taylor, John and Betty Stam: A Story of Triumph

Nothing can ever really hurt those that are the true friends of God.
　　　—Jonathan Edwards, Charity and Its Fruits

WHEN I WAS RUNNING the conference bookstores for Desiring God, the week before each conference was super crazy. All the books would come in, usually around eight thousand, I would estimate, and it would be time to price them. We had to organize the books into their categories, print off the pricing stickers for each of them, and put them on individually. Even with volunteers, this was a large task to manage along with all the other conference preparations.

So we frequently worked some pretty late nights. It was around one of these conferences that I pulled my record of three all-nighters in a row.

One night particularly stands out. Two of my coworkers and I were organizing and pricing the books two days before the conference, and we still had a long way to go. We were already pretty tired and looking at an all-nighter when one of my coworkers had the bright idea of joining up with some friends of his for a game of broom ball.

Broom ball, apparently, is a mostly Minnesotan or northern phenomenon. You are playing hockey on ice, but without skates. It's a pretty rigorous game, and being on ice means it takes even more effort to move.

So at about 11:00 that night, we took a break from our bookstore stuff, played a game of broom ball, and were back at work at 1:00 in the morning. We were able to get along well for a couple of more hours. But by 3:00 in the morning, we could barely move. It was one of the funniest things I've seen. It was almost like one of those dreams in which you keep telling yourself to move, but you can't. Only it was real life, and we still had a lot of work to do.

As always, we got everything done and the conference went great. And as always, the prep running up to the conference was fairly overwhelming—and compounded by that unfortunate broom ball game.

Here's the question: In pulling these long hours, were we just being bad stewards of our time?

I have no doubt we could have done many things better. I was recently out of seminary, and the bookstore operation was designed to run on as little manpower as possible. So we were short-staffed, and though we utilized volunteers, if we had been thinking (and had known how!), we would have sought out more volunteers and made better use of them (not necessarily an easy task, however).

So some of the need for excessive hours no doubt falls squarely on us. But does it entirely? I would say no. And I would also say that the need to work a lot, or simply the presence of other types of hardship in your work, is not necessarily a bad thing or the result of incompetence or, worse, sin.

SUFFERING IS MORE THAN WE THINK

We tend to make the same mistake with suffering that we do with good works. We tend to think good works are rare and spectacular things. Things we might do once in a while. But the ordinary things we do every day as we go about our lives? These are in a different category that is somehow detached from our spiritual lives.

And so it is with suffering. We think of suffering as extraordinary hardships that come upon us, such as moving to Africa for long-term missions or our house burning down or being persecuted for our faith.

We tend to see suffering as something that happens *outside of* our ordinary vocations. Suffering isn't what happens in the frustrations of our job or managing our homes. Suffering is only the big stuff that happens or the extraordinary stuff we do.

But in reality, the same thing we saw about good works is true of suffering. Just as good works are *anything* we do in faith, and just as our vocations of husband or wife, worker, student, or parent are the primary avenues in which we do good works, so it is with suffering. Suffering is not just extraordinary pain and loss that we endure; suffering is *any* hardship we endure, large or small. And the primary (though not exclusive) arena in which we experience suffering is our vocations—including, and perhaps especially, the workplace.

GOOD PRODUCTIVITY PRACTICES WILL NOT ELIMINATE ALL FRUSTRATION

There are two mistakes we often make in our work and personal lives when it comes to suffering. First, we tend to seek out better productivity practices and approaches as a way of reducing our stress and increasing our sense of personal satisfaction and comfort. Second, we tend to think that if someone is working a lot, finding their work highly challenging, and facing a bunch of dead ends or small failures, something is wrong. We suspect that they might be a workaholic or just are not being efficient enough, and we think that if they really knew how to work, they wouldn't be having these difficulties.

Both of these notions are wrong.

In relation to the first idea: it is a good thing to seek to reduce stress and increase our satisfaction in our work. The problem is that those goals are insufficient. Our true purpose in improving our productivity should be, as we have seen, to serve others. And ironically, this is the path to far greater joy.

In relation to the second idea: it is simply expecting too much from productivity practices. It assumes that if you just have everything figured out, having the right tools and work ethic and know-how, everything will go smoothly for you.

But it won't.

This is not to say that productivity practices don't matter. They do—immensely. But they will never solve everything, because the fundamental problem is not lack of knowledge or skill.

Good productivity practices will not eliminate all suffering because a measure of frustration—suffering—is inherent in all work because of the fall.

THE FALL: PRODUCTIVITY TAKES A HIT

After humankind fell into sin, part of the resulting curse was directed squarely at our productivity: "Because you have listened to the voice of your wife and have eaten of the tree of which I commanded you, 'You shall not eat of it,' cursed is the ground because of you; in pain you shall eat of it all the days of your life; thorns and thistles it shall bring forth for you; and you shall eat the plants of the field. By the sweat of your face you shall eat bread, till you return to the ground, for out of it you were taken; for you are dust, and to dust you shall return" (Gen. 3:17–19).

This is not simply a curse on working the ground. It is a curse on all work. Work itself is not the curse, but because of the curse, there is now inherent frustration in all the work that we do.

We can seek to overcome the effects of the curse in many ways. Helping the ground become more productive through improved farming methods, for example, works against the effects of the curse. But we cannot eliminate the effects; only the promised Messiah, Jesus, can do that (Gen. 3:15).

So the ultimate reason we experience so much hardship and frustration not only in our work but also in all areas of life is because of sin. This is what it is like to live in a fallen, sinful world.

And sin has some radical effects.

DOING THE RIGHT THING DOES NOT ALWAYS LEAD TO PROSPERITY

For example, it means that doing the right thing will not always lead to success.

Which is why, though the things we talk about in this book *will* help make you more effective, I want to make it clear that I am not promising a "successful life" or any such thing. First, I see true success as a matter of serving others for God's glory, not as individual peace and affluence.

But second, that reflects a sub-biblical view. The Bible does promise a measure of success—sometimes great success—to our wise and diligent efforts. "He who works his land will have plenty of bread" (Prov. 12:11). Our ordinary expectation should be that if we work hard, work wise, and are generous, things will turn out well.

But along the way, we will experience much hardship, difficulty, and even failure, because we live in a fallen world that is saturated with injustice.

So the last thing I want anybody to come away from this book with is the notion that biblical productivity means a life of unending success, as we typically define it. Not true. Not true in the slightest.

This is one of the great paradoxes of biblical effectiveness: often it doesn't produce any results; in fact, it seems to produce *counterproductive* results for at time. Spurgeon nails this:

> Let no man be deceived with the idea that if he carries out the right, by God's grace he will prosper in this world as the consequence. It is very likely that, for a time at least, his conscientiousness will stand in the way of his prosperity.
>
> God does not invariably make the doing of the right to be the means of pecuniary gain to us. On the contrary, it frequently happens that for a time men are great losers by their obedience to Christ.
>
> But the Scripture always speaks as to the long run; it sums up the whole of life—there it promises true riches. If thou wouldst prosper, keep close to the Word of God, and to thy conscience, and thou shalt have the best prosperity.[1]

YOU WILL SUFFER FROM YOUR WORK, AND IT'S NOT NECESSARILY SIN (OR INCOMPETENCE)

Another result of the fall, as we began to discuss earlier, is that we will find much inherent frustration in our work.

We often think that overwork, difficulty in work, and toil are signs of working too hard or workaholism or doing something wrong. But that is not necessarily the case. These things are not necessarily sin and will sometimes be necessary as part of the path of obedience in a fallen world.

This becomes clear when we look at some of the lists that Paul gives of the ways he has suffered. He lists many things that we wouldn't typically think of as suffering. In 2 Corinthians 11:23–28, for example, his list includes:

- Great labors: v. 23
- Persecution: vv. 24–25
- Accidents: v. 25
- Journeys: v. 26
- Danger (even apart from harm): v. 26
- Toil: v. 27
- Hardship: v. 27
- Sleepless nights: v. 27
- Hunger and thirst: v. 27
- Cold and exposure: v. 27
- Anxiety: v. 28

Accidents, hunger and thirst, cold and exposure, and persecution all fit neatly into our common categories of suffering.

But what's notable here are some things that we wouldn't typically think of as suffering.

Sleepless nights? Is that suffering? Yes. If you are up all night because your kids are sick, that is suffering. If you have to pull an all-nighter at work, that is suffering.

All-nighters are a form of suffering!

What about toil and great labors? Are those really suffering? Yes. Which means that if your work calls for unusual seasons of great exertion, don't first think, "I must be a workaholic." Instead, you may simply be enduring the regular path of suffering that God has appointed and which is just as necessary to your calling as Paul's toil and great labors were to his.

Even anxiety is included as a form of suffering. Which implies that if your work is complex and vague and you aren't always sure whether everything is going to work out, but it's really important and matters that it does, you might experience a legitimate form of anxiety. The peace of Philippians 4 is available here, but the point is that this concern is not to be discounted and is a real form of suffering.

Let's not fall into the notion that being a good worker who works unto the Lord means you will always be done with your work by 5:00 and ready to go home stress free. If your work is that easy, you probably aren't challenging yourself—or seeking the good of others—sufficiently.

The call to follow Christ is a call to radically spend ourselves for the good of others. Work is not the only arena in which we are to do that, and I'm not advocating unnecessary overwork or even prolonged periods of sacrificing family time. But the reality is that we too often have a pansy view of work. In contrast, as Ajith Fernando has said in his excellent article "To Serve Is to Suffer,"[2] "the New Testament makes it clear that those who work for Christ will suffer because of their work."

Suffering is not just persecution. As Paul's example shows, it is also the pain, tiredness (2 Cor. 6:5; even "sleepless nights," in which I would include all-nighters), seasons of extensive work (2 Thess. 3:8; 1 Thess. 2:9), confusion (2 Cor. 4:8), emotional pressure (2 Cor. 11:28; Gal. 4:19), and "non-mind-like-water" mental "weights" that come our way as we are simply being faithful. These are not automatically signs that we are working too hard. They are often part of the path, and they are *supposed* to be.

GOD DOES GIVE US MORE THAN WE CAN HANDLE

Another common fallacy is the idea that God won't give us more than we can handle.

The problem is that Paul says the exact opposite in 2 Corinthians 1:8–10: "For we do not want you to be unaware, brothers, of the affliction we experienced in Asia. For we were so utterly burdened beyond our strength that we despaired of life itself. Indeed, we felt that we had received the sentence of death. But that was to make us rely not on ourselves but on God who raises the dead. He delivered us from such a deadly peril, and he will deliver us. On him we have set our hope that he will deliver us again."

God *will* and often does give us more than we can handle, just like he did Paul. Why does he do this? So that we will rely not on ourselves but on him. God undercuts our inclination toward self-sufficiency by placing us in situations where we have no choice but to look to him for energy and strength and help.

Is God asking the impossible of us? God requires of us more than we can do. But he doesn't require of us more than we can do without his strength and power.

John Owen captures this well: "The duties that God, in an ordinary way, requires at our hands are not proportioned to what strength we have in ourselves, but to what help and relief is laid up for us in Christ; and we are to address ourselves to the greatest performances with a settled persuasion that we have not the ability for the least."[3]

WHY IT IS SO HARD TO EXECUTE GOOD ON A LARGE SCALE

Sometimes it is especially puzzling to understand why we encounter so many obstacles. Take, for example, a married couple that is seeking to go into missions, but experiencing setback after setback. Why does God allow that? They are trying to do a good thing. Why is it so often so hard to do good?

Aside from the fact that we live in a fallen world and that we encounter spiritual opposition (Ephesians 6), I want to suggest one other reason it is so hard sometimes to do good: The factors that make it hard to do good also make it hard to do evil. It is possible that if it were easier to do good, it would also be much easier to do evil, and more evil would be done.

But by allowing it to be so hard to do almost *anything* of consequence, God has made it so that you have to be highly dedicated to make much of an impact. This causes more good to happen, because it is the rare person who is highly dedicated to executing evil. There *are* such people. But evil often seeks termination in the self—improving our own lives at other people's expense, but not conceiving grand plans to do harm.

Those who seek to do good, on the other hand, are often highly dedicated and willing to persevere through obstacles. So it is very possible that by allowing it to be so hard to do anything, God is nonetheless enabling more good to be done overall because evil is that much harder to do on a large scale.

So persist. In your plans and ambitions to bring blessing to others, on both small and large scales, persevere in spite of obstacles. If you persevere, you will usually find that your plans will be accomplished (which is what Proverbs 16:3 indicates as well).

WHY WE'RE OFTEN FRUSTRATED AT THE END OF THE DAY

Most of us are concerned not only with the large scale but also with the everyday. Why do we so often get to the end of the day only to find ourselves frustrated by failing to have accomplished what we intended? Why do we so often find ourselves unfulfilled at the end of the day—or with our lives?

Some of the reasons are things we can control. I'll list just a few related to productivity and time management.

Internal Realities

- There is a gap between your compass and your calendar—between what is most important to you and how you are actually spending your time. In these cases, identifying your priorities and translating them into the fabric of your day will help.
- You are valuing the wrong things. There might be no gap between your compass and your calendar, but you still feel unsatisfied and adrift. In this case, it might be that your compass is altogether wrong—you are valuing the wrong things.
- You might be making basic technical errors. For example, perhaps you are overloaded because you consistently underestimate the amount of time things will take. In these instances, learning more about effective time-management tactics helps.
- Your tools may be wrong. You might have the right compass and tactics, but your tools are out of sync with how this should lead you to work. In these cases, you need better tools.
- You are trying to control too much. You might be seeking to exert an unrealistic amount of control over your time, setting yourself up for failure.
- You might be sabotaging yourself. I'm not into over-psychologizing this, but Seth Godin has some helpful things to say about "the resistance" we often experience when we try to do work that matters. His book *Poke the Box* is a helpful stimulus to get past this. See also his helpful little booklet *ShipIt*.

External Realities

There are also external pressures that often frustrate us:

- As Drucker points out, in many jobs it seems as though your time belongs to everyone else. Staying focused on accomplishing your priorities, therefore, is extra challenging.
- Many who are in strategic roles where the focus needs to be outward and on the future are hindered from giving their attention to the high level because of the pressure to keep operating. As long as you allow the flow of events to determine what you focus on, you will, as Drucker also points out, "fritter yourself away operating."[4] The solution is criteria that enable you to identify what is truly important and thus focus on "contribution and results, even though the criteria are not found in the flow of events."
- You might have inaccurate expectations which, therefore, are not being met. Frustration is often the result of unmet expectations. This is key in relationships as well. Whenever it looks like there's a chance of conflicting expectations, make the expectations clear.
- You might have certain intrinsic needs that are going unmet. I don't want to get psychological or turn our needs into an idol, but God has made us such that we have genuine human needs which are to be fulfilled in context with him. These stem from the four dimensions of our being: physical, social, mental, and spiritual. In *Ministries of Mercy*, Tim Keller does a good job of showing how in the fall, we were separated from God's means of fulfilling each of these four areas. Maybe you aren't interacting with people enough in your day. Maybe your job doesn't require the best of you and your talents. Or maybe you don't get paid enough. These are all real issues worth reflecting on.

RESPONDING TO SUFFERING

We are not fatalists. Though suffering is an intrinsic feature of the fallen world, we are to fight against it, both in our own lives and in the lives of others. And we will have increasing success. We will not have ultimate success until Christ comes, but we can indeed make a dent.

1. Minimize your suffering to the extent you can. This is obvious, but not to be neglected. When it is in your power to reduce your suffering, do so. Jesus assumes we will operate this way and that it is right to do so, because this inclination is the foundation of the Second Great Commandment: "Love your neighbor as yourself."

If we were supposed to be sadistic toward ourselves, this command would be unworkable. We treat ourselves well. That is as it should be. The problem is that we don't treat others this way as well. And it lies in the fact that we often put our own interests ahead of theirs when, like Christ, we are to do the opposite (Phil. 2:3–11; Rom. 15:2–3).

So do what you can to fix your suffering. In one sense, that's why this book exists: to help alleviate some of your suffering—the suffering of frustration in your work, not getting done what you need to get done, lack of peace of mind. The pressures toward nonresults I listed earlier— the reasons we are often dissatisfied at the end of the day, and the reasons it is often so hard to execute initiatives for large-scale good—are things we can do something about to a large degree if, in addition to faith and prayer, we get the knowledge and skill we need. That's one reason this book exists.

But as I've emphasized, I'm seeking not simply to do that for its own sake but to equip you more fully to spend yourself radically for the good of others. The alleviation of our suffering should not terminate with ourselves but should be a means of enabling us to advance in helping to relieve the suffering of others.

Which leads to the second point.

2. Embrace suffering for the good of others. We shouldn't simply alleviate our suffering so that we have more resources to devote to the good of others; we should *embrace* suffering in the pursuit of the good of others.

This is the example that Christ gives us to follow: "Let each of us please his neighbor for his good, to build him up. For Christ did not please himself, but as it is written, 'The reproaches of those who reproached you fell on me'" (Rom. 15:2–3).

We are to seek our neighbor's good because that's what Christ did. And further, in seeking our good, Christ endured hardship, for he took the consequences of our sin on himself. He pursued our welfare even to the point of suffering greatly himself to do it.

And Christ calls us to follow this same road, for his glory and for the good of his people and the world. Dietrich Bonhoeffer says it well: "The cross is not the terrible end to an otherwise God-fearing and happy life, but it meets us at the beginning of our communion with Christ. When Christ calls a man, he bids him come and die."[5]

The path of service is the path of suffering. We should not shrink from suffering, as though God intends an easy life on this earth for us. He intends a life of *true* fruitfulness for us (John 15:1–5), and this means giving up many earthly comforts and the allure of an easy life. "Whoever does not bear his own cross and come after me cannot be my disciple" (Luke 14:27). The needs of the world are so great, and the opposition to Christ and his kingdom is so great, that we cannot make an impact without spending ourselves radically in Christ's cause.

This doesn't make us sadists. We don't embrace suffering as if it is good in itself. It's not. That's what makes it noble to suffer for the sake of others. And that's exactly what makes it foolish to take it on needlessly (see Col. 2:16–23).

Here's how the first two principles fit together: Minimize your own suffering when you can, but embrace it when it's necessary for the good of others.

3. Recognize the great and unique privilege it is to suffer in faith for God's glory. It is an honor to suffer for Christ. After the apostles had been beaten for preaching the gospel in Acts 5, for example, "they left the presence of the council, rejoicing that they were counted worthy to suffer dishonor for the name" (Acts 5:41).

This really comes into perspective if you consider that we will never have the privilege of suffering for Christ again. It is only in this world, in the fight against sin and darkness to bring the light of the gospel to the nations and work for the relief of people from injustice and poverty and distress that we have the opportunity to endure hardship for Christ's name. I like how Mrs. Howard Taylor captures this in her account of the martyrdom of John and Betty Stam in China in 1934: "To all eternity we shall live and reign with Christ, but shall we ever be able to make sacrifices for him again? When sin and pain and death are no more, and all tears are wiped away, shall we ever have again the privilege that is ours now of sharing the fellowship of His sufferings 'to seek and to save that which was lost'?"[6]

ENCOURAGEMENT FOR THOSE WHO FEEL UTTERLY UNPRODUCTIVE

The question here is, What do you do if you are in the midst of great suffering?

There are some who perhaps are in a state in which they can do almost nothing I've suggested in this book. Their circumstances have rendered them almost unable to do anything at all.

Much can be said, and has been said, on this. I want to suggest just one thing here: that you wait, and in this waiting keep looking to Christ through prayer and reading the Scriptures.

This is something we all should do during any form of suffering, and all of the time. But it's especially important when we feel overwhelmed and even incapacitated.

There is also action to take, for sure. But when it feels like you can do almost nothing, waiting is something you still can do.

Waiting goes to the heart of what God requires: faithfulness to Christ. Over and over in Revelation 2–3, for example, Christ emphasizes faithfulness as the means by which we overcome the world and obtain victory.

Consider what he says to those who are powerless and unable to do anything:

> "I know your tribulation and your poverty (but you are rich)"
> (Rev. 2:9).
> "I know you that you have but little power, and yet you have kept
> my word and have not denied my name" (Rev. 3:8).

You can be poor in this world, and yet utterly rich before Christ (Rev. 2:9). You can be utterly powerless in this world, and yet highly regarded by Christ (Rev. 3:8). This is true riches.

While waiting, pray and read the Scriptures. You can do more through prayer than you can imagine.

If you can pray, you can change the world.

And while praying, keep obeying, right where you are. All biblical commands are things you can do in any circumstance. If it feels like your circle of influence has shrunk or even that you can hardly get out of bed in the morning because you are struggling with a terminal illness or deep depression, there is still much you can do. You can be kind and gracious to anyone who crosses your path (1 Cor. 13:5), you can call out to God for help (Ps. 18:6), and you can pray for the spread of the gospel among all nations (Matt. 6:9–10).

You can obey God wherever you are, whatever your circumstances, however small your capacity to do anything at all.

And if you are faithful, wherever you are, you will reign with Christ forever. "The one who conquers, I will grant him to sit with me on my throne, as I also conquered and sat down with my Father on his throne" (Rev. 3:21).

The path to productivity is not complicated. Look to Christ, stay faithful to the gospel and in testifying to his name (Rev. 12:11), and do justice, love mercy, and walk humbly with him (Mic. 6:8; all of this is summed up in Rev. 12:17 as "keep[ing] to the commandments of God and hold[ing] to the testimony of Jesus").

GOD TURNS ALL OF OUR SUFFERING FOR GOOD

In the midst of suffering for the good of others and waiting patiently for God to act, we find great encouragement in the truth that we will not be losers by any of our suffering. For God turns all of our suffering for good. "We know that for those who love God all things work together for good, for those who are called according to his purpose" (Rom. 8:28).

As Edwards said, "Nothing can ever really hurt those that are the true friends of God."[7] In all of our suffering, we are "more than conquerors" (Rom. 8:37), which means not simply that we will make it through but that God will turn all of our suffering and opposition to our benefit.

We will see this ultimately in heaven, but sometimes we see it in this life, as when the hall that housed William Carey's printing presses and all of his mission's translation work burned down, just when everything was at its height. Years of work were lost.

Here is Carey's response: "In one short evening the labours of years are consumed. How unsearchable are the ways of God. I had lately brought some things to the utmost perfection of which they seemed capable, and contemplated the missionary establishment with perhaps too much self-congratulation. The Lord has laid me low, that I may look more simply to him."[8]

Carey's response was to let the tragedy direct his focus and reliance even more fully on Christ.

And God didn't let their work languish. Not only were they able to rebuild within a few months and redo the translations that had burned up, but this fire also became a means of "making them and their work famous all over Europe and America as well as India."[9] This resulted in a surplus of funding for rebuilding and helped advance their work farther than it would have been possible otherwise.

Biblical productivity is productivity through suffering. If we respond in faith, times of hardship and low productivity can become our times of greatest productivity. For God turns all things for good.

And this is not the end of the story. One day, all suffering will be taken away forever.

SORROW *AND* SIGHING WILL FLEE AWAY

There is a remarkable statement in Isaiah 35:10: "And the ransomed of the Lord shall return and come to Zion with singing; everlasting joy shall be upon their heads; they shall obtain gladness and joy, and sorrow and sighing shall flee away."

Here's what's remarkable: The redemption of creation will be so comprehensive that not only sorrow will be gone but so will sighing.

Sorrow here refers, obviously, to the big things: sadness and grief over great losses, especially the loss of a loved one.

Sighing, on the other hand, refers to small frustrations. When you walk down the hall to get another bar of soap from the closet, for example, and the handle on the closet door breaks. That's a small frustration which has just created more work for you. When these sorts of small things happen, we often sigh.

And Isaiah is saying there won't even be the slightest hint of sighing in the new heavens and new earth. No sorrow, and no sighing either. Everything will always go just as it should.

THE FUTURE FOR THE PEOPLE OF GOD IS INCONCEIVABLY GREAT

The curse will be undone, in all of its dimensions. This includes the frustration and limitations and toil we encounter in our work and vocations.

In fact, the Bible often represents the reversal of the curse in terms of amazingly great productivity. For example:

"On this mountain the Lord of hosts will make for all peoples a
feast of rich food, a feast of well-aged wine, of rich food full of
marrow, of aged wine well refined" (Isa. 25:6).
"Then you shall see and be radiant; your heart shall thrill and exult,
because the abundance of the sea shall be turned to you, the
wealth of the nations shall come to you" (Isa. 60:5).
"'Behold, the days are coming,' declares the Lord, 'when the plow-

man shall overtake the reaper and the treader of grapes him who sows the seed; the mountains shall drip sweet wine, and all the hills shall flow with it. I will restore the fortunes of my people Israel, and they shall rebuild the ruined cities and inhabit them; they shall plant vineyards and drink their wine, and they shall make gardens and eat their fruit'" (Amos 9:13–14).

In the new heavens and new earth, we will still have the desire to work, but it will never involve any toil or hardship or pain or frustration. And neither will the fruit of our efforts seem so small and limited. We will live in the midst of utter, massive abundance, which we ourselves have a part in building up through the work we do in eternity, and it won't cause our hearts to swell in pride so that we forget the Lord.

And beyond this, as we have emphasized, abundance and material things are not the most important things. They will continue to be priority B in heaven. What is most important is Christlikeness, and this is guaranteed to us (Rom. 8:29). To be like Jesus—the Son of God himself—is the greatest privilege we can ever have. That is the ultimate blessing, and it is what everything is leading to.

In the meantime, because God is our ultimate treasure, we can say with Habakkuk in the midst of this suffering world, "Though the fig tree should not blossom, nor fruit be on the vines, the produce of the olive fail and the fields yield no food, the flock be cut off from the fold and there be no herd in the stalls, *yet I will rejoice in the Lord; I will take joy in the God of my salvation.* God, the Lord, is my strength; he makes my feet like the deer's; he makes me tread on my high places" (Hab. 3:17–19, emphasis added).

The Box

Core Point

Biblical suffering includes not just extremely difficult and challenging circumstances but also any hardship we encounter in the path of obedience, especially in our vocations of work and family. We ought to seek to minimize our own suffering when we can, but embrace it with joy when it is necessary for the good of others.

Core Quote

To all eternity we shall live and reign with Christ, but shall we ever be able to make sacrifices for him again? When sin and pain and death are no more, and all tears are wiped away, shall we ever have again the privilege that is ours now of sharing the fellowship of His sufferings "to seek and to save that which was lost"?

—Mrs. Howard Taylor, John and Betty Stam:
A Story of Triumph

Core Passage

Let each of us please his neighbor for his good, to build him up. For Christ did not please himself, but as it is written, "The reproaches of those who reproached you fell on me."

—Romans 15:2–3

Conclusion

YOU'VE NOW LEARNED why the discipline of personal productivity matters and how to increase your effectiveness in work and life.

Use what you've learned for good!

Make the goal of your life to show the greatness of Jesus Christ by doing good for others, and organize your life around this purpose.

In other words, as we have seen throughout this book: Be creative, competent, and audacious in doing all the good you can for the world, in big and small ways, both right where you are and in the cause of global good, to the glory of God, according to your gifts and abilities. Use technology and productivity practices to help you do *that*. And, as you do this in the power of the gospel, the world *will* change.

And as Spurgeon said, "Let us be on the watch for opportunities of usefulness; let us go about the world with our ears and our eyes open, ready to avail ourselves of every occasion for doing good; let us not be content till we are useful, but make this the main design and ambition of our lives."[16]

Toolkit

Recap

What's Best Next in 500 Words
Gospel-driven productivity in a nutshell

WE NEED TO LOOK TO GOD to define for us what productivity is, rather than to simply subscribe to the ambiguous concept of "what matters most." For God *is* what matters most.

When we do this, we don't enter a realm of spiritual weirdness, as we might fear. Good secular thinking remains relevant as a gift of God's common grace. Neither do we enter a realm of overspiritualization where the things we do every day don't matter.

Instead, the things we do every day take on even greater significance because they are avenues through which we serve God and others. In fact, the gospel teaches us that the good of others is to be the main *motive* in all that we do and the chief *criterion* by which we determine "what's best next." This is not only right, but also is the best way to be productive, as the best business thinkers are showing. More important, when we do this in God's power and as an offering to him, he is glorified and shown to be great in the world.

In order to be most effective in this way in our current era of massive overload and yet incredible opportunity, we need to do four things to stay on track and lead and manage our lives effectively:

1. Define
2. Architect
3. Reduce
4. Execute

The result of doing these things is not only our own increased peace of mind and ability to get things done, but also the transformation of the world by the gospel because it is *in* our everyday vocations that we take our faith into the world and the light of the gospel shines—both in what we say *and* in what we do (Matt. 5:16).

IF YOU TAKE ONLY FIVE PRODUCTIVITY PRACTICES AWAY FROM THIS BOOK

Learning and especially implementing productivity practices can be hard. It is easy to forget what we learned or forget how to apply it. One remedy is to keep coming back to this book. But if you can take away only five things from this book, take these:

1. *Foundation:* Look to God, in Jesus Christ, for your purpose, security, and guidance in all of life.
2. *Purpose:* Give your whole self to God (Rom. 12:1–2), and then live for the good of others to his glory to show that he is great in the world.
3. *Guiding principle:* Love your neighbor *as yourself.* Treat others the way you want them to treat you. Be proactive in this and even make plans to do good.
4. *Core strategy:* Know what's most important and put it first.
5. *Core tactic:* Plan your week, every week! Then, as things come up throughout the day, ask, "Is this what's best next?" Then, either do them right away or, if you can't, slot them into your calendar or actions list so that you will be sure to do them at the right time.

Getting Creative Things Done

Why it's so hard to get creative things done
and how to solve that

*When you're operating on the maker's schedule, meetings
are a disaster.*

— Paul Graham, "Maker's Schedule,
Manager's Schedule"

CREATIVE WORK ISN'T JUST ABOUT the stereotypical artist. If you are a knowledge worker, your job likely involves many tasks that require independent thought—preparing presentations, getting ready for meetings, writing articles for your company's website, and all manner of other such activities. These are all creative work because they involve creating new things. Hence, they require much thought, engagement, and emotional labor.

And, therefore, they require lots of focused time. Sometimes *long* stretches of consolidated time over several days.

This highlights a significant tension that most of us are feeling more and more. Creative work tends to require large blocks of uninterrupted time, yet it's often hard to make that time because of all the meetings and appointments coming our way.

This is true not only if you are a programmer, writer, blogger, or filmmaker but even if (especially if!) you are a pastor (needing sermon prep time), an executive (needing time to develop strategy and generally reflect), or even a homemaker (needing time free from pressing tasks to think through the vision for your family and home life). Hence, we need to give special attention to the issue of getting done creative things that require time to think new thoughts.

WHY IT'S SO HARD TO GET CREATIVE THINGS DONE

This brings us to the distinction between the maker's schedule and the manager's schedule, which Paul Graham explains effectively in his essay "Maker's Schedule, Manager's Schedule."[1]

The manager's schedule consists mostly of appointments. When operating in this schedule, you don't need to protect much time for creative work because your work is mostly meetings and appointments. If you have a long task to do, you just schedule it in.

The maker's schedule, on the other hand, consists of large blocks of uninterrupted time. Graham gives programmers and writers as two examples here. Makers "generally prefer to use time in units of half a day at least. You can't write or program well in units of an hour. That's barely enough time to get started."

The Innovation Process

Innovation is more likely to happen when you know a bit about innovation itself. It is helpful to know the innovation process and also the organizational culture that tends to foster innovative ideas.

In its simplest form, the innovation process is this: generate ideas (idea generation), determine which ideas to accept (idea acceptance), and then implement (idea execution).[2]

You harness this process not primarily by creating an innovation program but rather by creating a thriving innovation culture where this process happens frequently and spontaneously. The key mindset of this type of culture is to recognize the importance of harnessing the power of unplanned progress. This comes from following the principle of "try a lot of stuff and keep what works." If you have a "give it a try" atmosphere, lots of different things will be tried and some of those attempts will result in useful insights that can be built on and developed toward a solution.

Now, here's the problem: each of these schedules works fine in itself; the problem is when they meet. Here's how Graham explains it: "When you're operating on the maker's schedule, meetings are a disaster. A single meeting can blow a whole afternoon, by breaking it into two pieces each too small to do anything hard in. Plus you have to remember to go to the meeting. For someone on the maker's schedule, having a meeting is like throwing an exception. It doesn't merely cause you to switch from one task to another; it changes the mode in which you work."

Now, here's the key idea. The point is *not* that you are either a manager or a maker, and you better choose. Rather, it's that all of us, or at least most of us, are and should be both.

Which creates the problem: How do you handle the tension between the need for solo, uninterrupted time for creative work and the need for highly interactive, interrupted time for executing ideas and working with people?

RESOLVING (OR LESSENING!) THE TENSION

The solution is this: Don't try to do them at the same time. Have a routine that allows you consistent time for creative project work that is sectioned off in a part of the day (morning or afternoon or evening, in line with your energy cycles) different from your time for meetings. And in addition to this, sometimes keep entire days open only for project work.

This is Peter Drucker's concept of consolidating time, which arises from the fact that dribs and drabs of time are insufficient to get large things done, even if cumulatively the total amount is large.

So to get creative things done, you have to be disciplined to create large blocks of time for working on them. If you are diligent, you can do this even if you have a lot of meetings in a typical week. A helpful variation on the "Maker's Schedule, Manager's Schedule" for those whose work is especially filled with meetings is described by Cal Newport in his essay "Getting Creative Things Done: How to Fit Hard Thinking into a Busy Schedule."[3]

The Box

Core Point

To get creative things done, we need to distinguish the maker's schedule and the manager's schedule.

Core Quote

> [Makers] generally prefer to use time in units of half a day at least. You can't write or program well in units of an hour. That's barely enough time to get started.
> —Paul Graham, "Maker's Schedule, Manager's Schedule"

Action

If you don't have uninterrupted time structured into your week for doing your best creative work, figure out what you can do to schedule such time.

Knowing What's Best Next

The Easy Reference Guide

FOR THOSE WHO WANT IMMEDIATE HELP on some key issues in productivity, here are the places where this book addresses them:

Foundations

- Understanding knowledge work right: 36
- On superficial efficiency, and why it's bad: 43
- Finding meaning in your work: 77
- Why excellence should matter to Christians: 99
- What it means to live a gospel-centered life: 53
- The character ethic versus the personality ethic: 124
- What it really means to love your neighbor as yourself: 110
- The six horizons of work: 138

Define

- Developing a mission statement for your life that actually works: 147
- Creating organizational mission statements: 164
- Figuring out what to do with your life: 169
- How to define your roles and keep track of them: 179

Architect

- How to create a good weekly schedule: 195
- How to set up the right routines: 209

Toolkit

Reduce
- Why multitasking is bad: 241
- Why Facebook is productive: 248
- How to handle interruptions: 246
- How to overcome procrastination and use it for good: 243

Execute
- Planning your week in just a few simple steps: 257
- Utilizing repeating tasks and time-activating tasks: 283
- Creating simple project plans: 280
- How to manage workflow and get your email inbox to zero every day: 265

The Results
- Why we need to understand management and leadership: 304
- Why we need to understand economics: 306
- What to do with the time you save: 314
- How our faith relates to our work: 311

Recommended Reading

DEVELOPING A VISION FOR YOUR LIFE

John Piper, *Don't Waste Your Life*

Piper shows that God calls us to a life of radical obedience to him and love for others. There is to be something different about how we live. We are to live in a way that is salty and bright, that shows that God is supreme in our lives and more important than comfort, possessions, or pleasure. This is the harder path and involves risk (chapter 5 is titled "Risk Is Right: Better to Lose Your Life Than Waste It"), but this is the way not to waste your life—that is, to live the most meaningful life.

David Platt, *Radical: Taking Back Your Faith from the American Dream*

Platt shows us that we have often adopted the false values of safety and comfort in place of the way Jesus actually calls his followers to live. Jesus said his followers would leave behind possessions, comfort, and ease when necessary to advance the gospel and meet pressing needs, especially among the unreached.

Bill Hybels, *Becoming a Contagious Christian*

Hybels shows us how to point people to Christ in ways that are natural, respectful, and engaging. In giving concrete, practical, and helpful tips for how to effectively communicate our faith in Christ, Hybels also shows the excitement of the Christian life.

Gary Haugen, *Good News about Injustice: A Witness of Courage in a Hurting World*

The chief good works God calls us to are mercy and justice (Micah 6:8). As we have seen, we can do these (and are to do them) in all areas of life, especially our daily work. But this is not the only place we do them. We live in a world filled with injustice and need, and Haugen shows us

355

that having a global concern for those in need and seeking justice for the oppressed is an essential part of the righteousness God requires of us—and thus should be at the heart of how we envision our lives.

CHRISTIAN CHARACTER

Jonathan Edwards, *Charity and Its Fruits*
In my view, this is the best book ever written on the meaning of love according to the Scriptures. It can be a tough read, but don't let that deter you. As John Piper has said, "raking is easy, but all you get is leaves; digging is hard, but you might find diamonds."

Martyn Lloyd-Jones, *Studies in the Sermon on the Mount*
This is one of the best books ever written on how we are to live the Christian life. Lloyd-Jones takes us through the entire Sermon on the Mount, which is Jesus' charter on how to live the Christian life.

Tim Keller, *Generous Justice: How God's Grace Makes Us Just*
An excellent, short read showing us that justice is at the heart of the Christian life and how justice is brought about in our lives by God's generosity to us in the gospel.

GETTING THINGS DONE

Stephen Covey, *First Things First*
In my opinion, this is *the* best book on time management (though *Getting Things Done* is right up there with it) because it focuses not first on how to get things done faster but on the importance of determining whether we should do them at all. Covey takes a top-down approach, showing the importance of developing our mission, vision, and roles for being effective and living a truly meaningful life. One of the best things about Covey and his work is his emphasis on the character ethic as opposed to the personality ethic.

David Allen, *Getting Things Done*
Allen lays out the best process for managing workflow I have ever seen. Whereas Covey is strong at the higher levels (mission, vision, and roles), Allen is strong at the lower levels—what do you actually *do* with all this stuff that is coming your way? As I argue in this book, one of the most important needs is for an integrated approach that is strong at all levels—from the runway of next actions to the fifty-thousand-foot level of our life's purpose.

Scott Belsky, *Making Ideas Happen: Overcoming the Obstacles between Vision and Reality*
Belsky shows us that great ideas are not enough. The true work is making those ideas happen. Execution is a critical skill we need to develop

and is especially important because most great ideas die a premature death. We all lose out when this happens because some of the best ideas for new businesses, solutions to the world's problems, and artistic break-throughs never end up seeing the light of day.

Tim Ferriss, *The Four-Hour Workweek*
Ferriss' aim is to show us how to minimize the time spent working so we can maximize the time spent doing whatever we want. While I disagree with his view of work and the focus on "joining the new rich," the book is a fun read and Ferriss gives some of the most helpful productivity tips (which can be applied to many different purposes) in recent years.

Lynne Snead and Joyce Wycoff, *To Do, Doing, Done: A Creative Approach to Managing Projects and Effectively Finishing What Matters Most*
This book gives one of the best explanations for how to connect your projects to your daily work. It was written in the days of paper planners, but the concepts are still relevant.

Julie Morgenstern, *Time Management from the Inside Out*
Morgenstern helps us see that there is a correspondence between how we think of space and how we should think of our time, though we often miss it. This is one of the best books on understanding the place of a good schedule for your life and how to do it well.

Andy Stanley, *Choosing to Cheat: Who Wins When Family and Work Collide?*
This is a joy to read, as are all of Andy Stanley's books. In this book, Stanley focuses on how to preserve time for your family in the midst of competing demands of work and ministry.

MOTIVATION

Daniel Pink, *Drive: The Surprising Truth about What Motivates Us*
When it comes to motivation, there is a gap between what science says and what business tends to do. Most companies take the carrot and stick approach to motivation. Pink argues that intrinsic motivation is the most effective (and enjoyable) way to go about our work. The three ingredients for genuine motivation are autonomy, mastery, and purpose.

Marcus Buckingham, *Now, Discover Your Strengths*
We will be most effective in work and life when we seek to work in our strengths most of the time. Your strengths are not simply what you

are good at but what energizes you. Hence, there is a key connection between strengths and intrinsic motivation. Buckingham shows us how to discover our strengths and put them to use to maximize our effectiveness.

EFFECTIVENESS AT WORK

Keith Ferrazzi, *Never Eat Alone*

Ferrazzi explodes the common notion that networking is about selfishly pursuing your own ends. Instead, it is about connecting with others and seeking first what you can contribute. Understood in this way, networking is essential to effectiveness in our work and lives.

Tim Sanders, *Love Is the Killer App*

Tim was one of the first people to help me see that putting the other person first (while being smart—be smart *and* nice) is not only right but also the way to be most effective even in the business world. What love looks like in the workplace is continually seeking to share your knowledge, networks, and compassion.

Seth Godin, *Linchpin: Are You Indispensible?*

Everything Godin writes is excellent. Godin understands excellence perhaps better than any other writer at this time because he understands that it is not about being flawless or fancy. It is about doing work that matters, creating meaningful connections, and being remarkable in all that you do. The best way to spread ideas is to be remarkable, and this applies to people as well.

Jeff Jarvis, *What Would Google Do?*

Excellent on the new rules of the new economy, which are really old rules that have always been true. As Clay Shirky says, it is "an indispensable guide to the business logic of the networked era."

The Online Toolkit

You will find the following resources online for free at *www.whatsbest next.com/toolkit*:

Finding the Right Tools
- Recommended Electronic Tools
- Recommended Physical Tools

Core Productivity Checklists
- Weekly Planning
- Daily Workflow
- Resources for Fighting Global Poverty

Bonus Chapters
- Unconventional Productivity Practices
- Work within Your Strengths: Do What Strengthens You, Not What Weakens You
- Productivity and Leadership
- Plan Noble Things! Setting God-Centered Goals
- How to File in a Way That Is Not Annoying
- From the Cutting Room Floor (Great interview sections, chapter components, and quotes that there wasn't space to include.)

Five Short Articles
- Thinking Christianly about Technology
- In (Slight) Defense of the Guy Who Spent Too Much Time at the Office
- A Brief Word on Workaholism
- A Brief Word on Mistakes
- How *What's Best Next* Applies to Stay-at-Home Moms

Learn More and Pass This On

MY BLOG

For resources on living the Christian life, applying the Scriptures to all of life, theology, and improving our leadership, management, and productivity from an integrated Christian worldview, you can visit or subscribe to my blog: *www.whatsbestnext.com*.

THE SOCIAL WEB

I'd love to connect on Facebook and Twitter:

- Facebook: *facebook.com/mattperman*
- Twitter: *twitter.com/mattperman*

TWITTER SUMMARIES

If you tweet any quotes from the book, feel free to use this hashtag: *#wbn*. Here are a few summaries of the book in less than 140 characters:

- The best way to be productive is to put others first. This is both what the gospel teaches us and the most exciting life. #wbn
- We are to be creative, competent, and audacious in doing good for the world. Productivity practices exist to help us do that. #wbn
- You don't have to run to the hills to serve God. You can serve him in the things you do every day, when done in faith. #wbn
- The core principle of productivity is to put first things first. There are four steps to doing this: define, architect, reduce, and execute. #wbn
- Slack work is a form of vandalism (Prov. 18:9). #wbn
- Don't just be generous with the results of your work; be generous in your work. #wbn

Acknowledgments

I AGREE WITH WINSTON CHURCHILL: "Writing a book is an adventure. To begin with, it is a toy and an amusement; then it becomes a mistress, and then it becomes a master, and then a tyrant. The last phase is that just as you are about to be reconciled to your servitude, you kill the monster, and fling him out to the public."

And I say with Jim Collins: without the help from many, many gracious people, the monster would have won hands down.[1]

First, thanks to the Lord for saving a sinner like me and bringing me into his kingdom, making my life far better (and harder) than I ever could have imagined, and sticking with me and bearing me up to write this book.

Second, thanks to my wife, for standing strong through all the trials we've been through and taking infinitely more than her share of responsibility with the kids as I've sought to get this book written, and especially during those frustrating times when it felt like I was spinning my wheels all day. Those days almost exasperated both of us, and I know they frustrated her all the more.

To my kids, who have sacrificed in ways they don't even know. May the Lord give the time back to us.

To my parents for their support through the time of writing this book and all the challenges it involved.

To my brothers for providing the wisdom and encouragement to help me get this done.

To my friends Justin Taylor and Dustin Shramek, without whom this book would not have been possible. They took the initiative to help me, without being asked, at critical times in trying to cut this manuscript down, giving generously of their time and wisdom.

To my friends in DC, Josh Deckard, Phil Gallo, and Eric Simmons, for encouraging me to write and staying with me in prayer. And to Mike

Acknowledgments

Allen: Mike, you embody everything I talk about in this book. Your spirit of proactive generosity all day long, in everything that you do, is a model for us all.

To James Kinnard, who strongly encouraged me to get moving with this book and has been a good friend through the years.

To Matt Heerema, whose inspiration helped keep this book from dying.

To David Leonard, who kept encouraging me through the writing and then came in to proofread the manuscript in a pinch at the last minute.

To Mike Thate: thanks for all your encouragement.

To Chris Misiano: thanks for being such an excellent assistant and having so much patience through this process.

To Mike Wandling: thank you for transcribing the Wayne Grudem interview from the audio.

To Josh Etter, for stating so succinctly in a conversation we had several years ago that "we have to have a vision of God before we can have a vision for our lives."

To my neighbors, who started to think the book didn't even exist because it was taking so long!

To Steve and Linda Schwartz, for letting me use their house to write in the fall while they were waiting for it to sell.

To Glenn Brooke, for all of your prayers over the years.

To Jason Meyer and his wife, Cara, for their encouragement and support of Heidi and me through all the challenges of getting a book done.

To Lukas Naugle: you are a creative inspiration.

To Gary Steward, for your persistent encouragement.

To John Piper, for teaching me more about God than anyone other than my family.

To John Fonville, for your incredible gospel-centered example in all of life.

To Tim Challies, for providing early encouragement and help to get started (which you may not even remember).

To my agent, Andrew Wolgemuth, who was unflagging in his support, encouragement, and patience through the whole process. I couldn't have made a better choice for my agent.

To my editor, Ryan Pazdur. Thank you for all your input and for bearing with me. You are a fantastic editor.

And to dozens of other people: thank you for all of your support, encouragement, and help in making this book happen.

Notes

Introduction

1. Tim Sanders, *Love Is the Killer App* (New York: Random House, 2003), 11.
2. See, for example, my post "You Will Suffer from Your Work and It Is Not Sin" (*http://www.whatsbestnext.com/2010/08/you-will-suffer-from-your-work-and-it-is-not-sin/*) and my series "Suffering in Our Work and Everyday Lives," *http://www.whatsbestnext.com/2010/09/suffering-in-our-everyday-lives-an-introduction/*.
3. David Allen, *Getting Things Done: The Art of Stress-Free Productivity* (New York: Viking, 2001), xiii.
4. Scott Belsky, *Making Ideas Happen: Overcoming the Obstacles between Vision and Reality* (New York: Penguin, 2010), 4.
5. It didn't help my case, by the way, that I had just finished a series on how to set up your desk. You can read that series here: *http://www.whatsbestnext.com/2009/10/how-to-set-up-your-desk-an-introduction/*.
6. Peter Drucker, *The Effective Executive* (New York: HarperBusiness, 2006), ix.
7. Steven Hayward, *Churchill on Leadership: Executive Success in the Face of Adversity* (New York: Random House, 1998), 62.
8. Julie Morgenstern, *Never Check Email in the Morning: And Other Unexpected Strategies for Making Your Work Life Work* (New York: Fireside, 2004), 71.
9. David Martyn Lloyd-Jones, *Studies in the Sermon on the Mount* (Grand Rapids, MI: Eerdmans, 1999), 30–31.

Chapter 1: Why Is It So Hard to Get Things Done?

1. Peter Drucker, *The Effective Executive* (New York: HarperBusiness, 2006), 4. There is a role for managers, but the role of a manager is to be a catalyst in unleashing the individual's talents for the effectiveness of the organization, not to be a supervisor who tightly controls his people. For more on this, see Marcus Buckingham's *First, Break All the Rules: What the World's Greatest Managers Do Differently* and my article "Management in Light of the Supremacy of God" (*http://whatsbestnext.com/2011/01/management-in-light-of-the-supremacy-of-god*).
2. I'm not saying here that people are naturally lazy. They are not. I believe that most people want to do good work and will rise to the occasion when given responsibility. My point is that talent, ability, and effort are not in themselves enough to make us truly effective. Rather, we need to bring them together through a set of habits that enable us to unleash our effectiveness.
3. Drucker, *The Effective Executive*, ix.
4. Scott Belsky, *Making Ideas Happen: Overcoming the Obstacles between Vision and Reality* (New York: Penguin, 2010), 1.
5. Ibid., 9.
6. Tim Sanders, *Love Is the Killer App* (New York: Random House, 2003), 10–11.
7. Ibid.

8. David Allen, *Getting Things Done: The Art of Stress-Free Productivity* (New York: Viking, 2001), 4.

Chapter 2: Why Efficiency Is Not the Answer

1. Stephen Covey, Rebecca Merrill, and Roger Merrill, *First Things First* (New York: Simon and Schuster, 1994), 12.
2. Ibid.
3. For more on the counterintuitive notion that cost-cutting campaigns often undermine productivity rather than increase it, see my posts "Managing in a Downturn: Beware of Cost-Cutting Campaigns" (*http://www.whatsbestnext.com/2009/11/ managing-in-a-downturn-beware-of-cost-cutting-campaigns/*) and my comments on Seth Godin's excellent post "The Bad Effects of Smart Compromises" (*http://www.whats bestnext.com/2012/01/the-bad-effects-of-smart-compromises/*).
4. For more on this, see my post "Employees Are Not Overhead": *http://www .whatsbestnext.com/2008/10/employees-are-not-overhead/*. Tom Peters also takes this notion to task in his landmark book *In Search of Excellence: Lessons from America's Best Run Companies*. See especially chapter 2, "The Rational Model," and chapter 4, "Productivity through People."
5. Patrick Lencioni, one of my favorite management thinkers, makes this case very well in a recent article, "The Enemy of Innovation and Creativity." See also *Pat's Point of View*, "The Enemy of Innovation and Creativity": *http://www.tablegroup .com/pat/povs/pov/?id=30*.
6. Tim Sanders, *Love Is the Killer App* (New York: Random House, 2003), 33.
7. See Tom Peters and Robert Waterman, *In Search of Excellence* (New York: HarperBusiness, 2004). See especially chapter 6, "Close to the Customer," where they note that high-performing companies are "mainly oriented toward the value, rather than the cost, side of the profitability equation" (186), and chapter 2, "The Rational Model." See also my article "Against Over-professionalism in Management: Managing for the Human Side": *http://www.whatsbest-next.com/2013/05/against-over-professionalism-in-management*.
8. For more on this, see my post "Is Attending Conferences an Unnecessary Expense?": *http:// www.whatsbestnext.com/2010/03/is-attending-conferences-an-unnecessary-expense/*.
9. It also has a Christian form, where justification is made not just on the basis of efficiency but "good stewardship." One example of this is when people are forced to work with slow, old, and annoying computers because "it would cost too much to keep up with technology." In reality, however, if employees have faster computers, they will not only be able to do their jobs faster (there's efficiency) but will be more excited about their jobs (since their tools aren't annoying) and will be more knowledgeable at navigating the new economy (since they will be more current with technology). That would translate into much more effectiveness in the long run than the money saved by skimping on computers. The point: Treat your employees well. It's not only the right thing to do; but it will also serve your organization much better in the long term.

Chapter 3: Why We Need to Be God-Centered in Our Productivity

1. Stephen Covey, Rebecca Merrill, and Roger Merrill, *First Things First* (New York: Simon and Schuster, 1994), 50.
2. Which generation is GTD in (the system advocated by David Allen in *Getting Things Done*)? The answer is that it depends on how you use it. It can be utilized in accord with any of the generations, including the fourth. I think many people often settle for utilizing it within a second or third generation approach. One reason for this is that GTD easily inclines itself in this direction because it takes a bottom-up approach to getting things done rather than a top-down approach. *What's Best Next* advocates a fifth generation model and shows how you can utilize GTD within an effectiveness paradigm that seeks to go beyond being principle-centered to being God-centered.
3. As well as organizational and interpersonal leadership, as Covey fleshes out in his book *Principle-Centered Leadership*.

4. For a good discussion of what happens when we put something other than God at the center of our lives, see Timothy Keller's helpful book *Counterfeit Gods: The Empty Promises of Money, Sex, and Power, and the Only Hope That Matters* (New York: Penguin, 2009).

5. That's why, in one sense, this is a book on how to prepare for the final judgment. That is, how to live our lives so that on that day, the Lord will say "well done." For living a life that passes the final judgment is what it ultimately means to live a productive life.

6. It is interesting that the Scriptures frequently consider productivity in relation to the resurrection. For example, the exhortation here in 1 Corinthians 15 is given on the basis of the resurrection. That's the point of the "therefore." *Since* we will be raised, *therefore* we should be abundant in good works. Likewise, in Psalm 90, Moses asks God to "establish the work of our hands" (v. 17) right after alluding to the final resurrection (that's the meaning of v. 14; cf. also 30:5).

Chapter 4: Does God Care about Getting Things Done?

1. Wayne Grudem, *Business to the Glory of God* (Wheaton, IL: Crossway, 2003), 25–26.

2. Ibid., 27.

3. Peter T. O'Brien, *The Letter to the Ephesians* (Grand Rapids, MI: Eerdmans, 1999), 382.

4. Clinton E. Arnold, Frank S. Thielman, and S. M. Baugh, *Ephesians, Philippians, Colossians, Philemon,* Zondervan Illustrated Bible Backgrounds Commentary (Grand Rapids, MI: Zondervan, 2002), 33.

5. For more on how to think Christianly about seemingly "secular" areas of life, see the post by leading Christian blogger Justin Taylor "Is There a Distinctively Christian Way to be a Bus Driver?": *http://thegospelcoalition.org/blogs/justintaylor/2013/04/26/is-there-a-distinctively-christian-way-to-be-a-bus-driver/*.

Chapter 5: Why the Things You Do Every Day Matter

1. William Wilberforce, *A Practical View of Christianity* (1797; Peabody, MA: Hendrickson, 2006), 98.

2. Edwards makes this point well in *Charity and Its Fruits* (1852; Carlisle, PA: Banner of Truth, 2005), 103. Also see my blog post "The Christian Ethic," in which I expound on Edwards' statement: *http://www.whatsbestnext.com/2012/02/the-christian-ethic/*.

3. I have lots of stories I could tell. I should also add that though the trip was very meaningful, this particular trip was my first trip to Africa, and, as such, by the end I was ready to get home. The day the plane took off also felt like one of the best of my life!

4. And, of course, you really aren't safe if you do this. See John Fischer's very helpful book *Fearless Faith: Living beyond the Walls of "Safe" Christianity.*

5. I'm indebted to Merlin Mann for this analogy.

6. See chapter 24, on missions, for how we can all be involved now in solving large global problems and advancing the cause of the gospel for the sake of all nations.

7. Though if you are a professional mover, *that* takes lots of skill.

Chapter 6: Put Others First

1. Cf. also the updated version in John 13:34 (the New Commandment): Love one another as I have loved you.

2. Jonathan Edwards, *Charity and Its Fruits* (1852; Carlisle, PA: Banner of Truth, 2005), 181.

3. Ibid., 96.

4. Note also how Paul equates seeking the good of others that they may be saved with doing everything for God's glory in verses 31–33. To seek God's glory, in other words, is necessarily intertwined with seeking the good of others.

5. Stephen Covey summarizes this principle well as "seek first to understand, then to be understood." His chapter by this same name in *The Seven Habits of Highly Effective People* is one of the most helpful pieces on this subject that you will ever read.

6. Charles Spurgeon, *Counsel for Christian Workers* (Christian Heritage), 108.
7. Jonathan Edwards, *The Duty of Christian Charity to the Poor.*
8. Jonathan Edwards, *Charity and Its Fruits* (1852; Carlisle, PA: Banner of Truth, 2005), 168.
9. William Wilberforce, *A Practical View of Christianity* (1797; Peabody, MA: Hendrickson, 2006), 172.
10. See Francis Chan's book *Crazy Love: Overwhelmed by a Relentless God* and "Risk Is Right," chapter 5 in John Piper's *Don't Waste Your Life.*
11. For more on this, see my post "What Are Christian Values?": *http://www .whatsbestnext.com/2012/08/what-are-christian-values/.*
12. Edwards, *Charity and Its Fruits,* 58.
13. Ibid., 108.
14. If Christians are hesitant to embrace this concept, it is especially odd, because we aren't only ignoring the Bible but we are also decades behind on the best business strategy.
15. Tim Sanders, *Love Is the Killer App* (New York: Random House, 2003), 11.
16. Ibid., 12.
17. Ibid., 55.
18. Keith Ferrazzi, *Never Eat Alone* (New York: Crown Business, 2005), 9. Here are some other helpful statements he makes: "Over time, I came to see reaching out to people as *a way to make a difference in people's lives* as well as a way to explore and learn and enrich my own" (7); "I was, instead, *connecting*—sharing my knowledge and resources, time and energy, friends and associates, and empathy and compassion in a continual effort to provide value to others, while coincidentally increasing my own" (8).
19. Ibid., 7.
20. Ibid., 22.
21. This means, for example, if you are developing an online marketing campaign, you generally shouldn't use pop-up windows that open up automatically when people come to your site. Though that might result in more people seeing your ad, it will also tick that many more people off. Making people angry doesn't serve them and will undermine your marketing.
22. Edwards, *Charity and Its Fruits,* 184.
23. Edwards' book on love is one of the greatest expositions of 1 Corinthians 13 (the great chapter on love) ever. From what we've seen so far, it should be clear how the subject of Edwards' book (love) and the subject of this book (productivity) are ultimately one and the same, for productivity is ultimately about living a life of love for others.

Chapter 7: How the Gospel Makes Us Productive

1. John Piper, *The Roots of Endurance* (Wheaton, IL: Crossway, 2006), 119.
2. Ibid.
3. Ibid.
4. The best book ever written on justification is John Owen's *The Doctrine of Justification by Faith,* but it is very hard to read (much harder than his *Death of Death in the Death of Christ,* for which he is perhaps best known). After that is Jonathan Edwards' sermon *Justification by Faith Alone.* A much easier read, but just as comprehensive, is James Buchanan's *The Doctrine of Justification.* The best contemporary books on justification are R. C. Sproul's *Faith Alone* and John Piper's *The Future of Justification: A Response to N. T. Wright* and *Counted Righteous.* I hope to write a book on justification soon; in the meantime, I have some posts and articles you might be interested in checking out at *http://www.whatsbestnext.com/category/theology/justification/.*
5. Michael Horton, *The Gospel-Driven Life* (Grand Rapids, MI: Baker, 2009), 20.
6. Note also 2 Peter 1:9, which states, "For whoever lacks these qualities [the character qualities of vv. 5–7] is so nearsighted that he is blind, having forgotten that he was cleansed from his former sins." Letting the awareness of our forgiveness fall into neglect is one of the reasons some Christians live largely un-Christlike lives. It isn't that they believe the gospel too much; it's that they believe it too little. People who have fallen back in their Christian lives need more gospel, not less.

7. William Wilberforce, *A Practical View of Christianity* (1797; Peabody, MA: Hendrickson, 2006), 69–70.
8. Piper, *Roots of Endurance*, 158.
9. *The Gospel-Centered Life: A Nine-Lesson Study, Leader's Guide* (Greensboro, NC: World Harvest Mission, 2011), 42.
10. Robert Isaac Wilberforce and Samuel Wilberforce, *The Life of William Wilberforce*, in "An Excerpt from *The Life of William Wilberforce*" appendix 2 in *A Practical View of Christianity*.
11. John Pollock, "A Man Who Changed His Times," in *Character Counts: Leadership Qualities in Washington, Wilberforce, Lincoln, and Solzhenitsyn*, ed. Os Guinness (Grand Rapids, MI: Baker, 1999), 87–88.

Chapter 8: Peace of Mind without Having Everything under Control

1. Rick Warren, *The Purpose-Driven Life* (Grand Rapids, MI: Zondervan, 2002), 269.

Chapter 9: The Role of Prayer and Scripture in Our Productivity

1. Os Guinness, ed., *Character Counts: Leadership Qualities in Washington, Wilberforce, Lincoln, and Solzhenitsyn* (Grand Rapids, MI: Baker, 1999), 14.
2. Peter T. O'Brien, *The Letter to the Ephesians*, 369–70; 386. See also Douglas Moo, *The Epistle to the Romans* (Grand Rapids, MI: Eerdmans, 1996), 758.
3. See also Joshua 1:8, where Joshua is commanded similarly to meditate on God's law day and night, "for then you will make your way prosperous, and then you will have good success."
4. See the excellent summary of John Owen's view of Christian character in Sinclair Ferguson's *John Owen on the Christian Life*, 269–75.
5. Rick Warren, *The Purpose-Driven Life* (Grand Rapids, MI: Zondervan, 2002), 183.

Chapter 10: The Core Principle for Making Yourself Effective

1. I highly recommend Steve Krug, *Don't Make Me Think: A Common Sense Guide to Web Usability* (Berkeley, CA: New Riders, 2006).
2. Rick Warren, *Purpose-Driven Church* (Grand Rapids, MI: Zondervan, 1995), 87.
3. Peter Drucker, *The Effective Executive* (New York: HarperBusiness, 2006), 100.
4. Stephen Covey, Rebecca Merrill, and Roger Merrill, *First Things First* (New York: Simon and Schuster, 1994), 88.
5. For more information on the summit, see the website *http://www.willowcreek.com/events/leadership/*.
6. Note how we see both components of personal effectiveness right in Proverbs 6:6–8, where we are told to "consider the ant." The ant is, first of all, self-governing. She knows what to do "without having any chief, officer, or ruler." That's personal leadership. And she is diligent in actually doing what she determines. She "gathers her food in harvest." That's personal management.
7. Scott Berkun, *The Art of Project Management* (Sebastopol, CA: O'Reilly Media, 2005), 25.

Part 3: Define

1. John Piper, *Don't Waste Your Life (Group Study Edition)* (Wheaton, IL: Crossway, 2007), 48.
2. Because of space constraints, for the goals component, see the bonus chapter "Setting God-Centered Goals" online.

Chapter 11: What's Your Mission?

1. One of the best biographies on Edwards is Iain Murray's *Jonathan Edwards: A New Biography*. The book was so good that I didn't want it to end. A more recent and also very helpful bio is George Marsden's *Jonathan Edwards: A Life*.
2. Rick Warren, *The Purpose-Driven Life* (Grand Rapids, MI: Zondervan, 2002), 18.

3. Ibid., 317–18.
4. Note that to be able to think about this intelligently, you need to know something about God and his character. This comes not from speculation but from revelation, which means reading the Bible and understanding what he has said in his Word.
5. Jonathan Edwards, *Charity and Its Fruits* (1852; Carlisle, PA: Banner of Truth, 2005), 167.
6. Michael Horton, *The Gospel-Driven Life: Being Good News People in a Bad News World* (Grand Rapids, MI: Baker, 2009), 132.
7. David Martyn Lloyd-Jones, *Studies in the Sermon on the Mount* (Grand Rapids, MI: Eerdmans, 1999), 30–31.
8. Ibid., 32.
9. John Piper, *Don't Waste Your Life (Group Study Edition)* (Wheaton, IL: Crossway, 2007), 31.
10. For more on this, see my blog post "What the Sermon on the Mount Does Not Mean: Or, Don't Pull a Jim Marshall": *http://www.whatsbestnext.com/2011/06/what-the-sermon-on-the-mount-does-not-mean/*. See also Lloyd-Jones, *Studies in the Sermon on the Mount*, 42–43.
11. This phrase is from Stephen Nichols helpful book *Heaven on Earth: Capturing Jonathan Edwards's Vision of Living in Between* (Wheaton, IL: Crossway, 2006).
12. See *http://www.whatsbestnext.com/2011/06/the-resolutions-of-jonathan-edwards-in-categories/*.
13. *http://www.desiringgod.org/resource-library/articles/the-resolutions-of-jonathan-edwards*.

Chapter 12: Finding Your Life Calling

1. Charles Bridges, *Proverbs* (Wheaton, IL: Crossway, 2001), 38.
2. Dave Harvey, *Rescuing Ambition* (Wheaton, IL: Crossway, 2010), 62.
3. James Collins and Jerry Porras, *Built to Last: Successful Habits of Visionary Companies*, tenth anniversary edition (New York: HarperCollins, 2004), 93–94.
4. See Piper's sermon "Holy Ambition: To Preach Where Christ Has Not Been Named": *http://www.desiringgod.org/resource-library/sermons/holy-ambition-to-preach-where-christ-has-not-been-named*.
5. William Wilberforce, *A Practical View of Christianity* (1797; Peabody, MA: Hendrickson, 2006), x–xii. Note that "manners" = "morals" in Wilberforce's day; that is, the moral framework of Great Britain.
6. Charles Spurgeon, *Counsel for Christian Workers* (Christian Heritage), 10.
7. See his helpful book *The Adventures of Johnny Bunko: The Last Career Guide You'll Ever Need*.
8. Scott Belsky, "Finding Your Work Sweet Spot": *http://the99percent.com/tips/7003/Finding-Your-Work-Sweet-Spot-Genuine-Interest-Skills-Opportunity*.

Chapter 13: Clarifying Your Roles

1. Martin Luther, *An Open Letter to the Christian Nobility*.
2. Note also how "professional" includes a lot more than just doing my job. It includes things I do on my own, apart from formal employment, and also the support structures that my formal employment needs, such as career management and professional knowledge.
3. For insight on how to handle the tension between work and family, see Andy Stanley's excellent book *Choosing to Cheat: Who Wins When Work and Family Collide*.
4. And here's my brief summary of Keller's answer: *http://www.whatsbestnext.com/2011/08/tim-keller-on-discerning-your-calling/*.

Chapter 14: Setting Up Your Week

1. David Allen, *Ready for Anything: Fifty-two Productivity Principles for Work and Life* (New York: Penguin, 2003), 125.
2. Joseph Ellis' *His Excellency: George Washington* (New York: Random House, 2004).
3. Ibid., chap. 7.
4. Scott Belsky, *Making Ideas Happen: Overcoming the Obstacles between Vision and Reality* (New York: Penguin, 2010), 99.

5. Getting creative things done is one of the greatest new challenges in the era of knowledge work. Many have pointed out that the out-of-the-box approach of GTD doesn't give enough place to those whose work substantially consists of large blocks of time (the "maker's schedule," as Paul Graham calls it). The principles for getting creative things done are baked into Gospel-Driven Productivity. For some of the most helpful focused treatments on getting creative things done in the midst of busy, ever-changing schedules, see Paul Graham, "Maker's Schedule, Manager's Schedule": *http://www.paulgraham.com/makersschedule.html*. See also my post "How to Fit Hard Thinking into a Busy Schedule": *http://www.whatsbestnext.com/2010/12/how-to-fit-hard-thinking-into-a-busy-schedule/*, and Cal Newport, "Getting Creative Things Done: How to Fit Hard Thinking into a Busy Schedule": *http://the99percent.com/tips/6956/Getting-Creative-Things-Done-How-To-Fit-Hard-Thinking-Into-a-Busy-Schedule?utm_source=Triggermail&utm_medium=email&utm_term=ALL&utm_campaign=MIH+Dec+1+2010*.

6. "How to Better Control Your Time by Designing Your Ideal Week": *http://michaelhyatt.com/how-to-better-control-your-time-by-designing-your-ideal-week.html*. Also see Julie Morgenstern's discussion in *Time Management from the Inside Out*, chap. 5, "Time Mapping."

7. Julie Morgenstern, *Time Management from the Inside Out* (New York: Henry Holt, 2000), 79.

8. Quoted in Belsky, *Making Ideas Happen*, 77.

Chapter 15: Creating the Right Routines

1. See their blog, "Girl Talk" (*www.girltalkhome.com*) and "The Five O'Clock Club": *http://www.girltalkhome.com/resources#clubs*.

2. See some of my blog posts on why this is so important, such as "How Many Times a Day Should You Check Email?" (*http://www.whatsbestnext.com/2009/02/how-many-times-a-day-should-you-check-email/*), "An Example on Why You Should Not Check Email Continually" (*http://www.whatsbestnext.com/2009/02/an-example-to-show-why-you-should-not-check-email-continually/*), and "On Grasshoppers and Email" (*http://www.whatsbestnext.com/2009/10/on-grasshoppers-and-email/*).

3. See his excellent article "How to Mark a Book," *http://academics.keene.edu/tmendham/documents/AdlerMortimerHowToMarkABook_20060802.pdf*.

Chapter 17: The Art of Making Time

1. Peter Drucker, *The Effective Executive* (New York: HarperBusiness, 2006), 37.

2. Stephen Covey, *The Seven Habits of Highly Effective People* (New York: Free Press, 2003), 179.

3. I am indebted to Tim Ferriss' *The Four-Hour Workweek* for this very helpful observation.

Chapter 18: Harnessing the Time Killers

1. See Dave Crenshaw, *The Myth of Multitasking* (San Francisco: Jossey-Bass, 2008), 27.

2. Ibid., 18.

3. Ibid., 47. See also my blog post "The More You Multitask, the Worse You Get at It": *http://www.whatsbestnext.com/2010/03/the-more-you-multitask-the-worse-you-get-at-multitasking/*.

4. This is really incredible, if you think about it. The reason God can hear and answer millions of prayers at once, giving his full attention to each of us when we pray, is because he is multitasking. He is multitasking in the right sense, and it actually works for him: he is doing multiple things (trillions of things) at once.

5. See Daniel Pink's excellent book *Drive: The Surprising Truth about What Motivates Us*.

6. Eugene Greissman, *Time Tactics of Very Successful People* (New York: McGraw Hill, 1994), 73.

7. Kermit Pattison, "Worker Interrupted: The Cost of Task Switching," *Fast Company* (July 28, 2008), *http://www.fastcompany.com/944128/worker-interrupted-cost-task-switching*.

8. Ibid.

9. Ibid.

10. Wayne Martindale and Jerry Root, eds., *The Quotable Lewis* (Wheaton, IL: Tyndale, 1989), 335.

11. Stephanie Winston, *Organized for Success* (New York: Crown Business, 2004), 10.

12. Ibid., 197.

13. See my post "Stop Interrupting Yourself": *http://www.whatsbestnext.com/2008/12/stop-interrupting-yourself/*.

14. Scott Belsky, *Making Ideas Happen: Overcoming the Obstacles between Vision and Reality* (New York: Penguin, 2010), 112.

15. Farhad Manjoo, "Unchain the Office Computers!" *Slate* (August 25, 2009), *http://www.slate.com/articles/technology/technology/2009/08/unchain_the_office_computers.2.html*.

16. For more on this, see my blog post "The Tyranny of Corporate Computer Control": *http://www.whatsbestnext.com/2009/11/the-tyranny-of-corporate-computer-control/*.

Chapter 20: Managing Email and Workflow

1. David Allen, *Ready for Anything: Fifty-two Productivity Principles for Work and Life* (New York: Penguin, 2003).

2. David Allen, *Getting Things Done: The Art of Stress-Free Productivity* (New York: Viking, 2001), 216.

3. Ibid., 96.

4. For more on this, see my post "How to Get the Mail": *http://www.whatsbestnext.com/2008/10/how-to-get-the-mail/*.

Chapter 21: Managing Projects and Actions

1. If you have more large initiatives than you need to accomplish this quarter, you can time-activate them through your actions calendar or backburner.

2. For more on areas of responsibility, see chapter 13.

3. Note that, since it was written in the 1990s, it talks in terms of paper planners; however, the basic principles are easily transfered.

Chapter 22: Daily Execution

1. Scott Belsky, *Making Ideas Happen: Overcoming the Obstacles between Vision and Reality* (New York: Penguin, 2010), 64.

2. Stephen Covey, Rebecca Merrill, and Roger Merrill, *First Things First* (New York: Simon and Schuster, 1994), 168.

3. Scott Eblin, *The Next Level: What Insiders Know about Executive Success* (Boston: Nicholas Brealey, 2011), 19.

4. Peter Drucker, *The Effective Executive* (New York: HarperBusiness, 2006), 28–29.

5. Ibid.

6. Ibid., 100.

7. Ibid., 102–3.

8. Ibid.

9. Brian Tracy, *Eat That Frog: Twenty-one Ways to Stop Procrastinating and Get More Done in Less Time* (San Francisco: Berrett-Koehler Publications, 2007), 1.

Chapter 23: Productivity in Organizations and Society

1. Jonathan Edwards, *Charity and Its Fruits* (1852; Carlisle, PA: Banner of Truth, 2005), 169.

2. Daniel is a good example of this, and is likely intended as an example of how Christians are to relate to the secular arena while in exile—that is, prior to the return of Christ.

3. Edwards, *Charity and Its Fruits*, 169.

4. William Wilberforce, quoted in Chuck Colson's preface to William Wilberforce, *A Practical View of Christianity* (1797; Peabody, MA: Hendrickson, 2006), ix.

5. Edwards, *Charity and Its Fruits*, 171.

6. Peter Drucker, *The Effective Executive* (New York: HarperBusiness, 2006), 170–71.

7. Ibid., 170.

8. Ibid., 171.

9. Collins makes the same point in the following short video, where he goes so far as to say that Drucker contributed as much to the triumph of freedom over totalitarianism as perhaps even Winston Churchill himself: *http://www.whatsbestnext.com/2009/12/jim -collins-peter-drucker-contributed-as-much-to-the-triumph-of-freedom-over-totalitarianism-as-anyone/*.

10. Guy Sorman, *Economics Does Not Lie: A Defense of the Free Market in a Time of Crisis* (New York: Encounter Books, 2009), 1.

11. He lists several other examples as well: "The uncontrolled creation of currency produced runaway inflation that destabilized Germany during the twenties and facilitated the rise of Nazism. In 2007, hyperinflation devastated Zimbabwe. The nationalization of enterprises and the expulsion of entrepreneurs ruined Argentina during the forties and Egypt during the fifties. India's licensing regime froze the country's development from 1949 to 1991."

Chapter 24: The Greatest Cause in the World

1. Jonathan Edwards, *Charity and Its Fruits* (1852; Carlisle, PA: Banner of Truth, 2005), 170.

2. John Piper, *Don't Waste Your Life (Group Study Edition)* (Wheaton, IL: Crossway, 2007), 172.

3. See *http://joshuaproject.net/great-commission-statistics.php* for more statistics.

4. David Platt, *Radical: Taking Back Your Faith from the American Dream* (Colorado Springs: Multnomah, 2010), 70–71.

5. Note that term is "most foundational," not "most *important*." For the best explanation I've ever read on how evangelism and social action relate, see "Word and Deed: A Balanced Testimony," chapter 7 in Timothy Keller's *Ministries of Mercy*.

6. Charles Colson, preface to William Wilberforce, *A Practical View of Christianity* (1797; Peabody, MA: Hendrickson, 2006).

7. For more on the relation between the kingdom of God and the call to address the full range of human need, see Timothy Keller's excellent book *Ministries of Mercy*.

8. See Derek Kidner, *Psalms 1–72: An Introduction and Commentary* (Downers Grove, IL: InterVarsity, 1973), 179.

9. Classical Christian doctrines, especially the gospel, are thus actually the best grounds of social action. Christians often lost sight of this in the twentieth century.

10. See also Steve Corbett and Brian Fikkert's excellent book *When Helping Hurts: How to Alleviate Poverty without Hurting the Poor . . . and Yourself*.

11. On this, see my discussion of Worldreader.org's efforts to do this: *http://www.whats bestnext.com/2011/01/the-great-potential-of-low-cost-digital-book-distribution-for-overcoming -global-illiteracy/*.

12. Some of the best organizations, in my view, that are fighting large global problems in the name of Christ and also understand the opportunity presented by new technology are Food for the Hungry, Compassion International, World Vision, International Justice Mission, Live58.org, the PEACE Plan, and the Willow Creek Global Leadership Summit.

13. For more on this, see Peter T. O'Brien's very helpful discussion in *The Letter to the Ephesians* (Grand Rapids, MI: Eerdmans, 1999), 366–88.

14. Scott Belsky, "Finding Your Work Sweet Spot," *http://the99percent.com/tips/7003/ Finding-Your-Work-Sweet-Spot-Genuine-Interest-Skills-Opportunity*.

15. Scott Belsky, *Making Ideas Happen: Overcoming the Obstacles between Vision and Reality* (New York: Penguin, 2010), 220.

16. Charles Spurgeon, *Counsel for Christian Workers* (Christian Heritage), 108.

Chapter 25: Productivity in a Fallen World

1. Charles Spurgeon, *Counsel to Christian Workers* (Christian Heritage), 39.

Notes

2. See *http://www.christianitytoday.com/globalconversation/august2010/index.html*.

3. John Owen, *Works*, vol. 6, 94.

4. Peter Drucker, *The Effective Executive* (New York: HarperBusiness, 2006), 12.

5. Dietrich Bonhoeffer, *The Cost of Discipleship* (1959; New York: Touchstone, 1995), 89.

6. Mrs. Howard Taylor, *John and Betty Stam: A Story of Triumph*, rev. ed. (Chicago: Moody, 1982), 10.

7. Jonathan Edwards, *Charity and Its Fruits* (1852; Carlisle, PA: Banner of Truth, 2005), lecture 4.

8. Vishal Mangalwadi and Ruth Mangalwadi, *The Legacy of William Carey: A Model for the Transformation of a Culture* (Carol Stream, IL: Crossway, 1999), 62.

9. Ibid., 63.

Getting Creative Things Done

1. Paul Graham, "Maker's Schedule, Manager's Schedule," *http://www.paulgraham.com/makersschedule.html*. See also my post "How to Fit Hard Thinking into a Busy Schedule," *http://www.whatsbestnext.com/2010/12/how-to-fit-hard-thinking-into-a-busy-schedule/*. It links to Cal Newport's excellent article on the topic.

2. This conception of the process is from *FedEx Delivers: How the World's Leading Shipping Company Keeps Innovating and Outperforming the Competition* by Madan Birla. Birla goes into much more detail on the innovation process, and I recommend reading his book.

3. Cal Newport, "Getting Creative Things Done: How to Fit Hard Thinking into a Busy Schedule," *http://the99percent.com/tips/6956/Getting-Creative-Things-Done-How-To-Fit-Hard-Thinking-Into-a-Busy-Schedule?utm_source=Triggermail&utm_medium=email&utm_term=ALL&utm_campaign=MIH+Dec+1+2010*.

Acknowledgments

1. Jim Collins, *Built to Last* (New York: HarperCollins, 1994), v.